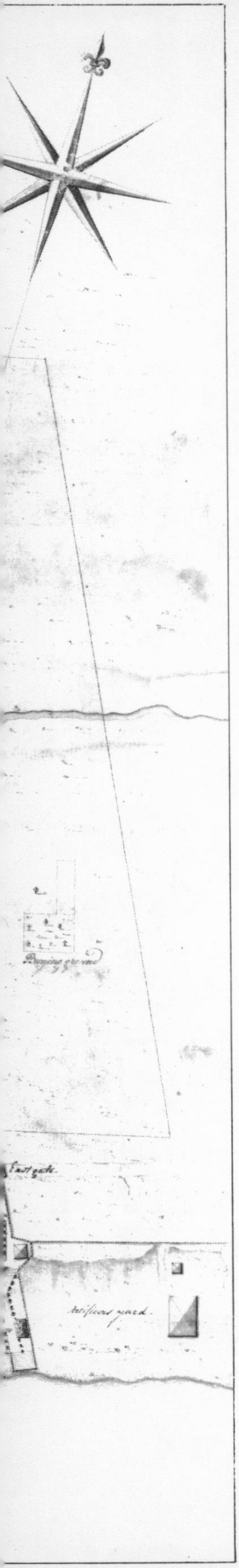

Fort Lernoult

(DETROIT)

by J. J. Rivardi, Niagara

March 29, 1799

The Detroit that greeted Father Richard when he arrived in 1798 looked like this. The map, dated March 29, 1799, is probably the earliest American map of Detroit. It "shows the old French town on the river (Fort Pontchartrain) and the fort built back of the town by the British during the American Revolution (Fort Lernoult)." Major John Jacob Rivardi of the United States Army Engineers drew the map.

Courtesy of the William L. Clements Library
Ann Arbor

GABRIEL RICHARD

Frontier Ambassador

GABRIEL RICHARD

Frontier Ambassador

Detroit in 1826

by FRANK B. WOODFORD

and ALBERT HYMA

with a Foreword by ROSCOE O. BONISTEEL
and an Introduction by EDWARD J. HICKEY

DETROIT - WAYNE STATE UNIVERSITY PRESS - 1958

WAYNE STATE UNIVERSITY PRESS
DETROIT 2, MICHIGAN
LIBRARY OF CONGRESS CATALOG CARD NUMBER 58-12331

Foreword ROSCOE O. BONISTEEL

THE opening paragraph of *Gabriel Richard, Frontier Ambassador* is apt to make you immediately turn to the nearest map of France to locate the town of Honfleur. If your modern atlas is complete, you should soon have your finger on Honfleur, right on the estuary of the Seine. Then, if you move your finger westerly along the northern coast of France, you will come upon two immediately familiar names—Omaha and Utah—the American names of the two beaches on which America and her allies landed to invade Europe in World War II. Your curiosity satisfied, you should return to the biography to become enthralled by the unfolding of Father Gabriel Richard's life. Dramatic scene follows upon dramatic scene. There is especially that touching portrait of Father Richard sailing from Honfleur on the ship *La Reine des Coeurs* on Easter Monday in 1792. Sailing with him are two other Sulpicians and a reverend father, their teacher. They look sorrowfully at the fading shores of France and the Church of Notre-Dame-de-Grâce, which overlooks the harbor from a promontory. They are sailing west to freedom, fleeing from the Old World and the Reign of Terror. As you ponder this picture, and all it implies, your mind encompasses another day some one hundred and fifty years later: assault troops landing on the beaches of France in the early morning of June 6, 1944. It is D-Day and Allied troops invade along the line of Carentan-Bayeux-Caen, with American troops landing on the west side of the line—yes, on Omaha and Utah beaches. There is a definite connection in these two scenes—Father Richard sailing west to fight for freedom and the American soldiers sailing east to fight for freedom on the shores of France, approximately fifty miles from Honfleur. Among these Americans were many direct descendents of the early parishioners of Father Gabriel Richard, and they, too, had the same spirit of courage as the great cleric when he invaded the wilderness of Illinois and Michigan.

Richard left France because he was ordered by the superior of the Sulpician Society. Without such an order he would have undoubtedly stayed in France; his life indicates more than enough fortitude to face the French Revolution, and more than enough courage to be martyred for his beliefs. His superior's decision to send him to America was a wise one. How wise, you will learn in the biography. Let us be thankful that he obeyed his superior's orders—all of us alike—Jew, Protestant and Catholic.

Time marches on. Soon a century goes by, then another, and the green memory of accomplishment rapidly fades—even the accomplishments of a "Gabriel Richard, gaunt, ascetic in appearance . . . a familiar figure in the streets of Detroit in his dusty, black soutane and shovel hat," as the authors describe him. If anything, this biography should bring him back—alive and vivid—standing before you. It seethes with human emotion, with patriotism, courage, intelligence, friendship, loyalties, and not the least, compassion and religion. It is filled with exciting episodes as, for example, the great Indian chieftain Tecumseh going before a conference of British leaders—his allies—demanding the release of prisoner Father Richard—or else. The good father was released, as you will read. So it goes throughout the book. After finishing the biography, you will feel you have met Lewis Cass, Augustus B. Woodward, William Woodbridge, the Reverend John Monteith, Father Michael Levadoux, and the others who participated in the drama of old Detroit.

Much research has gone into this book. The authors have left no stone unturned to go to original source material and present the book in such a way that the casual reader will enjoy it immensely, swept up in the adventures of Father Richard and his time. Father Richard, and his period, have been an attractive subject for many writers. In fact there is more material available in original notes, diaries, short articles and pamphlets than one would ordinarily expect. Many scholarly articles and books have been written concerning this period in Michigan history, and they have added to the authors' own original research. Readers should feel particularly indebted to Monsignor Edward J. Hickey of the Detroit archdiocese for his wide and reverent contributions to the field of Richard research. His deep interest in Father Richard is amply revealed in the Introduction and in a bibliographical note. Further acknowledgment should be extended to other Richard scholars, especially to Father George Paré for his book *The Catholic Church in Detroit, 1701-1888* and to Sister Mary Rosalita, professor of American history at Marygrove College, Detroit, for her well written book *Education in Detroit Prior to 1850*.[1]

Father Gabriel Richard was a remarkable man, and clearly within the definition of the exceptional man given by Louis Untermeyer when he was writing of that distinguished American poet, Robert Frost: "The creator, the artist, the extraordinary man, is merely the ordinary man intensified: a person whose life is sometimes lifted to a high pitch of feeling and who has the gift of making others share his excitement."[2] There can be no doubt that Father Richard was such an extraordinary man—a man of God, whose life was lifted to a high pitch because of his beliefs.

"He has the talent of doing, almost simultaneously, ten entirely different things," wrote Quebec's Bishop Joseph-Octave Plessis of Richard.[3] The recorded events of Richard's life bear the good bishop out. We know Richard had a restless, inquiring mind that always functioned in high gear. From his disembarkment at Baltimore in 1792, until his death in Detroit in 1832, he was a busy priest and a pioneer on many fronts.

Few people today realize as they drive along Detroit's Michigan Avenue that this great route to Chicago was brought about through Father Richard's vision. His arguments as a territorial delegate in the House of Representatives swayed governmental support in its behalf. Among those convinced was House Speaker Henry Clay, the great "Harry of the West," who became a close supporter of Richard's roadway plan. Also helping Richard's endeavors at different times were such men as Daniel Webster and Thomas Jefferson.

He had staunch supporters in the hierarchy of the Catholic church. But he never became bishop of Detroit, and it is difficult to say why. Was it because of his interest in politics or his insistent enforcement of church law as in the Labadie case? Or was it a combination of both, including jealousy on the part of others because of his Territory-wide influence and leadership? Whatever the reason, or reasons, Richard was not deterred from giving of himself to causes to his fullest extent. His entire career was devoted service-beyond-self.

Among the many things that caught his interest was education. This goes back to his early schooling in France and a belief that in due course he would make teaching his life work within the framework of the Sulpician Society. One of his early efforts in Michigan was to provide the means of education for deaf-mutes; moreover, he is generally regarded as the father of modern Indian education. Richard was never at a loss for something to do; but always his active mind came back to programs of education—for the Indians, for the children of his parishioners, for anyone who needed it, for that matter.

Education was a part of the bloodstream of this cultured refugee from revolutionary France. You cannot disassociate the idea of formal education at any level from Father Richard, and a most casual research will soon convince you that he was interested in primary, secondary and vocational education. Though he was practical in his approach, as he had to be in the wilderness of Michigan, nevertheless he saw beyond it the framework of higher education. Beyond the primary, secondary and vocational schools, he envisioned the university level. In 1817, Lewis Cass and General Duncan McArthur signed the Treaty of Fort Meigs with the Indian chief Tontagini who represented the Chippewa, Pottawatomie and Ottawa tribes. The treaty gave six sections of Indian land to Richard's Church of St. Anne in Detroit and the newly established "College of Detroit." One can easily see the influence of Father Richard behind this land grant to the two causes closest to Richard's heart—religion and education. Undoubtedly, the dynamic priest had influential support from Lewis Cass, an early advocate of higher education.

Walking down the long corridor which leads to the main dining room of the Michigan Union at Ann Arbor, you can see today pictures of the former presidents of the University of Michigan. The first picture is of the Reverend John Monteith. Next to him is Father Gabriel Richard, the only vice-president in the line, followed by succeeding heads of the university. The biographical sketch underneath Richard's picture is clear and concise, keeping alive the memory of one of the state of Michigan's great educational leaders. At the inauguration of President Harlan H. Hatcher a few years ago, a Presbyterian minister and a Catholic priest officiated, recalling to the historically-minded the establishment of the legal predecessor of the University of Michigan, the Catholepistemiad of Michigania in 1817. Father Richard's contributions are not easily forgotten.

Further evidence of Richard's continuing interest in higher education is offered in the memorial he presented to the Territory's Governor and Judges in 1808. Wilfred B. Shaw, historian of the University of Michigan, recently pointed out in a paper read before the faculty group Azazels that the memorial "contained the first formulation of the term, 'college of literature, science, and the arts' in the expression 'The Hon. Legislature partly knows what has been done by the subscriber for the encouragment of literature, scientific knowledge and useful arts.' "[4]

The people of Michigan and particularly the alumni of the University of Michigan know Gabriel Richard as one of the two founders of the university. He was the first vice-president of the Catholepistemiad—or University—of Michigania, which was founded by an act of the Governor and Judges of the Territory of Michigan on Tuesday, August 26, 1817. This act was signed by William Woodbridge, secretary of Michigan and acting governor; by A. B. Woodward, presiding judge of the Supreme Court of the Territory of Michigan; and by John Griffin, one of the judges of the Territory of Michigan. It was the culmination of conversations extending over the previous years between the educational leaders of the period and the subsequent incorporators of the institution. Augustus B. Woodward was ostensibly the draftsman of the act, but there must have been numerous conferences about this idea of creating a system of education before the actual writing of the act. Disregarding whether the education plan was borrowed from France or suggested by the charter of any of the earlier state universities of this country, historians generally agree that its enactment was an advance in educational thinking. Policy was to be made on a state-wide scale with a central core of public support. No one can say with certainty who advanced this central idea, since the over-all plan came about as a combination of ideas, experiences and backgrounds.

Historians know that the first or true creator of a plan or program is often lost in the limbo of time, and often one can only assert an opinion drawn from isolated facts.[5] In spite of the grandiose plan stated by Woodward in words generally not understood by his contemporaries, it is not hard to envision the broad idea of territorial education as coming from the active mind of Richard. The discussions between those early frontier patriots as they planned the education of Michigan youth is easily imagined. Guided by records of the time, plus diaries and other miscellaneous materials, the overtones in this plan of education indicate the concrete influence of the great Sulpician priest. We at Michigan are pleased to think of the part played by him in the early days of the university. Even though the titles he held were largely of a passive nature, he remained as vice-president and professor from the beginning until the end of the Catholepistemiad, afterwards continuing as a trustee of the university established by the Act of 1820. The names of those with whom he worked and served in educational endeavors sound like an early *Who's Who of Michigan.*

Richard's generous spirit was surcharged with a desire to serve people and protect their rights. Wishing everyone to have an equal chance, his activities covered a wide range of political, intellectual and social activity. He brought to Detroit its first organ and its first continuous printing press. He established the Richard Press, printing Detroit's first home-town newspaper, *The Michigan Essay; or Impartial Observer,* and such works as *The Child's Spelling Book; or Michigan Instructor* and the *Cass Code.*

One realizes that the many-sided Richard must have been an acute student of human nature. He had to be to survive. His activities made him a target for criticism and abuse, but he emerged with his reputation spotless, his prestige undimmed. Nevertheless, both in church and in public life, Richard had his ups and downs. As issues arose he tried to settle them by arriving at the truth. He never wavered in what he believed to be the truth or his duty as man and priest. Father Richard was "every inch a priest, . . . each of these inches was thoroughly patriotic and American," Sister Mary Rosalita discloses.[6] Today, as in times past, men seek something to which they can cling for moral support when doubts and anxieties confuse them. The example this man of the cloth gave, particularly when under fire, serves to remind us that the loss of self in service to God and humanity is one of the great sources of personal strength and courage.

Real tolerance is born in emergencies. Religious differences are forgotten for humanity's sake, particularly when men are fighting for self-preservation. There were many examples of this in both World Wars and in Korea. Jewish and Catholic soldiers risked and gave up their lives for their Protestant comrades, and the reverse was true. While it is too much to say that Father Gabriel Richard was the first American exponent of such tolerance, he certainly was one of its pioneers. It was he who extended a helping hand to the Protestant groups migrating into the wilderness territory. This fact is recorded in early Michigan Protestant memorabilia. Apparently Father Richard's actions so impressed those who did not belong to his faith that they thought it important enough to preserve for future generations. Chase S. Osborn, former governor of Michigan and regent of the University of Michigan—a man well known for his dedication to the principles of freedom—could write about Father Richard thus:

"If we wish to split hairs about dates, October 15, 1764 could be given as the day of his birth (instead of 1767) because of a claim made in some records that he was born in the earlier year. That is not important. The fact is he was born, and that carries it all. There was no big city in the province of Charente-Inférieure where he was born, it being a pastoral region. That made and kept him simple in his tastes and practical in his thinking. As a rector of St. Anne's he loaned to the Reverend John Monteith the premises where were held the first meetings of the Protestant Society. The attitude of Richard was the first great exhibition of religious tolerance in America. This might be the biggest single thing that Father Richard ever did."[7]

Many will agree with this conclusion.

As is indicated above, we gain insight into the true character of a man by his acts; and often, too, from the things he writes. In the case of Father Richard, all we need do is glance at his letter of appreciation to his father for the sacrifices he made in order that Richard might obtain a formal education, and the sequel —Richard's promise to make good use of it. "How happy you are to have thought that a good education is worth more than money," Richard was able to write, "and is the best inheritance you could leave us after death."

A few years ago a friend gave me a book; in it he placed a marker on which was printed a prayer of Saint Francis Assisi, a prayer I have read many times. I quote that part which truly exemplifies Father Gabriel Richard and his life:

"O Divine Master, grant that I may not so much seek to be consoled as to console; to be understood as to understand; to be loved as to love; for it is in the giving that we receive; it is in the pardoning that we are pardoned; and it is in dying that we are born to eternal life."

Preface

THOUGH a preface to this book will not add a cubit to Gabriel Richard's stature, it does help to orient the reader of the book and provide a suitable place for the authors' acknowledgments. Obviously, no apologies need be made for writing a book on Richard, for he is of local, national and international interest, and his accomplishments are being more and more recognized.

This biography began in the scholarly studies and historical interests of A. H. and then was taken up by F. B. W., whose interests lie also in the time and place of Father Richard. Monsignor Edward J. Hickey, pastor of St. Mary's of Redford, Detroit, and former Chancellor of the Archdiocese of Detroit, who has spent many scholarly years in collecting Richard materials in Detroit, was then called in as contributor and collaborator. He is the source of many of the illustrations, and we acknowledge our debt to him for the captions to all the illustrations as well as for the Introduction. We are grateful, also, to the Hon. Roscoe O. Bonisteel—a member both of the Board of Governors, Wayne State University, and the Board of Regents, University of Michigan—for his pertinent Foreword. The staff of the Burton Historical Collection, Detroit Public Library, was, as always, most accommodating in seeking out and making source material available.

Finally, the book has profited from the very careful editorial handling of the editors of Wayne State University Press and the enthusiasm displayed by the Press designer for the subject. The artistic and stylistic success is due largely to them.

F. B. W.
A. H.

Introduction MSGR. EDWARD J. HICKEY

THROUGHOUT my life I have had a continuing interest in Father Gabriel Richard, and it is very gratifying to see this biography published, and equally gratifying to write the Introduction to it.

I first became interested in Richard in 1919, as a graduate student at the Catholic University of America, while studying church history. When the time came to choose a subject for my dissertation, I seriously considered the life and activities of Father Richard; however, my major professor, Dr. Peter Guilday, advised against the choice. He stressed the dearth of printed source material and original documents,[1] pointing out that Richard's diverse activities in the religious, political, educational and social spheres of his time required more than a beginner's maturity of judgment and perspective. Also discouraging, Dr. Guilday pointed out, were the multitudinous strands of Richard's life that led far afield—to Propaganda, Rome; to the Society for the Propagation of the Faith; to Saintes, Richard's birthplace; to Issy; perhaps to Quebec and Montreal; and most certainly to distant parts of the United States.

In short, I was forced to choose a narrower subject. Fortunately, however, I was able to select one which, on occasion, had some relationship to Father Richard and his manifold activities. In the course of my later studies on the Continent, I stayed a year in Paris, studying at the École des Chartes, the Sorbonne, and the Institut Catholique de Paris. In the archives of the Society for the Propagation of the Faith, I examined, translated, and made hundreds of transcripts of missionaries' letters begging the Society for men and money for the struggling church in America. And here again—despite the lack of heat in the archives and light only from a kerosene lamp—Father Gabriel Richard fired my imagination.

I was attracted to Gabriel Richard for two reasons. First, he appealed to me as something of a hero. He was able to overcome difficulty in pursuit of worthy objectives. Without flinching, he could face danger. Neither poverty, disease, nor disaster deterred him. He did not weaken in the face of trouble or retreat from responsibility. To me, he was man enough to oppose difficulty with strength, danger with courage, and even face death without fear. He reminded me of that earlier American priest, a Sulpician like himself, who was probably the first white man to set foot on the site of Detroit, Dollier de Casson, a giant in stature and in strength, who with his companion René de Bréhant de Galinée had demolished the Iroquois' stone idol, Manitou, and planted in its place the Cross and the fleur-de-lis of France.

And then there was a second, and deeper, reason for my interest in Richard. During my studies abroad, I tried to evaluate the moral significance of America and its relationship to the ideas of human dignity and human liberty and how Father Richard and his fellow priests had understood and contributed to this relationship.

Why did the idea of human dignity and freedom in France result in a reign of terror, while in America this same idea inspired a new era of religious liberty? Undoubtedly, the outstanding significance of America is its freedom of religion, the inalienable right to worship God according to the dictates of conscience, without civil control or interference. For centuries prior to the American experience, the common man of Europe had groaned under a contrary concept—the state had the right and duty to interfere in religious matters. But with the founding of America, this principle was rejected.

Religious factors had been prominent in the establishment of the English colonies of Massachusetts, Maryland, Rhode Island and Pennsylvania. A desire to avoid the religious quarrels and persecutions that followed in the wake of the Protestant Reformation prompted these colonists to found new homes in America. And it was in the colony of Maryland that the principle of religious toleration was first formally inaugurated within the limits of the United States. The colony was founded to give a religious haven to Catholics fleeing the persecution of their homeland. However, the rules laid down by Leonard Calvert, governor of the colony, ordained that no one was to be persecuted for his religious convictions, thus providing a refuge for people of all Christian beliefs. It was not publicly announced that religious freedom would be extended to Catholics for fear they would be prevented from departing. Accordingly, two ships, the *Ark* and the *Dove,* left England in November 1633 and established the settlement of St. Mary's near the mouth of the Potomac River in March 1634. Andrew White and John Altham, two Jesuit priests, were the Catholic chaplains for the new settlement; ministers were also provided for Protestants. This policy of religious toleration—Maryland's chief claim to distinction in American colonial history—was further strengthened legally in 1649, with the Maryland assembly's enactment of the famous Toleration Act.

America owes the general acceptance of this principle of religious freedom to the political genius of the great men who invoked that new charter of human rights—the Declaration of Independence. We can be eternally thankful to them, and especially to the foremost of their number, Thomas Jefferson, who pridefully declared in his epitaph that he had accomplished three outstanding things: The Declaration of Independence, the Virginia statute of religious liberty, and the University of Virginia. And when this message of religious freedom in America was heard across the Atlantic it was as if a brighter and bigger sun had dawned, promising a new day—clean and fresh and sweet—which would drive away the darkness of denied human rights—rights so long refused in the name of religion. It was truly a revolution, a revolution stating that henceforth within the newest and richest of states, God's sun would shine daily over millions of men to whom religious freedom would be the first word of the new gospel of hope, a hope long denied them at the point of the sword or exile, but now built into the convictions and the daily life of a new people and a new world.

The new republic pressed onward across its vast regions, frontier succeeding frontier, until the continent was harnessed and made serviceable to all the arts of man, until its mountains and valleys, its limitless prairies, inland seas and lordly rivers, were written into such a geography as had never before been imagined. In those early days, the Catholic church rendered an incalculable service to the young republic in the way of unifying the undisciplined and eager multitudes who poured in through every port. These multitudes were in no way homogeneous in language, education, ideals or habits and customs. They still smarted under immemorial oppression and injustice; ignorant as yet of the divine purpose that was guiding the new state and shielding it from grave errors, political and social. Whenever in these early days the Catholic priest set up his altar, the immigrant children of many peoples and nations gathered about him to learn from his discourse and example the meaning of America. Here one missionary held back the abused and incensed savage along the new and loosely drawn borderline; there another saved an immense territory for America; there still another pierced the forests with roads, set up a printing press and helped create a university. Elsewhere, they were the first, and long the only ones, to open institutions of education and charity along the far flung lines of western immigration. Which brings me to Father Gabriel Richard's contribution, a contribution which, if it is not the most heroic part of American Catholic history, certainly is its most interesting.

In Paris I often saw sites that figured in Richard's life—the Church of St. Sulpice and adjoining it what was formerly the Grand Seminaire of St. Sulpice, where members of the clergy had been persecuted at the time of Richard's ordination and escape; the corridor in the convent of the Carmes where officers of the Revolution had demanded under the penalty of death priests' signatures to the Civil Constitution. In the adjacent garden stands the sign *Hic ceciderunt* ("Here they fell") marking the site of the massacre of scores of nonjurors, priests who preferred death to being traitors to the divine constitution of the church. I was also able to visit the building in which Richard had taught, and the seminary at which he had studied at Issy. At least three of the priests in Detroit diocese around 1800 had left France to escape the guillotine, the most prominent being Gabriel Richard.

In 1791, Bishop John Carroll, the first Catholic bishop in the United States, had arranged to have several Sulpicians come from France to Baltimore to form the faculty of St. Mary's Seminary and Georgetown College at Washington, D.C. Among these was Father Richard. Later Richard served an apprenticeship in the missions, laboring for six years with the French and the Indians on the difficult Illinois missions near the present site of St. Louis. The earliest missionary activity in this area was the establishment of a mission at old Kaskaskia in the Illinois country by Father Jacques Marquette in 1675. This mission was transferred in 1700 to the present site of Kaskaskia. The Jesuits even founded a college there in 1721. When the Jesuits were expelled from France, Father Pierre Gibault left the Quebec seminary and came to Kaskaskia, Vincennes, Peoria, Cahokia and other Illinois missions. His devoted labors eventually made him the most influential individual in the locality. Later, Father Gibault and George Rogers Clark became closely associated in the contest between the British and the American forces for the possession of Kaskaskia, Prairie du Rocher, Cahokia and Vincennes; and it was largely through the influence of Father Gibault that these pivotal posts in the Northwest were secured for the United States. Father Richard, while in the Illinois country, may very well have caught his fever of loyalty to American free institutions from Father Gibault.

Detroit, which until 1796 had been a military outpost and fur trading center under French and British domination, was indeed ready for someone to introduce those cultural foundations which would make it a more civilized community; it was also ready for someone to lay the foundations of the new American institutions. And Father Gabriel Richard was the man who took the lead, a man with vision, a man with enough unselfish, steadfast devotion to accomplish what had to be done. For not only was there physical poverty to overcome, but worse—mental and spiritual ignorance and indifference. Fire, famine, plague, and military occupation also visited the city in his time. In addition, he was often involved in controversy and litigation, continually suffering from narrow-mindedness in the community which discouraged both him and other leaders of the city.

Yet he was able to embrace all this and persevere. Until a few years previous to his entrance into the College of Saintes, both the Benedictine Fathers and the Jesuits had successively made up its faculty. Was it the work of these Benedictine monks in Christianizing and civilizing Europe that inspired Richard to do so much for Detroit? Or was it the memory of the Jesuit fathers coupled with their heroic missionary tradition embodied in the *Jesuit Relations* that stimulated him? Perhaps it was the peaceful accomplishments of the Jesuit Reductions in Paraguay that gave him his pattern. Or was it the visit to the seminary at Angers of the prince of Cochin-China that sparked his zeal to work among the savage tribes of America? And what of the vision of culture and civilization that Gabriel had known in Paris—the universities, libraries, schools, institutions for the blind, deaf, dumb, the orphaned and the sick? Did that keep him laboring to build a new Paris at Detroit?

"God knows," Richard said, "how many plans, great and small, for schools and missions pass through my head, for the Indians, for the deaf-mutes, for the children of the poor. My mind, my imagination, and still more, my heart are full of projects which remain forever sterile. . . . How many castles in Spain have I not built in America during these years!"[2]

And what of Richard's devotion to liberty? Let his accomplishments at Detroit be our guide. This whole-hearted champion of liberty was not found lacking. But how great must have been the strain on Richard, brought up under the *ancien régime* and accustomed to the union of church and state, to witness the fury of the Reign of Terror and the enthronement of the wanton Goddess of Reason at Notre Dame! Yet, he also recognized that this same philosophy, this same love of liberty had also inspired the American Revolution; and, paradoxically, he was able to sincerely embrace this philosophy, eventually becoming one of its most valiant and foremost supporters.

Such then were the thoughts my studies had provoked. After I had finished my graduate work abroad and returned to Detroit in 1922, Father Richard came to my mind once more as an object for further study because of the wealth of Richard associations in Detroit. The Richard statue, sculptured in stone on the façade of the City Hall along with those of Cadillac, La Salle and

Father Marquette, impressed me. I discovered that John A. Russell of the Detroit Library Commission had made an impressive address at the dedication of a branch library to the memory of Gabriel Richard; that a board member of the Detroit Historical Society, T. A. E. Weadock, himself once a member of Congress, had written a paper on Richard's work in the House of Representatives; and that Richard R. Elliott, a local historian, had published an impressive magazine article on Richard.[3] These were men of mature judgment, scholars; and if they, like Dr. Guilday, my major professor, held Father Richard in such esteem and thought his work so important, I felt he must indeed be a worthwhile subject for further study. Clarence M. Burton, who spent a fortune acquiring, classifying and housing source material bearing on Detroit history, also admired Richard, so much so that he seriously recommended his canonization. Mr. Burton gave me gracious encouragement in my studies as did George Catlin, former librarian of *The Detroit News.*

Eventually it was my good fortune to become instructor of history at Detroit's Sacred Heart Seminary and it seemed proper for me to begin a collection of historical works for my own library, to subscribe to the historical reviews, to attend sessions of the American Historical Association, and in a minor role, to help found the American Catholic Historical Association. My interest in the life of Father Richard also continued to mount.

Although I found it necessary to decline an invitation to participate in writing the history of the church in Detroit, because of the press of clerical duties not dissimilar to those listed by Gabriel Richard when he declined to make the annual address before the Michigan Historical Society at the time of its foundation, I followed closely the work of my confrere, the Reverend George W. Paré, and assisted where I could, particularly in matters concerning Father Richard. In preparing his history of the church in Detroit,[4] Paré carried on intensive work at the Quebec chancery archives, the Baltimore archdiocesan archives, Mount St. Mary's Seminary in Cincinnati, Notre Dame University, and St. Louis University, and collected a large number of photostats of documents which have proved invaluable to Richard scholars. Other Richard students, too, have made important contributions. Sister Mary Rosalita, of Marygrove College, Detroit, has made exhaustive studies of Richard's plan for Indian missions and schools, and has contributed articles to the reviews on almost every phase of Richard's activities.[5] Albert Hyma of the University of Michigan has done extensive work at Ann Arbor, Washington, Baltimore, Paris, Issy and Saintes, primarily in preparation of the present biography.[6] Sister Mary Dolorita, of the Baltimore archdiocese, has done painstaking research at the National Archives, the Library of Congress in Washington and at the Detroit Public Library's Burton Historical Collection.[7] And Mildred Connely, until recently of the English Department at Wayne State University, has devoted a dozen years to exploring Richard materials with the intention of publishing a fully documented and definitive biography.[8] Clarence M. Burton, of course, assisted by Gracie B. Krum and Elleine H. Stones, has helped immensely, as has the Honorable Joseph A. Murphy, Probate Judge of Wayne County, Michigan, who made available the detailed inventory of Richard's library and possessions at the time of Richard's death.

So great has been the impact of all this Richardiana on Detroit, that for the last twenty years Richard's birthday has been the occasion of a rather elaborate annual celebration. There have been programs in both public and parochial schools, feature articles and news stories in the metropolitan and Catholic press, banquets, radio programs and college dramatic presentations, all of which were promoted by the Gabriel Richard Committee headed by James E. Frazer. Numerous pamphlets and articles have been published, notably those by Randolph Adams, Chase S. Osborn, George W. Paré, Stanley Pargellis, Andrew A. Polscher, Milo M. Quaife, Mildred Connely, Albert Hyma and Sister Mary Rosalita.[9] Pargellis would make Richard the patron saint of Detroit, and Osborn and Catlin would have the University of Michigan erect a monument to his memory.

The Richard Press and the imprints issued by it have commanded special attention and treatment in the very excellent bibliography of early Michigan imprints by Douglas C. McMurtrie. There are also the bibliography of the Richard Press by Norman E. Clarke and *A Bibliography of Father Richard's Press in Detroit* by A. H. Greenly.[10] There have been tangible results from this recent civic interest. Two public schools have been named for Richard, one in Detroit and one in Grosse Pointe. There is the Gabriel Richard Park on Jefferson Avenue, adjacent to the Belle Isle bridge approach, where stands the Jungwirth statue of Richard in granite; the Gabriel Richard Council of the Knights of Columbus building on Amity Avenue; the ten story Gabriel Richard Building at Michigan Avenue and Wayne Street; and the tile crypt at the present St. Anne's, which enshrines Richard's hitherto neglected tomb. The 1837 date on the seal of the University of Michigan has been corrected to read 1817, the date when Richard and others first collaborated in the founding of the university. The National Catholic Educational Association, which helps keep alive Richard's memory, sponsors annual Gabriel Richard lectures, and at the University of Michigan there is the Gabriel Richard Student Center.

Thus public interest in the life of Father Gabriel Richard continues to grow. A moment's reflection can easily account for this phenomenon, even though a century and a quarter has rolled by since Richard's death. No one can doubt that there is a felt need for Richard's spirit in our own times. For we realize that without a belief in a supreme being and his wise providence, all that we cherish and hold sacred—the spirit of free inquiry, the practice of free speech, the free way of life, the world's heritage of art, the aspirations of science and the spiritual ideals of religion—may be destroyed. Godless materialism can wreck our civilization. Today, God's law has, in a literal sense, become the law of survival. In the immortal words of the Northwest Ordinance, "religion, morality and knowledge" are, indeed, "necessary for good government and the happiness of mankind."

Contents

Illustrations

GABRIEL RICHARD

Frontier Ambassador

Chapter 1

The Émigré

THE QUAY AT HONFLEUR

SITUATED on the estuary of the Seine, Honfleur looks out upon its harbor sheltered from the buffeting winds that sweep out of the west and race down the English Channel.

An ancient port which has seen the long black ships of the Vikings, Honfleur has lived through much history. Once the chief port of Normandy, it was a center of medieval traffic between France and England. Part of the invasion fleet of William the Conqueror assembled there in 1066; the Plantagenets of England trod its quays when they visited their domains, which in the twelfth century included about half of modern France.

Honfleur's sons knew the ways of the sea. Year after year they set forth on long voyages that took them to fishing grounds off the Grand Banks and the waters of the Gulf of St. Lawrence long before the Pilgrims founded their colony on Massachusetts Bay. Ships manned by hardy Honfleur seamen went faring early in the seventeenth century on notable journeys of adventure and exploration; later they carried with them the Normans and Bretons who founded Quebec and gave France an empire in the New World.

Honfleur's cobbled streets were busy with the traffic of a commerce that reached to such far-off places as Java and Sumatra. On occasion, these same streets echoed to the rhythmic tread of armies. In times long gone by, it had seen the passing of ships, great lords and humble men-at-arms on their way to the Holy Land in the Crusades of Richard the Lion-Hearted of England and Louis IX of France. In other less stirring times, the moonless nights bore silent witness to the secret comings and goings of small, swift craft, manned by smugglers carrying forbidden cargoes down the harbor, then setting their weathered sails for the English coast.

Like most cities which know the perils of the sea, Honfleur was a curious mixture of rough manners and pious ways. High on a promontory overlooking the harbor was the venerable church of Notre-Dame-de-Grâce, built by Duke Robert the Magnificent in 1034. It had become a shrine for seafarers. Before its altar, sailors knelt for their last devotions before putting out to sea; it was there they went first after reaching home port to give thanks for a safe voyage.

But in 1792 a different air pervaded Honfleur—an air of tension, of furtiveness. Its taverns and inns received visitors who came quietly out of the night and who departed just as stealthily down to the wharves, where they slipped aboard waiting ships. No one spoke much about these matters. Honfleur had become accustomed to intrigue and conspiracy. In a town which lived, to a great extent, by the dubious trade of the smuggler, questions were not asked, information not freely offered. The townsfolk turned their eyes away, kept their mouths tightly closed, and if a few pieces of gold were occasionally dropped into their hands by some stranger seeking passage on one of the ships in the harbor, they accommodated him and then conveniently forgot about it.

For those were troubled days in France. The Revolution was tearing the old familiar fabric of the nation asunder, and terror walked the land. In Paris, the guillotine was busy, counting a frightful toll among the aristocrats and those members of the clergy who steadfastly refused to foreswear their first duty to the church and acknowledge the state as the supreme authority. Thousands fled for their lives to Honfleur and other Channel ports. They were the émigrés who sought sanctuary in England or elsewhere, some even in America, that distant, virtually unknown quantity across the sea.

It was in such an atmosphere as this that on Easter Monday, April 9, 1792, four men appeared in Honfleur. Of their arrival and movements, of the accommodations they sought and the arrangements they made, there are no specific historic details. Against the dark backdrop of troubled times there can only be speculation.

The four men, inconspicuously garbed, quietly determined, yet troubled in spirit at the thought of leaving their homeland, were clerics. Three of them were of the Society of St. Sulpice, fugitives from the quiet, cloistered academic life of the seminary at Issy, near Paris. The fourth was a reverend professor who had taught with them. They had chosen as only they could choose: duty to God before allegiance to a revolutionary government which proclaimed the ascendancy of reason over divine authority. Each would willingly have stayed and accepted martyrdom, but their superiors had directed them elsewhere.

It is not beyond the bounds of probability that they knelt together, these four, in Notre-Dame-de-Grâce before quietly making their way to the waterfront.

There, it is known, they boarded the waiting brigantine, *La Reine des Coeurs*. When the tide was full, at eleven o'clock, the mooring lines were cast off and the sails were unfurled. The vessel moved away, pointing its stub nose into the slate-gray waters of the Channel, westward for America. On deck, straining their eyes for a last look at the sailors' shrine on the height above the town, stood four black robed figures. One of them was Father Gabriel Richard.

It was the last time he was to see his native land. Ahead lay a destiny of which, at the moment, he could not dream—a destiny that was to take him to the American Northwest to transform him into a great and venerated historical figure of that strange young nation beyond the seas. For him it was the beginning of an adventure which would lead him into the forests and settlements of a vigorous frontier. There, in inauspicious surroundings, he would help erect the framework of one of the world's great educational institutions; there he would find a path leading, ultimately, to a seat of honor in the halls of the national legislature.

But those things still lay far ahead.

A CHILD OF SAINTES

Gabriel Richard was born in the city of Saintes, October 15, 1767, the son of François Richard and Marie Geneviève Bossuet, or Baussuet, as the name occasionally appears in the records.[1] The Richard family took note that Gabriel was born at 10 a.m.; and that he was carried to the cathedral church of St. Peter by Jacques Bardon and Marie Vaujour, "our domestics." That designation suggests, as was in fact the case, that the family was of more than average means and position.

Saintes was a pleasant little city in a pleasant part of France, a good place to be born in and in which to live. Its people were industrious, trading in [illegible] the iron products which came from its small foundries. The sur[illegible]yside was noted for its vineyards, and the region's wines were [illegible]hoice. Much of the crop went into the making of brandy of [illegible]ts name from the nearby village of Cognac.

[illegible]ntury, before the French Revolution, Saintes was more important than it is today. Situated on the Charente River, it lies inland a few miles, forming the apex of a three-city triangle whose other two points are the seaports of Rochefort at the north and Bordeaux at the south. Accessible to the coast by its little river, Saintes has a traditional feeling of kinship with the sea.

Although now included in the department of Charente-Inférieure, at the time of Gabriel's birth Saintes was the capital town of the ancient province of Saintonge. Far back in dim antiquity, it was the tribal city of the Santones, from whom it takes its name. It was well known to the Romans who left a number of their monuments, including the ruins of an arch and an amphitheater. Charlemagne passed through Saintes with his armies, pausing long enough to build its cathedral. The wild, fierce Norsemen were frequent visitors in the ninth century, coming in their long ships, sacking and killing, and leaving behind ruin and desolation.

After the fall of Rome and the emergence of the medieval duchies, Saintonge gradually merged into that region of southern France known as Aquitaine, and its people acknowledged the suzerainty of the powerful Aquitaine dukes. In return, they shared, in the Middle Ages, in a movement of cultural awakening, receiving from northern Italy those first impulses of what eventually became the Renaissance. Saintes listened entranced to the songs and stories of the great minstrels of the langue d'oc. She had her heroes and her saints. King Richard, who in time would be dubbed the Lion-Hearted, was besieged behind the walls of Saintes by his father, Henry II of England. Richard's mother, Eleanor of Aquitaine, one of the great women of history, visited Saintes often with her retinue of knights, ladies, troubadours and jongleurs; and there, no doubt, she sometimes held her famous Court of Love. Long before most of Europe had stirred out of its Dark Age, Saintes knew and gloried in the beginning of that colorful, exciting episode of history marked by the rule of chivalry.

In Gabriel's day these things were but memories. Saintes had more tangible relics of its past—its churches. Most venerable of these was St. Eutropius, dating from the sixth century. In it was entombed Saintes' first bishop and its patron saint, the martyr Eutropius. There were also Notre-Dame and St. Peter's, built in the eleventh and twelfth centuries, respectively. The latter, a
tradition, initiated the practice of the angelus. Besides its chu
had its hospital, seminary and other religious houses. It co
see until its last bishop, Pierre Louis de la Rochefoucau
Revolution's clerical purge and died under the guilloti

Early portrait of Gabriel Richard by an unknown artist. Painted at Chantilly, France, while Richard was vacationing in the summer of 1790 from his theological studies at Issy, a suburb of Paris. It is now located at St. Mary's of Redford rectory, Detroit. Its authenticity is still in question.

Painting of Richard by James O. Lewis, now hanging in the rectory of St. Anne's Church, Detroit. It was painted posthumously from a study made of Richard immediately his death on September 13, 1832, at 65. The ravages of cholera, mediate cause of his d ntier missionary 's conception d twelve

Photograph by Sylvester Lucus

The church of Notre-Dame-de Grâce, in Honfleur, France. It was from this port that Richard sailed to America on April 9, 1792, on orders from his superiors. The church is a famous shrine dedicated to the patroness of sailors and was one of the last scenes that Richard saw of his native France as he fled aboard the brigantine *La Reine des Coeurs*.

Courtesy of Ministére des Travaux Publics des Transports et Tourisme, Paris

The Cathedral of St. Peter, Saintes, France, built in the twelfth century. Gabriel Richard, the son of François Richard and Marie Geneviève Bossuet, or Baussuet, was baptized here on October 15, 1767, the day of his birth.

Courtesy of Ministére des Travaux Publics des Transports et Tourisme, Paris

2, 1792. Thus it was said that Saintes' list of bishops closed, as it had opened, with a martyr.

In Saintes, amid the old and new, the currents of the natural provincialism of the French flowed in deep channels of piety and romance. These were blended in the character and consciousness of Gabriel Richard.

The father, François, was a native of Rochefort, the son of Jean and Marguerite Guerineau Richard. The latter was the daughter of a merchant who prospered by supplying the French navy with ammunition and supplies; his success earned him high standing in Rochefort where, before his death, he was known as "the first alderman." He claimed the title of Sieur de la Fontaine. Jean Richard evidently was successful, too, for François seems to have had most of the advantages available to members of his class at that time, including a good education at the Collège de Beaupréau at Vendée. He secured a position as a civilian naval clerk at Rochefort, and in 1751 he was promoted to the rank of "écrivain," or chief accountant and secretary. This would imply that he had a sound business training and considerable administrative talent.

It was while François was so employed that he become acquainted with Geneviève Bossuet, who also lived at Rochefort. She was the orphaned daughter of Jean Bossuet. The father was a descendant of a family which had pretensions (apparently not well founded) to noble lineage, claiming distant kinship to Jacques Bossuet, Bishop of Meaux, who at one time had been court preacher to Louis XIV.

Geneviève's grandfather, Olivier, had inherited the title of Sieur de Beausejour, along with a substantial fortune from his father, Sebastian Baussuet, Sieur de la Folatière. Unfortunately, the family wealth was dissipated by Olivier, and the estates which passed to Jean were seized by creditors soon after he inherited them. Jean's position then seems to have declined from that of great landowner to the role of small merchant, a matter of unhappy concern to his relatives. He died when Geneviève was a child, and her upbringing was left to a guardian and tutor, M. Huon de Rosnes, Sieur de Rosne en Saint-Hippolyte de Biard, who managed to retrieve some of the Bossuet money. When Geneviève wed she was able to bring François a decent dowry. The couple were married at Saujon in 1764. Geneviève was at that time thirty-four years old.

Within a year or two after his marriage, François left the naval service, apparently in comfortable circumstances, and he and Geneviève settled down in Saintes. Six children were born to them, the first two dying in infancy. Gabriel was their third and the first to survive. He was followed by two daughters, Catherine Elizabeth and Geneviève. The latter lived only a month.

Then, when Gabriel was five years old, his brother Charles Abraham was born. When this youngest child was taken to the church to be baptized, Gabriel and Catherine were his godparents.

In 1772, François moved his family to an estate of one hundred and fifty acres which he had acquired a short distance outside of Saintes on the road to Saint Denis du Pin. Known as the Jallet manor, or La Jallet, it was described as a pleasant place, situated in a rolling countryside whose hills were cloaked with woods and vineyards. While not pretentious, the house was attractive and comfortable—a typical manor in which a man could dwell with pride in his station. House and garden were enclosed by a high stone wall, pierced by a portal above which, cut into the masonry, were the words from the Psalm: "O Lord, open thou my mouth, and my tongue shall proclaim thy rightousness and sing thy praise." Prophetic words they proved to be in their influence on young Gabriel's life![2]

Above the portal rose a large square pigeon house with a pointed roof of tile. Spacious, well-tended lawns surrounded the house, adjoining which were the usual farm out-buildings. Eventually, La Jallet passed into the hands of Catherine's husband, François de Meshinot, and it remained in the possession of their descendants for more than a century.

Here, knowing the affection of a closely-knit family life, sheltered from the ferment of unrest that was beginning to disturb the world outside the garden wall, Gabriel Richard spent his early childhood in almost idyllic surroundings.

"A VERY ORDINARY STUDENT"

Gabriel Richard's childhood was like that of most normal youngsters in a well-adjusted household in which there is a happy balance of affection and discipline. He was a vigorous, energetic child, sometimes described as flighty and boisterous. There were occasions when his father despaired of him, but that is often the way with fathers and their high-spirited offspring.

The elder Richard had the Frenchman's healthy respect for learning. Fortunately, he was in a position to provide a good education for his children. In later years, Gabriel came to appreciate this, and in a letter to his father, written when he was seventeen years old, he said:

"I am amazed at all the sacrifices which you have made for my education.

Impossible as it is to be worthy of such goodness, I can only promise that by hard and continued application I shall give you all the satisfaction that lies in my power."[3]

But before that was written, there were some doubtful years.

Gabriel's first schooling was at the hands of a tutor; there is no evidence that he made considerable progress or was more than an indifferent student. When he was eleven or twelve, it became necessary to provide him with more formal education, and he was sent to Saintes and enrolled in the Collège, a kind of high school under the direction of the Reverend Louis-Augustin Hardy, curé of St. Peter's. There he remained for six years, going through a well-rounded curriculum which included literature, rhetoric, philosophy, botany and geography.

His introduction to schooling was not auspicious. One of his early companions recalled that he was "proud in exhibiting to his fellow students his provision of nuts, apples, pears and jelly." Abbé Hardy, at first look, saw little in Gabriel to impress him favorably.

"A good father like you cannot feel very easy about a boy like your son," he wrote François a month after Gabriel had entered the Collège. "He surpasses all the other students in the college in sprightliness and light-mindedness. . . . He is a very ordinary student. However, I hope time will make his fire subside. . . . His health is good and his spirit very gay, in spite of the little troubles he brings upon himself."

A few months later, in a following report, there were no signs of marked improvement. "Your boy," declared the Abbé in a mood of resignation, "is about the same. He enjoys excellent health, and he is fat and happy. His progress is not apparent, but he is a good child."

By the time the first school year ended, however, Abbé Hardy was more encouraged. "I believe I notice some change for the good in your son," he wrote with cautious optimism. "He is less peculiar than he was in the beginning. He is a diligent student, and if he does not lead his class, he is at least not at the bottom. His liveliness gives us reason to fear for him, but he gives evidence of being kind-hearted."

Gabriel's liveliness did, indeed, give cause for concern. It led him into an accident which, except for the guiding hand of a providence that protects adventurous boys, might have been fatal.

During his second year at the Collège, when he was in his twelfth or thirteenth year, some masons were working on a new chapel. Despite warnings not to do so, Gabriel climbed the scaffolding, and began to bother the workmen, disobeying their orders to get down. One of the masons threatened him with a stone. Gabriel dodged, lost his balance, and toppled backward to the ground from a height of about twenty-five feet, suffering serious injuries to his face which left a permanent scar and structural disfiguration. As a result, "when he spoke or ate, the lower jaw was deflected slightly from right to left." This trifling deformity won for him the nickname of "Wrymouth" from his schoolmates.[4]

This escapade stretched the patience of the school authorities almost to the breaking point. There was some discussion of expelling him. However, it was decided that he had been punished sufficiently by his injuries, and Abbé Hardy wrote to François that "this accident may help him to overcome a defect which does not affect his heart."

Many years later, his facial scar caused speculation among his parishioners and fellow townsmen in Michigan and became the subject of a highly romanticized story which was long current. A venerable citizen of Detroit, whose reminiscences are preserved in the *Michigan Pioneer and Historical Collections*, insisted he had the following account from Richard himself:

"I was a priest in France at the time of the Revolution directed by Robespierre. I saw some of the soldiers near my house one day, and heard them asking for me. I knew what that meant, and I jumped out of a rear window. As I landed on the ground a woman in an adjoining house threw a teapot at me. It broke on my check, inflicting a deep wound. I ran out on the street until I was exhausted. Seeing some men digging a ditch, I jumped into it. They were friends and covered up my priest's garb with their coats and vests. I was not seen, and my pursuers passed by. I worked in that ditch until I got a chance to leave for America in a vessel."[5]

While Richard may have lived for a while in constant danger from the civil authorities, there is no evidence that he ever was actually mistreated.

The fall from the scaffold very obviously frightened Gabriel and had a sobering effect upon him. It marked a turning point in his young life. His wild, harum-scarum ways changed, and he became a quiet, serious and ambitious student. From that moment he began to progress in his studies, quickly attaining a high level of proficiency. About this time too—June 14, 1781 to be exact—he wrote his parents announcing he was to make his first communion the following Sunday.

"Consequently," he said, "I beg your forgiveness for all my disobediences to you and for all the sins I have caused you to commit." Then, with a hint of superciliousness, he added the hope that he would be pardoned for "all the quarrels you have had, of which I have been the cause through my misbehavior."

At the end of the second school year he begged to be permitted to remain at the Collège to make up work instead of going home for summer vacation. By the time his third year ended, his reformation was so complete that his principal had only the highest praise for him.

"I confess," Hardy declared, "he is a much more lovable child than I had been inclined to believe at first. He leads his class; he is full of good sense and emulation. . . . He is a model for his fellow students, and he gives me as much consolation as he formerly gave me anxiety, and that means a great deal. I deem you fortunate to have such a son." Hardy rewarded his pupil with a copy of a geography textbook which Richard prized throughout his lifetime and which always occupied an honored place in his personal library. Pasted inside its front cover may still be seen the certificate attesting that he had advanced to the third class, except in Latin poetry. In that course he had been moved forward into the second class. He displayed unusual facility in the composition of Latin and French verse. His notebooks, which have been preserved, reveal a keen, interested mind.

His scholastic progress continued. In 1783, he expected to win honors and wrote his mother, urging her to attend the exercises. She did so, only to share his disappointment when his name was not called out. It was consolation to mother and son, however, that he stood close to the top of his class.

During Gabriel's last two years at the Collège, his letters reveal an awareness of what was occurring in the outside world. He commented, January 30, 1783, on the Treaty of Paris which concluded America's Revolutionary War and which was greeted with almost as much rejoicing in France as in the United States. He expressed concern at the news that his brother Charles was suffering severe eye strain which interfered with his studies; he spoke with fraternal interest of his sister's education at a girls' school at La Rochelle. He mentioned with enthusiasm the consecration of the new bishop of Saintes, Monsignor de la Rochefoucauld. He described a particularly severe storm which created panic among the people of Saintes and which his principal compared to the day of Last Judgment. "This picture I have given you," Gabriel wrote, "must inspire us with the fear of it. . . . You can read of it in the latest newspaper."

In the autumn of 1783, after a summer at La Jallet, Gabriel returned to the Collège for his final year. His thoughts turned to the future and a consideration of his further education. Along with several of his classmates, he favored the idea of pursuing classical studies at the University of Paris. "You know," he informed his father, "that I should take my course of study of philosophy in a university, and it is nearly time to come to a decision, if we want to find a place." He added that he was determined to take Greek because "it offers the greatest advantages; there is an infinity of Greek authors who equal the Latins in every way and from whom one can draw the most useful knowledge."

Unfortunately, François had suffered some financial difficulties, and he told Gabriel he would be unable to stand the expense of sending him to the University of Paris. If this was a disappointment, Gabriel accepted it with good grace and without complaint. Abbè Hardy was hoping that his pupil might find his vocation in the clergy and suggested that he enter the seminary conducted by the Sulpician Society at Angers. Young Richard accepted this proposal, pointing out to his father that he could spend a year or two there at little cost and without committing himself to enter the priesthood. This latter suggestion evidently was to block any objections François might have to his son prematurely deciding to become a churchman. There is reason to believe that François hoped Gabriel might enter either the field of medicine or law.

So the year passed, and graduation time arrived. On this important occasion, there were to be no disappointments. Both François and Geneviève were on hand to applaud their son as he was awarded first honors in rhetoric, French oration and Latin poetry, and second honors in Latin oration. Indeed, it was with difficulty that Gabriel, on the journey home, restrained the proud François from exhibiting his laurels to the other passengers in the stage.

The program of those graduation exercises, with the name of Gabriel Richard heading the scholastic list, remains a cherished memento in the archives of St. Anne's Church in Detroit.

THE SEMINARIAN

The summer of 1784 was spent at La Jallet, with the Richard family united. It was not entirely a vacation of idleness for Gabriel. There was work to be done in the fields and vineyards, but there were also pleasures to enjoy, visits to relatives and friends in Saintes. And above all, there were books to read and hours to spend in study and contemplation.

The holiday passed all too quickly. In October, Gabriel set out for Angers to enter the Sulpician seminary. He went by way of Rochefort and La Rochelle, stopping at each place to visit members of the family. At La Rochelle he was forced to wait for the Angers stage which made the trip only once every two weeks. The distance measured in miles was not far, but the road was uncertain and time-consuming. It was a week after leaving La Rochelle before he arrived at his destination.

Angers was an ancient, picturesque city in the storied Loire Valley, renowned in olden times as the seat of the counts of Anjou, who gave England its Angevin dynasty. The seminary, located near the cathedral, consisted of two buildings. In one was the minor seminary for students of philosophy; the other, the major seminary, housed the advanced theological students. It was to the former that Gabriel reported with one hundred and thirty-four fellow students. One of them, he discovered, was also named Gabriel Richard, and to avoid confusion he thereafter signed himself Gabriel Richard of Saintes.

The seminary belonged to the Society of St. Sulpice, which had been established in 1642 in Paris by Jean-Jacques Olier, administrator of the Parisian parish of St. Sulpice. Olier had founded his own seminary primarily to train priests for his own parish, which was one of Paris' largest and contained some of the most vicious criminal elements of the city. So successful were Olier's efforts that before long bishops throughout France, and even in faraway Canada, were calling for graduates of his seminary to aid them in their dioceses. In more precise terms, the Society of St. Sulpice was founded "for the purpose of providing directors for the seminaries" established by Olier; its object "was to labor in direct dependence on the bishops for the education and perfection of ecclesiastics."[6] The Society was a success from the outset and was generally credited with raising the level of the French clergy. Besides Angers and the mother house at Paris, the Sulpicians had seminaries in the principal cities of France in Gabriel Richard's day, and these were regarded as among the front rank educational institutions of the kingdom.

Gabriel entered into the life at Angers with enthusiasm, but still uncommitted. He undertook a full course of studies, which included logic, metaphysics, physics and, most important to him, mathematics, which had not been part of the curriculum at Saintes. The first scholastic year passed without incident. The winter was bitterly cold that year; the seminary was austere, and Gabriel found it necessary, in addition to his classroom work, to exercise vigorously in order to keep warm. Summer came, but instead of going home, he remained at work at Angers. His superior reported to François that "your son is doing well in his classes, and he also makes good progress in piety. His character is excellent and everybody likes him." He did not write home often enough to satisfy his family; he excused himself by saying that he was extremely busy. Among other things, he was preparing to defend a thesis in logic.

His diligence aroused the admiration of his fellow students, one of whom, a cousin with whom he shared a room, wrote to his family stating that young Richard "must have an iron temperament to work as he does." This letter was passed along to La Jallet, eliciting from Geneviève an alarmed admonition against injuring his health by overwork.

"You reproach me in your letter that I work too hard," Gabriel replied, "but I am very far from deserving that reproach which in a sense would be a compliment." He explained that he was actually at his books only four hours a day and that a seminary rule forbade night work. He added that he had made no "indiscreet vows."

"You urge me not to allow myself to go to excess in my zeal," he wrote on another occasion. "I recognize your tender affection for me in this important advice. . . . As for study, you need not fear lest work should make me ill, for we have less time for study than I had in the Collège at Saintes." He often expressed, at this period, his satisfaction with his life and his gratitude to his parents for making it possible. "How happy you are," he told his father, "to have thought that a good education is worth more than money, and is the best inheritance you could leave us after death." This suggests that François and Geneviève had made important sacrifices for their children's education.

By the end of his second academic year at Angers, in 1786, Gabriel defended a difficult thesis in physics, a copy of which is still in existence, and he was awarded the degree of Master of Arts. This marked an important crossroads in his life. Not only had he now won high academic standing, but he had reached the point where it became necessary to decide what direction he would henceforth take.

Actually, the decision already had been made. During the previous two years he had given much thought to the matter of a career and gradually had made up his mind. At the beginning of his second academic year, he informed his father that he was determined to enter the priesthood, despite apparent parental misgivings. "I am always very docile to you, dearest Father," he wrote François at this time. "I respect and will always respect you. However, I think it is my duty to request again your permission for me to take tonsure." To this the elder Richard replied that he was not concerned with making Gabriel a priest rather than a lawyer or physician, "but only a good Christian and a faithful servant of God in whatever state you might be called." This seemed to settle the matter, and a family friend told François that "your elder son is now well on his way to the priesthood. All that remains to be done is to secure for him a good benefice in one of our districts." The only question remaining in Gabriel's own mind was whether he should become a missionary or a parish priest, and he begged his parents to help him to decide. As it happened, events then in the shaping would determine his course for him.

Meanwhile, having accepted his vocation, his next step was to begin his theological studies. To this end he entered the major seminary at Angers in the autumn of 1786. There he was destined to spend the next three years. He became more dedicated to his scholastic work, and his thoughts were more concerned with the future he had planned. He became a scholar of considerable stature. During this period he started to acquire a library, which became fairly extensive for its time; it has been preserved virtually intact.

Taking his own calling seriously, Gabriel began to exhibit deep concern for the spiritual state of his family. The unsettled times led the people of France to inquire more analytically into their social and political organization, and some of this searching spread into the field of religion and morality. One hundred years before, a revival movement within the Roman Catholic church had been started by Cornelius Jansen, bishop of Ypres. The basis of Jansen's philosophy, stated in the most simple terms, was that theology was weakened when based wholly on logic and required a closer relation to spiritual experience. In this his ideas were closely parallel to those of Calvin. Some of Jansen's precepts were rejected by the church as heretical. Nevertheless, his writings were widely circulated, and in eighteenth century France they received fairly wide popular attention.

Much to his distress, Gabriel learned that his own father had been reading a Jansenist book, the *Exposition of the Christian Doctrine*. In a letter to François, dated May 11, 1787, he warned him against being too much influenced by this work.

"There will always be Jansenists," he declared, "because the simple-minded will be impressed by their austere virtue. . . . The only fault of this book is that it is too severe, and, instead of representing God as the kind Father that he is, pictures him on the contrary as a hard imperious master."

Other ideas, then current in literature, also worried Gabriel. He suggested to François that another book, *Historical and Critical Dictionary*, by Pierre Bayle, apparently then very popular and included in the elder Richard's library, be kept under lock and key, "for it tends to undermine the foundations of religion and therefore of morals." He was afraid of the effect of this work, which subtly attacked orthodox Christianity, on the mind of his sister. If she must read anything, he suggested it be *The Disorders of Reason,* a proper book which in thirteen years had gone through seven editions.

"I can tell you that I will never tire of reading it, and that it is written particularly for ladies and people in the world," he told his sister, Catherine. He mentioned that among the interesting authors quoted in it were Voltaire and Rousseau, and that it "is full of fine feelings and gives the most beautiful extracts from the best authors who have written on religion." His references to Voltaire and Rousseau suggest that Gabriel may even then have had a feeling for the need of social reform and liberal thought which he displayed later in life. It was only when the philosophers and advocates of change invaded the precints of theology that he rejected them.

Gabriel's success at the major seminary matched that which he had enjoyed as a student in the general studies division of the institution. He won the respect of his masters and superiors. "I am not surprised by the evidence of his virtue . . . for his conduct here has always been perfectly good," his superior remarked.

His life in the major seminary, while all business, was not austere in the sense of having a monastic quality. It was, in many respects, much like that of the ordinary university student. He was free to spend his vacations at home, and he did so in the summer of 1787. The following year, however, he informed his family that he would remain near Angers, the guest of an elderly canon of the local cathedral, then living in retirement in a country house. Gabriel had agreed to tutor the canon's nephew. He told his parents that this arrangement would save them money, and he suggested they donate some of it toward the reconstruction of an old church near Saintes.

In the late fall of 1788, Gabriel was eligible to receive minor orders which, conferred upon ecclesiastical students during their seminary period, are the first steps toward elevation to the priesthood. Because of the severity of the weather, travel was impossible and the conferring ceremony was delayed until the spring of 1789 when the bishop's authorization was received. Soon after that he went home to La Jallet, spending the summer with his parents. Autumn came once more and he returned to Angers. It proved to be his last visit to La Jallet; it was the last time he was to see his father and mother.

For now his work at the seminary was drawing to a close. On April 10, 1790, he put the world behind him and entered the Society of St. Sulpice as a candidate. This involved, at the same time, his entering a house of the Society known as a Solitude, where he would complete his preparation for priestly orders for which he would be eligible in about a year. He was sent to Issy, a suburb of Paris, where his theological training not only became intensified, but where he also was given charge of a preparatory school.[7] The summer of 1790 he spent in relative quiet and contemplation at Senlis, near Paris, in the company of a distant relative, a M. de Dournon, who reported that Gabriel "was fine in every way." He was admired by all who knew him, although he did not seek much company, preferring to live a remote and somewhat ascetic life, said M. de Dournon, who further explained: "He would rather spend his time in his room or with clergymen." He did, however, visit Chantilly where he sat for a portrait. A local priest described him in these words:

"His face reveals a sanguine temperament and his strong lips remind one of him whom Abbé Hardy called 'that fat boy.' His eyes are eager and mobile, in spite of the stillness required for posing, and they suggest without any question the vivaciousness for which the child had often been reproached. But a certain reserve in the eyes and the lips shows that this native fieriness has been subdued and bridled."

An examination of this portrait, which has been preserved, suggests an austerity, tempered by kindliness. Gabriel Richard, his features somewhat disfigured by his childhood accident, was by no means a handsome man. He was tall, angular, and especially in later life, his general mien and appearance were typical of the popular conception of the country schoolmaster.

Richard had a tremendous capacity for self-application to his labors. He had become a complete academician. A fellow student, François de Meschinet, observed that "he made a thorough study of the most arduous problems, consulting the highest authorities to reach an enlightened opinion. He knew how to make the best use of his time, even of his recreation periods. You could see him discussing interesting problems with his fellow-students. All admired his judgment and the moderate and becoming tone in which he delivered his opinions. . . . Students flocked around him."

Certainly his mind was eager and grasping for knowledge; moreover, combined with his inborn inquisitiveness, was a fine analytical ability. He read widely and he wrote extensively during the time spent at Issy. His books and manuscripts, which have long reposed in the library and archives of the archdiocese of Detroit, attest to the universality of his interests and studies. He wrote, literally, on scores of subjects. He had a number of his papers bound to better preserve them. Their range covers theology and philosophy, as would be expected. But there are other papers which reveal him as a serious student of the sciences, particularly mathematics and botany. It is a safe assumption, derived both from his entering the Society of St. Sulpice and the direction of his interests, that he envisioned a teaching career within the church. The later events of his life, and his accomplishments, reveal that, at heart, he was always the pedagog.

THE ROAD TO EXILE

While Gabriel Richard was quietly preparing himself for the priesthood at Issy, more or less sheltered from the turbulence of the times, France was being shaken to its ancient foundations. What was happening in France was, to a degree, what was happening elsewhere in the world. Stirred by the writings of such men as John Locke, Voltaire, Rousseau, and even Thomas Jefferson and Thomas Paine, to mention but a few, men were arriving at a new concept—a concept which recognized the dignity and the liberty of the individual and proclaimed him the master, not the docile servant, of the sovereign, regardless of whether the latter was represented by the state, a monarch, an oligarchy or a parliament.

Revolution shook the Western world in the eighteenth century. American colonists, aroused by the words of the same philosophers whose ideas were penetrating the minds of Frenchmen, threw off the yoke of colonialism and established a free nation, dedicated to the proposition that all men were created equal. In England the political revolution was more orderly, consisting of social and economic reforms achieved gradually over a longer period of time through legal and constitutional methods.

The seeds of discontent sown by the philosophers found fertile soil in France. While for a time, under a strong, almost absolute monarchy, the germination was barely evident, it was, nevertheless, taking place below the surface. Oppressive taxation, the need for social and economic reform largely ignored by the ruling classes, brought the seed to flower. In the spring of 1789, the Estates-General was convoked at Versailles, partly for the purpose of seeking relief from an oppressive system of government, partly to devise the means of helping the peasant and lower classes, who were suffering from the effects of a severe winter and a short food supply.

What began as a moderate and constitutional reform movement quickly got out of hand, due to the inability of the king and his ministers and to the emergence of demagogs, who quickly took over the masses. Soon there was revolution, followed by a period of complete anarchy, first in Paris and then throughout the provinces. Hand in hand with anarchy came the Terror, and a frightful blood-letting that shocked the world and left France debilitated for years.

During the internal struggle, which reached the peak of its fury about 1790, old institutions were swept away—many of them, such as the feudal system of land tenure, almost overnight. This attack on national establishments spread to the church, which, in some of its administrative aspects, was as corrupt as the government. In an attempt to forestall a call for change even more drastic than was taking place, the clergy agreed to the discontinuance of tithing provided some other source of revenue was made available for the support of the church. This and other concessions, however, were not enough. The upsurge of nationalism brought with it a demand that the church be brought under the domination of the state and that the church's ties with Rome be broken.

Under the chaotic conditions which prevailed, civil administration collapsed. Stirred by the Declaration of the Rights of Man, and shouting "Liberty, Equality, Fraternity," the people refused to pay taxes. Desperate for revenues, the revolutionary leaders looked to the church. Its lands were confiscated in 1789; in 1790 the monastaries were suppressed. With church property as security, a new currency known as assignats was issued. With this paper money the clergy were to be paid regular salaries. This led to the abolition of sinecures, which were a very real evil. Gradually, more assignats were issued until inflation made them virtually worthless.

Meanwhile, in its continued campaign to weaken the position of the church, the National Assembly, which had replaced the Estates-General in August 1790, adopted the Civil Constitution of the Clergy, making that body almost wholly subservient to the state. It proclaimed that members of the clergy without exception were to be given the status of what amounted to civil servants. Moreover, it was decreed that in January 1791, the clergy would have to swear their allegiance to the state and indicate their acceptance of the Civil Constitution or lose their standing. The Pope condemned this order and forbade the French clergy to comply. As a result, only four bishops and a handful of the lower clergy took the oath. About fifty thousand, led by one hundred and twenty-eight bishops, refused to swear. "Nonjurors" was the term applied to them, and their steadfastness brought them perilously close to outlawry. Their salaries were cancelled; their private property was confiscated. Measures were even taken against their relatives. After Gabriel Richard had fled the country, his parents were forced to give affidavits stating that it had been his intention, before adoption of the Civil Constitution, to become a missionary. Had it been proved that Gabriel was actually a fugitive, his family's property probably would have been forfeited. Many of the clergy were arrested and imprisoned, and a number of them, particularly the bishops, paid with their lives on the guillotine. Yet, despite the threats and the pressures, not a single member of the Society of St. Sulpice took the oath.

Naturally, Richard felt strongly about these matters. Like many of his brethren of the clergy, he was sympathetic to the need for general reform, but as a loyal churchman he could not accept those decrees which made the church subject to the state.

"All that which is being pretended to be done today in the Civil Constitution of the Clergy comes down to this, that all power of the church and the clergy depends absolutely on the people and their sovereignty," Gabriel wrote as he uneasily watched the unfolding of events. "They depose more than one hundred and thirty bishops and put others in their places, and they declare that the deposed clergy have no power of jurisdiction whatsoever. . . . This power of opening heaven to sinners, to administer sacraments, is contrary to the text: *'Nemo dat quod non habet'* [One cannot give that which he does not have]."

Challenging the power of the people to choose their own pastors, or that of the civil authorities to appoint them, Richard continued: "The choice of ministers, the granting of powers attached to clerical offices, those are certainly acts that appertain to the government of the Church. Jesus Christ, and not the people, instituted bishops for governing the Church."[8]

These opinions were not publicly stated, but merely by holding them Gabriel was placed in jeopardy. His position was doubly difficult because of the fact that in 1791 he reached the age of twenty-four and became eligible for ordination. In 1791 he had received the subdiaconate, the first of the sacred orders, and he looked forward eagerly to being vested with the full habiliments of priesthood. That highly anticipated event would be one of the most exalted moments of his life. Now, however, there was doubt that, as a nonjuror, he could be ordained. He would not accept the rites from a bishop who had sworn allegiance to the Civil Constitution; a nonjuring prelate dared not administer them openly. What had to be done had to be done surreptitiously.

Not far from the parish church of St. Sulpice stood a private house, the property of the Society. One room had been made into a chapel. On October 9, 1791, Gabriel Richard slipped unobtrusively out of the seminary and inconspicuously made his way to that house. There he was received by Msgr. de Bonal, Bishop of Clermont, who administered the rites of ordination in the absence of the Archbishop of Paris, who dared not be present.

The joyfulness of the occasion was tempered by disappointment. It was Gabriel's fondest dream to return to Saintes as a priest and in his native city, in the church of his childhood, with his family and close friends present, celebrate his first mass. It was not to be. To have applied for a travel permit would, under the circumstances, have been folly. It would have resulted almost certainly in his arrest, and his name might have been added to that list of priests being massacred for their refusal to submit to political authority. Instead, the day following his ordination, Gabriel—Father Gabriel, at last—offered mass for the first time at the Shrine of Our Lady of Loretto, on the grounds of the seminary at Issy.

Immediately thereafter, he was transferred from Issy to the community of the Robertins, in the Rue Cassette in Paris. This was the annex of a clerical school, and his assignment there was to teach mathematics. His stay was brief and uneasy. From Saintes came word that the Collège, where his brother Charles was a student, had fallen into the control of clergy who had accepted the Civil Constitution. Gabriel took prompt steps to have him transferred to Issy.

It must have seemed to him, at this time, that the world was closing in on him, and he must have experienced deep concern, not only for himself, but for his friends, his family, and above all, his beloved church. An expected gloriously fulfilling career now had turned into a life of disappointment. He could not serve his church openly but had been forced instead into what amounted to an "underground" existence, with death and persecution ever lurking. In December 1791, the government created a Committee of Surveillance to hunt down nonjuring priests as if they were dangerous animals. Almost daily there were whispered reports of friends and colleagues being taken; the death toll would soon begin to mount. There was nothing that Gabriel and his associates could do to help except offer their prayers. They, too, had become fugitives.

The Sulpicians were ready—even willing—to suffer the fate of the others. Martyrdom held no terrors for them. But their superiors had different ideas.

Father Jacques Emery, the superior-general of the Society, had been contemplating a refuge for the Sulpicians in other climes and places. A group of émigrés had negotiated for the purchase of a tract of land in America, located on the north bank of the Ohio River in what was then the Northwest Territory. This site, soon to be settled by a colony of expatriates, would have the name of Gallipolis. Father Emery thought about establishing a Sulpician house there. The plan was laid before the papal nuncio at Paris, Archbishop Dugnani, who made a counter-proposal. He suggested sending a group of members of the Society to Baltimore which had shortly before been designated as the first see in the United States. The idea was, apparently, that a seminary would be needed there, and the Sulpicians would be the best suited to conduct it.

Acting as Father Emery's representative, Father Francis Charles Nagot, the superior of Richard's community of the Robertins, was sent to London to discuss the plan with John Carroll. The latter had gone to England in 1790 for the purpose of episcopal consecration, having been appointed the first bishop of the United States. Bishop Carroll gladly accepted Father Nagot's offer to establish a seminary at Baltimore. Accordingly, all arrangements having been made, the first group of Sulpicians from France reached the United States on July 10, 1791. All friends and associates of Father Richard, they were Anthony Garnier, Michael Levadoux, John Tessier, and their superior, Father Nagot.

Arriving at Baltimore, they purchased a tavern on the outskirts of the city and, dedicating it to better purposes, opened its doors in October to five students who had accompanied them from France. This was the beginning of St. Mary's Seminary, the first of its kind in the United States.

These men were the advance guard, and others soon followed them. Bishop Carroll had need of them, and of many more, because prior to their arrival his extensive diocese, reaching from Canada to Georgia and from the Atlantic to the French settlement in Illinois, was served by only thirty-five priests. With a substantial, if widely scattered, Catholic population in the Great Lakes region and around Vincennes, Kaskaskia and Cahokia, there not only was immediate demand for trained pastors, but also an imperative need to recruit and train young men specifically for the American priesthood.

Thus it happened that in the spring of 1792, the second contingent quietly left Issy for Honfleur, on the first leg of their journey to self-imposed exile. There were four in the group—Fathers Gabriel Richard, François Matignon, Ambrose Maréchal and François Ciquard. Some of these, as well as some of their predecessors, were destined for high and important places in the American church.

The brigantine *La Reine des Coeurs,* which bore them to America, was a slow, lumbering vessel. Their passage, which began at Honfleur on April 9, 1792, consumed nearly ten weeks. It was an uncomfortable voyage, and the hearts of the little company of Sulpicians were heavy at leaving their beloved France behind them. It was particularly depressing for Gabriel, who had had no opportunity to bid farewell to his parents. His solace was his faith and the prospect of serving God in a new land, dedicated to freedom of life and thought. In his heart undoubtedly was the hope that someday he might again see his homeland.

On April 12, the ship cleared the English Channel; a few days later the Azores were left behind, and on June 18 the passengers caught their first glimpse of the American coast. Slowly and laboriously, the vessel worked its way up Chesapeake Bay. On Friday, June 22, Richard and Maréchal went ashore to purchase provisions. On Sunday, June 24, they debarked at Baltimore.[9]

It was the first stop, in this new world, of a journey that was to take Gabriel Richard far into the American Northwest, leading him to a new, undreamed of life in the service of God, and to an honored place in the annals of the United States.

Chapter 2

The Missionary

SHEPHERD IN FAR PASTURES

WHEN Gabriel Richard came to the United States in 1792, he found a young nation which had not grown much beyond the limits of its original thirteen colonies. The Revolutionary War had been over less than ten years; the Constitution had been in effect for less than five. George Washington was President; Thomas Jefferson, who was to be Richard's friend and advocate, was Secretary of State.

The continental limits of the new nation in the west were at the Mississippi River. Beyond it lay Louisiana, a possession of Spain. Over the Alleghenies, north of the Ohio River, was the Northwest Territory. In name it was American; in fact, the British continued to occupy part of it, particularly the area around the Great Lakes. The center of their control was Detroit. From there they exerted influence upon the Indians, most of whom remained uncivilized and who roamed virtually unmolested through their vast tribal hunting lands. The fur trade was primarily in the hands of the British at Detroit, Mackinac and a post or two in what is now northern Ohio and Indiana, and along the western shores of Lake Michigan and the rivers of what is now Wisconsin. The Ottawas, Chippewas, Wyandots, Pottawatomies, Miamis, Winnebagos and a few other tribal groups made up the aboriginal population, which was numerous only by comparison with the size of the comparatively small white population.

The white settlements were mainly Detroit, a small village, but still the largest inhabited place in the Northwest; Vincennes on the Wabash; Kaskaskia, Cahokia and Prairie du Rocher in the country of the Illinois along the Mississippi above its juncture with the Ohio. Retaining the language and customs of France, these places were more French than English or American. A few white Americans had drifted into the neighborhood of Kaskaskia, while others were gradually, almost tentatively, feeling their way, crossing the Alleghenies, or coming up from Kentucky and building their cabins along the north bank of the Ohio. The territory was still mostly primeval forest whose resources remained largely unsampled by American settlers, although there were signs that the tide of immigration was ready to start flowing.

The new Northwest country, sparsely settled as it was, had its problems. Many Indians, influenced by the British who were reluctant to give up the land, were hostile to the Americans. A good many Yankee lives would be lost before the Northwest was safely and securely under United States control. The French habitants held no strong political convictions. Their preference was to be left alone, although it may be said that they were more favorably inclined toward the Americans than the British. Where the latter had lost control of the French settlements at Vincennes, and around Kaskaskia, the bishop of Quebec had yielded his jurisdiction, recalling his Canadian priests from their parishes. These were now the pastoral lands of Bishop Carroll in far away Baltimore, and it became his responsibility to find pastors to minister to this remote flock. The Sulpician émigrés, of whom Richard was one, proved to be the answer to his problem.

The general attitude of the United States in 1792 was pro-French, the result of the Revolutionary War alliance. Hence, Richard and his colleagues, upon their arrival, found themselves in an atmosphere which, while alien and strange, was still tolerant and friendly.

Richard's first experience, however, was one of disappointment. On leaving France, he had assumed that in Baltimore he would have a teaching assignment as professor of mathematics, either at the new Seminary of St. Mary's, or at its off-shoot, Georgetown Academy. The latter, as a matter of fact, had become, at least temporarily, of greater importance than the seminary. The academy had been established for the purpose of providing preliminary education for those who were to enter the seminary. Instead, it was competing with it. The few seminary students who were available went to Georgetown to teach. There were too few incoming scholars to make St. Mary's a success. The result was that when Richard and his fellow-passengers appeared on the scene there was no need or demand for additional professors.

The newcomers answered Bishop Carroll's immediate need, however, for he quickly found employment for them. But in doing so, he broke up their little band, and they became widely separated. Ciquard was sent to Maine to minister to the Abnaki Indians; Matignon was established in Boston and from there gave service to much of New England. Maréchal remained in

Baltimore; in time he would become its archbishop. The group which had preceded Richard to the United States had also been scattered. One of them, Father Michael Levadoux, after spending a year at St. Mary's, had been sent westward as vicar-general to the Illinois missions. He set out to his post there on January 15, 1792, thus being far away at the time Richard arrived in Baltimore.[1]

The break-up of this little group of ten or a dozen priests was almost like breaking their last tie with home. Disciplined as they were, they accepted their assignments without complaint, reconciled to the loneliness which, for a while, was certain to assail them. Richard had known Levadoux in France. Although Levadoux was twenty years Richard's senior, a strong attachment existed between them. The relationship was almost like that of a younger and an older brother. Levadoux was a man of strong personality, brilliance of mind and great physical energy. He had the reputation of being an able administrator, a quality which his superiors, Father Emery and Bishop Carroll, felt was strongly needed among the French-American outposts on the Mississippi.

Richard must have experienced a profound sense of personal loss when he learned that Levadoux no longer was at Baltimore. But the separation was not to be for long. Levadoux discovered that the three parishes of Kaskaskia, Cahokia and Prairie du Rocher were too widely separated and the duty of administering them too great for one man. He sent a plea to the bishop, requesting the assistance of one or more additional priests. Bishop Carroll acquiesed, and on September 30, 1792, Richard set out from Baltimore to join his friend in the west.

His route took him across the mountains to Pittsburgh, down the Ohio to its confluence with the Mississippi; thence north on that great river to his destination at Kaskaskia. Unfortunately, he left only the most meager account of this journey into what was for him an unknown land. How useful and informative would it have been had he described by what means he traveled, what he saw, and what were his sensations and impressions! The only thing he had to say was included in a letter to his father, written in the spring following his arrival in Illinois. This was dated April 30, 1793, and in it he tells of his departure from Pittsburgh "after having waited for more than one month for favorable waters."[2] The usual Ohio River conveyance of that day was a flatboat, and undoubtedly it was on one of these that he rode, at least until he reached the Mississippi.

He reported that he and his companions (we do not know for certain who they were) passed the town of Gallipolis, "the new settlement of Frenchmen which is being developed on the Scioto River about thirty miles higher up." He must have been somewhat confused about the exact location, because the town of Gallipolis is situated on the Ohio, many miles above the point where the Scioto flows into it. It was, indeed, a settlement intended as the home of a large colony of French émigrés. As has been disclosed, it was once considered for the site of a Sulpician seminary. It was, perhaps, fortunate that Baltimore was selected instead, for the French immigrants who had bought their Gallipolis lands from the Scioto Company found their titles defective. The group of original settlers, most of whom were of the French upper class, scattered into Ohio, Kentucky, Pennsylvania and other states. Some made their way to Detroit. Their presence in the United States added a distinguished element to the sparse Catholic population.

Before reaching Gallipolis, Richard passed Marietta, the first organized settlement in Ohio, founded in 1788 by New Englanders. Below Marietta and Gallipolis, he may have seen Fort Washington, the most advanced American army post, situated where Cincinnati stands today. Somewhere along the Ohio he was met by Levadoux, who had gone part way to meet him. At the Falls of the Ohio—Louisville—they were overtaken and joined by Father Flaget who was on his way to Vincennes.

Together Richard and Levadoux passed the mouth of the Wabash, where they probably parted from Flaget, continuing on to the Father of Waters. Richard stated that he "entered the Mississippi about 400 leagues from Pittsburgh" on December 5, "and on the 16th of the same month we reached the village of the Kaskaskians. It has taken us about the same number of days, thirteen to fourteen, to cover thirty-five leagues on the Mississippi as it took to make 400 leagues on the Ohio."[3]

Gabriel Richard had penetrated deep into the heart of the continent, discovering as others have before and since, that America is truly a land of magnificent distances. Moreover, there, in the wilderness, he found his duty awaiting him.

Having set out from far distant shores to find sanctuary in a seminary, he had been led by Providence to the life of a missionary among primitive and savage people on the very edge of civilization.

DISILLUSIONMENT

Richard arrived at Kaskaskia on December 16, 1792. He was happy to be reunited with his good friend Father Michael Levadoux. But beyond that, his introduction to the frontier and the people among whom he was to live and work resulted in some disillusionment. As a student, he had read Rousseau and had become impressed, as many of his contemporaries had, with the idea that nobility of mind and soul was to be found close to nature; that the savage state was one of fundamental purity. Rousseau was perhaps the first to conceive of "the noble red man," an impression he gained without ever having seen an Indian, at least in his natural surroundings.

Here, now, was Gabriel Richard in as natural a setting as could have been found anywhere, and he saw little in it that was pure or noble or that mirrored Rousseau's flights of philosophic fancy. The country, particularly in the season of his arrival, was harsh. The Indians were barbaric, slothful, intemperate and from the white man's standpoint, incredibly filthy. Through contact with the whites they had been exposed to civilization, but little of it rubbed off on them; what did usually consisted of the worse vices and few of the virtues. They offered an unlimited challenge to a missionary. Most of them, like so many of the Indians whom the French missionaries tried to convert, preferred being Indians to Christians. When they accepted the faith, it was often for some immediate material advantage and not from deep understanding and conviction.

There were three stations or parishes in the territory served by Levadoux and Richard. They were Kaskaskia, Cahokia and Prairie du Rocher. These were already old establishments, having been the sites of early French strongholds. After the loss of Canada to the British in 1763, control of the area on the east bank of the Mississippi passed to the English. They held it until the American Revolution when George Rogers Clark led his daring expedition to capture Vincennes and Kaskaskia, establishing American supremacy over the strategic triangle formed by the juncture of the Ohio and Mississippi Rivers.

The Illinois district, like some other parts of the Northwest, remained French in social character, probably politically also, under the Stars and Stripes. The population around the three mission stations consisted, at best, of a few hundred white families. French Catholics predominated, although there was the beginning of an American Protestant immigration comprised mostly of new settlers from Kentucky. Richard's activities were twofold: He was missionary to the Indians and curate for the established French families. Across the Mississippi was Louisiana, a Spanish possession in 1792. The west side of the river was referred to by Richard as "the Spanish bank." It too had its settlements, more French than Spanish in character. Chief of these was St. Louis, opposite Cahokia. Its parishes were under the juridiction of New Orleans, and while some of the priests at St. Louis and other places in Louisiana were known to Richard and Levadoux, there is little evidence of much intercourse between them.

At first, Richard made his headquarters with Levadoux at Kaskaskia, and on February 17, 1793, he first signed the parish there as "prêtre curé de la paroisse." Three months later his name appeared on the Prairie du Rocher register as "prêtre curé de St. Joseph," indicating that he was dividing his attention between the two stations.[4]

Levadoux and he had great plans. Together they built a new church (still standing) at Cahokia. They heard reports that a French nobleman, the Marquis de Marnesia, was contemplating establishing a colony of twenty thousand émigrés in the Illinois country. This prompted the two priests to look ahead to the time when new parishes would be necessary, as well as a sufficient clergy to serve them. Being seminarians themselves and Sulpicians always, they began to discuss an academy which might be expanded into a seminary at some future time. On March 1, 1793, Richard wrote about this project at "Kackackiac" (*sic*), stating that funds were being collected, and that one person had promised a donation of twenty-five hundred pounds. Richard acquired a tract of two hundred acres of land near Kaskaskia in his own name, with the probable intention of using it for the site of this proposed educational institution.

This scheme of the two priests may have been somewhat grandiose in view of actual conditions. The colony of the Marquis de Marnesia did not materialize. There may have been an effort to start an academy, but the project certainly did not flourish. Instead, Richard seems to have devoted most of his attention after mid-1793 to Prairie du Rocher, although he was constantly traveling back and forth between that place and Cahokia and Kaskaskia.

"As for me," he wrote Bishop Carroll some time later, "I am fairly content with my little village of Prairie du Rocher, although at times there are grave scandals in it. I derive my greatest consolation from 5 or 6 English-speaking families who live 10 to 15 miles from my place of residence. They are surrounded by other families who were Protestant, but among whom I could doubtless make some converts if I had a greater facility in speaking English."[5] He asked that he be sent a book which had been written by an English convert, along with a book of English hymns set to music. Several Englishmen had asked him for devotional books, he said. He stated a need, also, for catechisms and spelling books.

Richard worked diligently during this period to perfect his English; on occasion he wrote to Bishop Carroll in that language, apologizing for his imperfections, but pointing out that it gave him a useful opportunity to improve himself. He asked Carroll to reply in English.[6]

His life on the frontier was vigorous. He was constantly on the move, visiting the other missions as well as the people directly under his charge. Most travel was by water, both for short and long distances, and it can easily be imagined that Richard became a proficient canoe-man, although on longer trips he undoubtedly employed Indian paddlers. On such occasions, he can be pictured sitting in one of the frail craft reading his breviary, while two or more stalwart braves sped him toward his destination. The hardships of frontier travel made the cassock an impractical garment at times, and, like most others, Richard would lay it aside for the more utilitarian uniform of the voyageur.

There were many disappointments. Even the French habitants among whom he labored were a wild, unruly lot, and Richard complained on more than one occasion about their drunkenness, indolence, and failure to attend mass rgularly. He spoke of one priest who had lived at Kaskaskia for a while and was supported chiefly by the generosity of a Protestant who took pity on him. Richard referred to "the great vices of the inhabitants" and the bad habits of the Indians. Both he and Levadoux commented somewhat bitterly that of all people the white Illinoisans were the worst. To make matters worse, some of his parishioners, having sampled the delights of political freedom under American rule, were occasionally inclined to challenge the authority of the church. Specifically, they insisted on the right to choose their own pastors, a tenet which Richard, understandably, emphatically rejected.

Some of his disillusionment was noticeable in his letters to Bishop Carroll, for whose prayers and remembrances "at the altar" he called to sustain him. There was no sound of complaint, no suggestion of insubordination in all this. It was simply the expression of a lonely young man whose planned life had been radically altered, and who had no reason to feel that he was accomplishing anything of importance. This state of mind, while far from being morbid, was partly the result of occasional pangs of homesickness; a longing once more to see his family and his homeland. This was reflected in his letters and in plaintive inquiries about mail from France. He had received no letters from his parents since his arrival in America. He begged the bishop to see that his own letters to his parents were forwarded with dispatch.

"I owe much to my father," he told Carroll in one of his letters, "for he gave me an education that cost him a great deal of money, too much for me to forget. God, in calling me to go and labor in a country far removed from my own, has not deprived me of natural sentiments. He is not offended by my being sensible. . . . I am anxious to receive some news of my family."[7] He considered himself expatriated, and, with many of his Sulpician colleagues, he looked toward the day when he would return to France and the relative peace and quiet of an academic existence in a seminary. Nevertheless, he was faithful in his duties and a historian said of him: "Father Richard, who was in the Illinois country with Father Levadoux, is without a doubt the greatest name in the missionary annals of the Sulpicians."[8]

For four years Richard and Levadoux worked side by side in the Illinois country, and then came a change.

The Treaty of Paris, signed in 1783, gave the Northwest Territory, including that part known as Michigan, to the United States. The metropolis of this Lakes district was Detroit, originally a French settlement which passed to British control following Wolfe's capture of Quebec and the fall of Canada. But after the Revolution, Britain was loath to give Detroit up. Commanding the passage between the upper and lower Great Lakes, and being the center of a thriving fur trade, it was strategically important, both militarily and economically. A number of English and Scots families had settled at Detroit and prospered through trade. The allegiance of many of them remained with Great Britain. On the pretext that the Americans had not fulfilled all of their treaty obligations, the British continued to occupy the post with a garrison. Efforts to settle this issue peaceably were made, agreement for British withdrawal finally being reached by a treaty negotiated for the United States by John Jay in 1794. Under its terms, the British agreed to evacuate all frontier posts in the Northwest Territory by June 1, 1796. They were further persuaded to live up to this contract by General Anthony Wayne's decisive defeat of the Indians at Fallen Timbers in 1794. As the result of this victory, the British position became untenable. In 1796 they withdrew into Upper Canada and built a new fort at Malden, commanding the mouth of the Detroit River. On

July 11, the town and fort of Detroit were formally taken over by a detachment of American troops under Colonel John Francis Hamtramck.

As long as the Union Jack flew over Detroit, the bishop of Quebec exercised ecclesiastical jurisdiction over the town and all of Michigan. Immediately after the establishment of the American see at Baltimore, the Canadian bishop wrote Carroll, stating: "As for Detroit, I shall continue to send missionaries there as heretofore." But when the political jurisdiction changed in 1796, so did the ecclesiastical. Early in the year, he wrote Carroll again, informing him that Detroit and the other American possessions henceforth would be recognized as part of the Baltimore diocese. "The city of Detroit," he stated, "and its outskirts form a large enough parish of Catholics to deserve to have a resident priest." The "outskirts," in this instance, included the settlement at River Raisin, twenty-five or thirty miles below Detroit; Mackinac Island, the focal point of the northern fur trade; and several other small communities of French and Indians scattered from the southern shore of Lake Erie to Prairie du Chien on the upper Mississippi in what is now Wisconsin. The bishop of Quebec recalled his priests serving the area and handed over the responsibility of administering it to Carroll.[9]

The news of the impending change reached Richard's ears at Kaskaskia and evidently aroused his interest. Detroit was an old city; by 1796 it had a comparatively large French population of well-instructed Catholics. Its church, St. Anne's, which dated from 1701, was firmly established. To Richard, in the Illinois country, Detroit must have seemed like a most advanced, civilized community. In a letter to Bishop Carroll, dated January 24, 1796, at Prairie du Rocher he pointed out:

"You need several priests in various places, and particularly in Detroit and Michel-Machina [Michilimackinac, or Mackinac Island], which have some three or four thousand inhabitants."

If this wistful suggestion was an attempt to achieve transfer to either of those places, he apparently relied only on it to influence Carroll's mind; he did not, as far as is known, pursue it further. Possibly he was thinking that it offered a useful field for himself and Levadoux. At least, he included in his letter the statement that Levadoux was in excellent health and "in every way most flourishing." By this time Richard was being assisted by at least one other priest, a Father Pierre Janin. He was afraid, he said, he might lose the latter because "Mr. Jannin, who is working among the Kaskaskians, wants to accept a position in Spanish territory, where the governor of the Natchais [Natchez], who came here last fall, will send him to New Orleans."

This, plus the fact that Father John Rivet, at Vincennes, was planning to leave, meant, "I fear I shall soon have to revert to my original position of having to serve two parishes, and perhaps even more."[10]

Bishop Carroll needed no hint; he had made plans which, for the moment, included Levadoux, but, unfortunately, not Richard. On March 30, 1796— it must have been almost immediately after receiving the letters from the bishop of Quebec and Richard—he wrote Levadoux, proposing that he take the Detroit post. He made it clear this was not an order; he suggested that Levadoux visit Detroit and the other Lakes missions to inform himself about them and decide if he could be useful and happy there. Levadoux and Richard carefully weighed this request; together they signed the reply in which Levadoux agreed to make the inspection trip, but added that he preferred not to remain in Detroit because that would separate him from Richard.

Thus it came about that on June 15, Levadoux set out, leaving Richard behind. Neither anticipated, obviously, that they would long be apart. Levadoux traveled across Illinois to a village on the shore of Lake Michigan named "Chicagou." From there he crossed the lake to Michigan's western shore and proceeded northward, "a painful experience" lasting sixteen days. Eventually he arrived at Mackinac where "everybody, Englishman, Frenchman, and Indian, all tried to surpass themselves in expressing the joy my coming gave them." From Mackinac he reported, "It is absolutely necessary for the good of religion that a missionary be stationed there." After a stay of several weeks, he departed for Detroit, arriving on August 14, to find the town garrisoned by American troops. He was cordially received by the inhabitants, by Colonel Hamtramck, and by General Wayne himself. He promptly ingratiated himself with Wayne and the military by announcing that "after vespers, I and my parishioners will sing a solemn *Te Deum* in thanksgiving for our union with a free people, and at the same time will pray heaven to preserve the hero who so wisely presides over the United States, and who by his victories has delivered us from the fury of a barbarous people."[11]

If Levadoux referred to George Washington, that may well have been the first occasion on which the President of the United States was commended to God by the prayers of a Roman Catholic congregation.

Levadoux was impressed by the need and desire of the people of Detroit for a spiritual leader, and despite his original intention to return to Illinois, he found he could not do so in good conscience. Within a short time he made his decision known to Carroll.

"I see that I cannot return to the Illinois," he said. "I hope that my letter reaches you early enough to enable you to replace me before winter. . . . The people here are better instructed and much more religious than in the Illinois country. I can not but praise their piety and good manners. I do not dare give them hope that they shall have the pleasure of seeing you. For them, as for their pastor, that would be the height of happiness. They have charged me to convey to you their gratitude for having been provided with a pastor. Please, my Lord, accept mine for all the kindness you have shown me, and believe that it will last as long as the life of him who is with most profound respect, of your Lordship, the most obedient servant."[12]

It was obvious that if he and Richard were to be reunited, it would have to be at Detroit.

ON DESTINY'S STAGE

With Levadoux gone, Richard's responsibility increased. Father Janin, who had been looking after Kaskaskia, had left that station. Richard was forced to divide his time and attention among Prairie du Rocher, Cahokia and Kaskaskia. There is evidence that for a short period in 1797 he also served the missions at St. Genevieve and New Madrid in what is now Missouri. His burden was made greater by the separation from his friend. And those to whom he ministered made his task still more difficult by their unruly, undisciplined conduct. At Kaskaskia, Richard became involved in a dispute with a colleague named Sievre concerning who should celebrate mass and under what conditions. The parishioners supported Sievre. All this, and more, Richard had to report to his bishop, and in doing so his feeling of inadequacy and failure must have grown more intense.

Conditions might have been intolerable for him had it not been for the calm, judicious and understanding letters he received from Carroll. They must have given him comfort and encouragement. In his reply to one such letter, Richard added this postscript:

"I have not had time to write you that long letter in English, however, my Lord, as I begin to writt the English tolerably, I pray please you to writte me in your native tongue. I am your most humble and obedient servant, G. Richard, pr. Please to remember me at the altar."[13]

His troubles with the Illinoisans were not limited to Kaskaskia. At Cahokia he had a more serious matter with which to contend. Upon returning after an absence from the parish, he learned that one of his people, a man named Thomas Brady, had married. Apparently Brady was in a hurry, and could not wait for Richard to come back to perform the ceremony, so he had called on a local civil official to marry him in the church. Upon learning of this, Richard, on the following Sunday, made some sharp and caustic comments regarding Brady and the official for this irregular procedure. Brady was offended, and either he, or one of his friends, carried a garbled report of what Richard had said to the magistrate. The latter promptly cited Richard to appear before him to give an account of his critical remarks and then ordered him to apologize for them.

Richard, at the time, was boarding at the home of Nicolas Jarrot, an influential member of the French community. He appealed to Jarrot for advice about what to do, and was advised not to appear before the magistrate, because "if he did he would be doing irreparable harm to religion." It is not known for certain whether Richard followed this counsel, but it is likely that he did. At any rate, the affair caused so much commotion that Jarrot thought it wise to write a detailed account of it to Levadoux. Levadoux, in turn, passed the story on to Bishop Carroll who, it has been assumed, supported Richard's actions. At least there is no indication that Richard was disciplined in any way.[14]

Meanwhile, Levadoux was having his own problems in Detroit. His territory was much too extensive for him to handle alone. He could serve St. Anne's in Detroit, but the other missions—those at River Raisin, Mackinac, Sault Ste. Marie and elsewhere—were being sadly neglected through lack of manpower. For a while, Levadoux ministered to the people of Sandwich, on the Canadian side of the Detroit River. Their priest had died and his replacement had not yet appeared.

"The town of Detroit itself is not much," Levadoux wrote Carroll, explaining his plight. "English traders form practically the entire population. But the shores of the river are inhabited for twelve leagues on both sides making this parish extremely difficult to care for. I have already partially covered it. The River Raisin is a new establishment on both sides of the river of this name, which empties into Lake Erie. The nearest of its settlers are at least fourteen leagues from Detroit. There are about 110 families, nearly all farmers. They came to me there, and gave me a very kind reception. A plot of 120 acres has been set aside for the use of the priest on which they have built a pretty rectory whose upper storey serves as a church. They have already written you concerning their ardent desire to have a priest sent them."[15]

To this petition of the River Raisin people, Levadoux added his own appeal.

"If you could only replace Mr. Richard so that he would be free to join me! I need his help badly. . . ."[16]

There were, from time to time, other suggestions by Levadoux that Richard be sent to aid him. Carroll was anxious to send help, but he, too, faced a dilemma. If he reassigned Richard, who would look after the Illinois stations? At one time, Carroll considered sending a Father Cheverus to Detroit, and he wrote the trustees of the River Raisin church, stating his intentions.

"I am writing him [Levadoux] today to arrange for your being given an excellent priest at present living in the Illinois country; or, if that be impracticable, to advise me as promptly as possible so that I may have one start from here as soon as I have the means to defray the expenses of his journey."[17]

Possibly, one of the references here was to Richard, but the plan did not immediately work out for fairly obvious reasons. A few months later, Levadoux proposed that Bishop Carroll use two hundred dollars, sent him from Detroit, to pay the travel expense of Father Cheverus. He included in this message directions for reaching the town. But this arrangement also failed. Richard, who was quite willing to leave Illinois and join Levadoux, again became the most likely candidate.

It has been suggested that the bishop's decision to shift him was prompted by the trouble which had been caused by the Brady marriage. Possibly Carroll desired to avoid any further ill-feeling which might cause a rift in the Illinois church, and limit Richard's usefulness. This, however, is only speculation and there is no evidence to support it. It is quite likely that Carroll was influenced most by Levadoux's importunities to send Richard to him, and by a sympathetic desire to reunite the two friends. Richard was still a comparatively young man and certainly he was not yet an experienced priest. It is highly probable that there was a feeling in Baltimore that he could become more useful under the supervision and tutelage of an older, wiser head.

Fortunately for all concerned, the problem solved itself. Two young French priests, brothers, volunteered to go to Illinois, opening the way for Carroll to transfer Richard. Early in 1798, the latter received his instructions—it must have been with joy—to proceed to Detroit and report to Levadoux. These instructions reached Richard in February or early March because on February 4, 1798, Carroll wrote Levadoux that Richard was being transferred and that a second priest, Father Jean Dilhet, was also being sent to him. Richard did not delay his departure. He left Illinois on March 21. Instead of taking the circuitous route followed two years earlier by Levadoux, he chose the shortest way—the heavily traveled trail followed from time immemorial by the Indians—up the Ohio and Wabash Rivers, portaging from the latter to the Maumee, and thence to Lake Erie, near the present site of Toledo, and from there, probably by vessel, to Detroit.

An account of part of his trip was included in a quaint letter to Carroll, written from Vincennes on April 20. Richard used the opportunity to exercise his English, and also to report on other matters of general interest, including some further troubles with the civil authorities at Kaskaskia. These references may pertain to the Brady episode, in which event complaints about Richard's conduct therein may even have been carried up to the federal government.

"Most Reverend Sir," he wrote, "as I am in way to go to Detroit in pursuance of the orders I received from you, I will send you words from this place. I started from Illinois the 21st of last months and I came here by Ohio and Wabsche Rivers. It is of my duty to give you some notice of event that has happened in the performing my mynistry as pastor of the Illinois country. Conformably to your directions I did give the benediction of marriage to two certain persons, both Catholics which had been married by a justice of the county of Randolf where Kaskaskia is. This same judge (Cownel yohn Edgard is his name) made me some reproaches about it, however very civilly, and said to me he was obliged to write on that subject to the Secretary of the States, alledging that my conduct was contrary to the Laws which should be vane if a second marriage as he said before Catholic priest be necessary. I have explained to him our opinion on the present matter in the better manner I could, and with the most fit politness and the most suitable to the friendship that has allwais existed between him and me. I have distinguished the Sacrament from the contract and moreover the civil contract from the Ecclesiastic contract, so that the civil contract could have all its effects, though at the same time the ecclesiastic contract might be invalid before our church. No more upon that matter.

"I found Reverend Mr. Rivet but little better. Since fifteen months he has been almost allwais sick, and I am affraid very much that he will never live long while.

"I will set out from this place immediately and I hope to be at Detroit in at least a month. There is already a month I left Prairie du Rocher. The Ohio was rising so much and the wind blewd hard so often, that I could not go fast. Before I may conclude this letter, I must beg you as much earnestly as I can, to provide a good pastor to Prairie du Rocher. It was a little flock but grateful and faithful. I was too much happy with that people, but alas! what do I say? I must resing [resign] me entirely to the supreme will of God. I rely on his promises, and I hope he will not cease to assist me and to be my comfort. I beg you the assistance of your prayers, I have never been in a so much need of (them) as I am and I will be in the new poste where you send me. I remain your most obedient and perfectly devoted servant."[18]

Despite Richard's assurance that he was about to leave Vincennes, it appears likely that he tarried there a while longer. If not, his progress across Indiana and Ohio was remarkably slow.

Although Carroll's letter to Levadoux (notifying him that Richard and another priest, who turned out to be Dilhet, had been ordered to Detroit) was sent early in February, it did not reach Detroit until mid-May. When Levadoux received it he became seriously concerned because neither priest had made an appearance, nor had there been any word from them. On May 21, he wrote Carroll, expressing his anxiety and impatience, stating that other travelers had not reported seeing them on the way.

But his worry was unnecessary. On June 3, Richard entered the stockaded village of Detroit. It is easy to imagine the warmth of the embrace with which he was greeted by Levadoux, who immediately notified Carroll of his arrival. Richard's coming, he said, brought joy to the whole parish. A few days later, he reported that Richard "has won the confidence of all, and I hope that his services here will be of the greatest value. His knowledge of English, which he speaks passably well, will entitle him to much consideration."

The joy of Richard and Levadoux at being together again was increased by the appearance on June 27, of Dilhet.[19] A Sulpician from Issy, he had arrived from France in January. After a brief training period in Baltimore, he had set out for the Northwest with instructions to report to Levadoux and take charge of the River Raisin parish.

But more important, Gabriel Richard at last was on the scene where, for the next thirty-four years, he would play a memorable role in shaping the development of the American region of the Great Lakes.

EXTRAIT

DU REGISTRE

DES DÉLIBÉRATIONS

DE L'ADMINISTRATION CENTRALE

DU DÉPARTEMENT

DE LA CHARENTE-INFÉRIEURE.

***PARTAGE** fait entre la République et la citoyenne* **Geneviève Bossuet**, *femme* **Richard**, *ascendante d'émigré.*

AUJOURD'HUI 6 Prairial, an 6me. de la Republique française, une et indivisible, l'administration centrale du département de la Charente-Inférieure, assemblée au lieu ordinaire de ses séances, en présence du Commissaire du Pouvoir exécutif,

A été rapportée et déposée sur le bureau la déclaration de la citoyenne *Geneviève Bossuet*, femme *Richard*, ascendante d'émigré, fournie aux fins de partage en exécution des lois des 9 floréal an 3 et 20 floréal an 4, visée tant par l'administration municipale du canton de Soubise que par le directeur de la régie de l'enregistrement et du domaine national.

Examen fait de ladite déclaration et des pièces y jointes, il a été reconnu que l'actif de la partageante se compose ainsi qu'il suit :

Mobilier.

Trente-huit articles évalués séparément, et dont les évaluations réunies s'élèvent à la somme de 5,892 fr., dont moitié pour la déclarante, attendu sa communauté avec son mari, ci. . . . . 2,946 fr.

Six bœufs, deux vaches, soixante-dix-huit brebis, deux charrettes, un versoir et une charrue, ce qui forme et le bétail et cheptel du bien de Lajallette; le tout évalué 1,096 fr., deduction faite de la portion afférante au métayer, dont moitié pour la partageante, ci. . . . . 547 fr.

Deux bœufs, deux veaux, deux vaches, et les fruits en provenant, une taure, une mauvaise charrette et un versoir; le tout composant le cheptel du bien de Lagrève, évalué la somme de 730 fr., dont moitié pour la partageante, ci. . . . . 365 fr.

TOTAL du mobilier. . . . . 3,858 fr.

IMMEUBLES.

Biens patrimoniaux.

Le domaine de Lagrève, situé commune d'Échilais, canton de Soubise, consistant en maisons de maître et de métayer, granges et servitudes, cour et jardin, soixante-sept journaux de terres labourables en six pièces, vingt-quatre journaux de prés et marais en trois pièces; le tout évalué par articles séparés, et dont

3,858 fr.

Ci-contre. . . . . . . 3,858 fr.

les évaluations réunies s'élèvent à la somme de. . . . . 12,437 fr. 50 c.

Acquêts de communauté.

Le domaine de Lajallette consistant en maison de maître, trois maisons de bordiers, deux maisons de métayers, jardin, cour et servitudes, une petite garenne d'un quart de journal, vingt-deux journaux ou environ de prés en neuf pièces, un journal un quart de mottes en quatre pièces, cent soixante journaux ou environ de terres labourables en trente-cinq pièces, vingt journaux ou environ de vignes en quatre pièces, en outre une rente foncière de 1,000 fr au capital, attachée audit domaine; le tout évalué par articles séparés, et dont les évaluations réunies s'élèvent à la somme de 29,058 fr., dont moitié pour la déclarante, ci. . . . . 14,529 fr.

TOTAL de l'actif. . . . . 30,824 fr.

Passif à déduire.

Une rente de 26 fr. 25 c. au capital de 525 fr., dûe au citoyen Ouzanneau, et établie par acte d'acquisition du domaine de Lajallette, en date du 14 novembre 1771, dont moitié est à la charge de la partageante, ci. 262 50

A déduire également le préciput accordé par la loi, ci. 20,000 »

} 20,262 fr. 50 c.

RESTE en partage. . . . . . 10,562 fr.

La déclarante est mère de trois enfans, Charles et Elisabeth Richard, ayant légalement constaté leur résidence sur le territoire de la République,

Et Gabriel Richard, émigré, ce qui donne à la nation droit au quart dans le partage formant la somme de. . . . . 2,640 fr. 50 c.

Et procédant à la fixation et réglement des objets qu'il convient d'attribuer à la nation pour la remplir de cette somme, il a été arrêté ce qui suit.

ARTICLE PREMIER.

Il appartiendra à la République et sera réuni au domaine national,

Une maison de maître située dans la commune d'Echilais, canton de Soubise, avec un chais et autres bâtimens en dépendans, estimés. . . . . 1,000 fr.

Seize journaux et demi de terres labourables faisant partie de la pièce de vingt-trois journaux détaillés dans la déclaration, lesquels seize journaux et demi seront pris dans la partie la plus approximée de la maison ci-dessus mentionnée, et sont estimés à raison de 100 fr. le journal, ci. . 1,650 fr.

TOTAL. . . . . 2,650 fr.

II.

Au moyen du réglement ci-dessus, l'administration déclare, au nom de la République, expédier et abandonner en toute propriété à la citoyenne *Geneviève Bossuet*, femme *Richard*, tant pour le préciput accordé par la loi que pour sa portion et celles de ses enfans républicoles, le surplus des biens déclarés, tout séquestre sur iceux demeurant en conséquence définitivement levé; déclare également lesdits biens déchargés de l'hypothèque de la Nation, et ladite *Bossuet* entièrement quitte envers le trésor public, à raison de l'émigration de son fils.

III.

L'administration centrale rappelle aux administrations municipales, aux commissaires du Directoire exécutif et aux receveurs de l'enregistrement et du domaine national, les dispositions de l'art. VI de la loi du 9 floréal an III, pour les soustractions et estimations frauduleuses qui auraient pu être faites dans la déclaration.

IV

Le présent arrêté sera imprimé et affiché; copies en seront adressées au ministre des finances et au directeur de la régie nationale des domaines.

Fait à Saintes, les jour, mois et an que dessus.

Signé au registre, BOUISSEREN, *Président*; BARTHELEMY, Louis FLORNOY, LÉRIGET, BOICHOT, *Administrateurs*;

LAGAROSSE, *Commissaire du Directoire Exécutif*;

ROY, *Secrétaire-général*.

A SAINTES, de l'Imprimerie de CORINTHE, JOSSERAND et HUS, Imprimeurs du Département, maison du ci-devant Doyenné.

Courtesy of St. Mary's of Redford Church, Detroit

The writ of attachment, May 26, 1797, on the property of Gabriel Richard's mother was secured by the revolutionary, anti-clerical French government because of Richard's escape to the United States. As an ascendant of an émigré priest, Geneviève Richard, a resident of the Department of Charente-Inférieure, was required to pay 2,650 francs, or one-fourth the value of her property.

THE

CHILD'S SPELLING BOOK;

OR

Michigan Inſtructor:

BEING

A COMPILATION,

FROM THE MOST APPROVED AUTHORS.

SELECTED BY A TEACHER.

PART I.

DETROIT:

PRINTED BY JAMES M. MILLER.

1809.

Courtesy of Burton Historical Collection

The Child's Spelling Book; or Michigan Instructor, was the first item that Gabriel Richard printed on his press, one of the first presses in Detroit. No matter in what work he was engaged, Richard's pedagogical interests inevitably came forward.

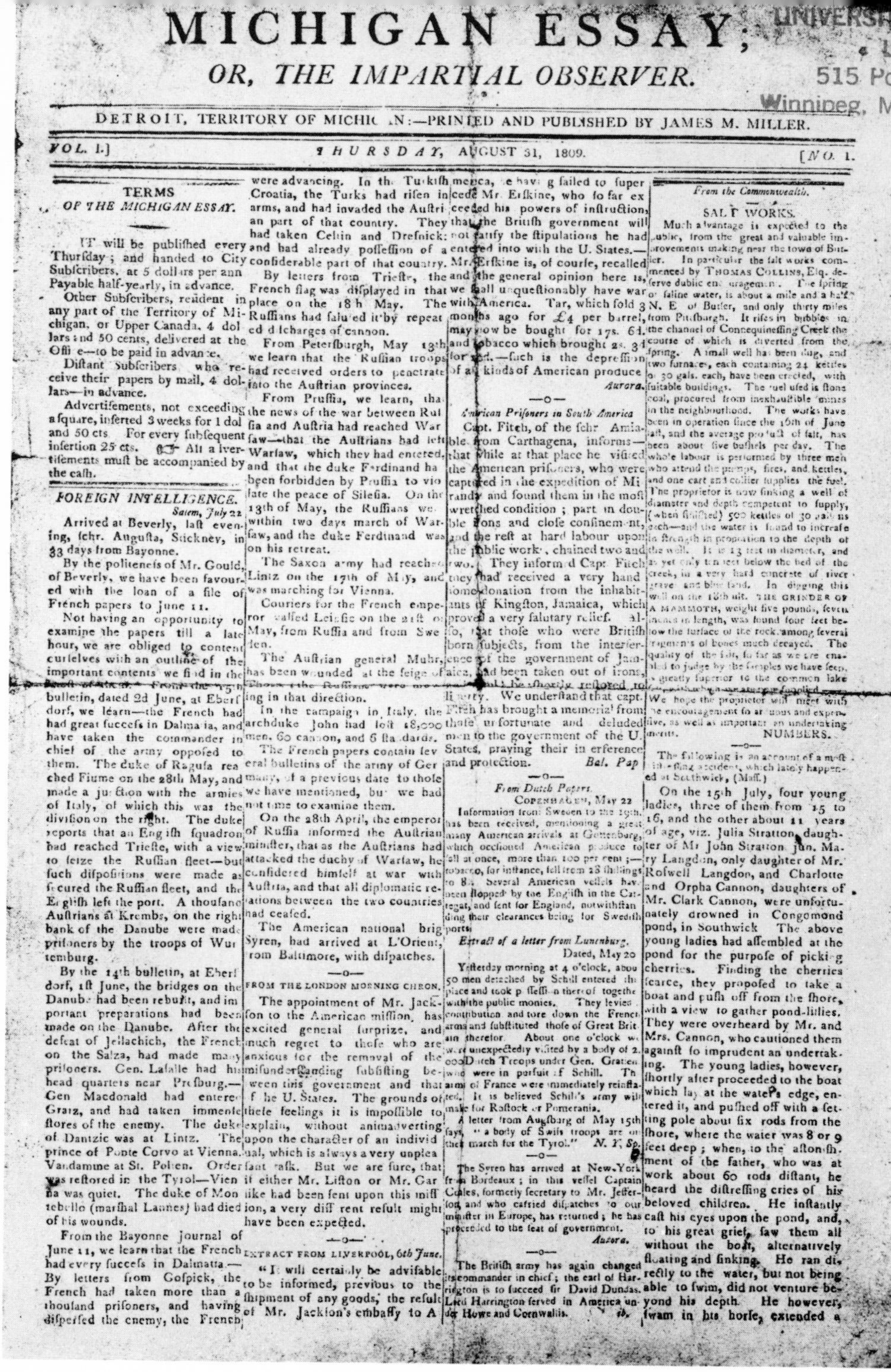

MICHIGAN ESSAY;
OR, THE IMPARTIAL OBSERVER.

DETROIT, TERRITORY OF MICHIGAN:—PRINTED AND PUBLISHED BY JAMES M. MILLER.

VOL. I.] THURSDAY, AUGUST 31, 1809. [NO. 1.

TERMS
OF THE MICHIGAN ESSAY.

IT will be publiſhed every Thurſday; and handed to City Subſcribers, at 5 dollars per ann Payable half-yearly, in advance.

Other Subſcribers, reſident in any part of the Territory of Michigan, or Upper Canada, 4 dollars and 50 cents, delivered at the Office—to be paid in advance.

Diſtant Subſcribers who receive their papers by mail, 4 dollars—in advance.

Advertiſements, not exceeding a ſquare, inſerted 3 weeks for 1 dol and 50 cts. For every ſubſequent inſertion 25 cts. All advertiſements muſt be accompanied by the caſh.

FOREIGN INTELLIGENCE.

Salem, July 22.

Arrived at Beverly, laſt evening, ſchr. Auguſta, Stickney, in 33 days from Bayonne.

By the politeneſs of Mr. Gould, of Beverly, we have been favoured with the loan of a file of French papers to June 11.

Not having an opportunity to examine the papers till a late hour, we are obliged to content ourſelves with an outline of the important contents we find in the ... From the 15th bulletin, dated 2d June, at Eberſdorf, we learn—the French had had great ſucceſs in Dalmatia, and have taken the commander in chief of the army oppoſed to them. The duke of Raguſa reached Fiume on the 28th May, and made a junction with the armies of Italy, of which this was the diviſion on the right. The duke reports that an Engliſh ſquadron had reached Trieſte, with a view to ſeize the Ruſſian fleet—but ſuch diſpoſitions were made as ſecured the Ruſſian fleet, and the Engliſh left the port. A thouſand Auſtrians at Krembs, on the right bank of the Danube were made priſoners by the troops of Wurtemburg.

By the 14th bulletin, at Eberſdorf, 1ſt June, the bridges on the Danube had been rebuilt, and important preparations had been made on the Danube. After the defeat of Jellachich, the French on the Salza, had made many priſoners. Gen. Lalalle had his head quarters near Preſburg.—Gen Macdonald had entered Gratz, and had taken immenſe ſtores of the enemy. The duke of Dantzic was at Lintz. The prince of Ponte Corvo at Vienna. Vandamme at St. Polten. Order was reſtored in the Tyrol—Vienna was quiet. The duke of Montebello (marſhal Lannes) had died of his wounds.

From the Bayonne Journal of June 11, we learn that the French had every ſucceſs in Dalmatia.—By letters from Goſpick, the French had taken more than a thouſand priſoners, and having diſperſed the enemy, the French were advancing. In the Turkiſh Croatia, the Turks had riſen in arms, and had invaded the Auſtrian part of that country. They had taken Cetin and Dreſnick; and had already poſſeſſion of a conſiderable part of that country.

By letters from Trieſte, the French flag was diſplayed in that place on the 18th May. The Ruſſians had ſaluted it by repeated diſcharges of cannon.

From Peterſburgh, May 13th we learn that the Ruſſian troops had received orders to penetrate into the Auſtrian provinces.

From Pruſſia, we learn, that the news of the war between Ruſſia and Auſtria had reached Warſaw,—that the Auſtrians had left Warſaw, which they had entered, and that the duke Ferdinand had been forbidden by Pruſſia to violate the peace of Sileſia. On the 13th of May, the Ruſſians were within two days march of Warſaw, and the duke Ferdinand was on his retreat.

The Saxon army had reached Lintz on the 17th of May, and was marching for Vienna.

Couriers for the French emperor called Leipſic on the 21ſt of May, from Ruſſia and from Sweden.

The Auſtrian general Muhr, has been wounded at the ſeige of ... the Ruſſians were ... ing in that direction.

In the campaign in Italy, the archduke John had loſt 18,000 men, 60 cannon, and 6 ſtandards.

The French papers contain ſeveral bulletins of the army of Germany, of a previous date to thoſe we have mentioned, but we had not time to examine them.

On the 28th April, the emperor of Ruſſia informed the Auſtrian miniſter, that as the Auſtrians had attacked the duchy of Warſaw, he conſidered himſelf at war with Auſtria, and that all diplomatic relations between the two countries had ceaſed.

The American national brig Syren, had arrived at L'Orient, from Baltimore, with diſpatches.

—o—

FROM THE LONDON MORNING CHRON.

The appointment of Mr. Jackſon to the American miſſion, has excited general ſurprize, and much regret to thoſe who are anxious for the removal of the miſunderſtanding ſubſiſting between this government and that of the U. States. The grounds of theſe feelings it is impoſſible to explain, without animadverting upon the character of an individual, which is always a very unpleaſant taſk. But we are ſure, that if either Mr. Liſton or Mr. Garlike had been ſent upon this miſſion, a very different reſult might have been expected.

—o—

EXTRACT FROM LIVERPOOL, *6th June.*

"It will certainly be adviſable to be informed, previous to the ſhipment of any goods, the reſult of Mr. Jackſon's embaſſy to America, he having failed to ſuperſede Mr. Erſkine, who ſo far exceeded his powers of inſtruction, that the Britiſh government will not ratify the ſtipulations he had entered into with the U. States.—Mr. Erſkine is, of courſe, recalled and the general opinion here is, we ſhall unqueſtionably have war with America. Tar, which ſold 3 months ago for £4 per barrel, may now be bought for 17s. 6d. and tobacco which brought 2s. 3d. for 9d.—ſuch is the depreſſion of all kinds of American produce *Aurora.*

—o—

American Priſoners in South America

Capt. Fitch, of the ſchr Amiable, from Carthagena, informs—that while at that place he viſited the American priſoners, who were captured in the expedition of Miranda, and found them in the moſt wretched condition; part in double irons and cloſe confinement, and the reſt at hard labour upon the public works, chained two and two. They informed Capt Fitch they had received a very handſome donation from the inhabitants of Kingſton, Jamaica, which proved a very ſalutary relief. Alſo, that thoſe who were Britiſh born ſubjects, from the interference of the government of Jamaica, had been taken out of irons, ... liberty. We underſtand that capt. Fitch has brought a memorial from theſe unfortunate and deluded men to the government of the U. States, praying their interference and protection. *Bal. Pap*

—o—

From Dutch Papers.

COPENHAGEN, May 22

Information from Sweden to the 19th has been received, mentioning a great many American arrivals at Gottenburg, which occaſioned American produce to fall at once, more than 100 per cent;—tobacco, for inſtance, fell from 28 ſhillings to 8. Several American veſſels have been ſtopped by the Engliſh in the Cattegat, and ſent for England, notwithſtanding their clearances being for Swediſh ports.

Extract of a letter from Lunenburg.

Dated, May 20

Yeſterday morning at 4 o'clock, about 50 men detached by Schill entered the place and took poſſeſſion thereof togethe with the public monies. They levied contribution and tore down the French arms and ſubſtituted thoſe of Great Britain therefor. About one o'clock we were unexpectedly viſited by a body of 2,000 Dutch Troops under Gen. Gratien who were in purſuit of Schill. The arms of France were immediately reinſtated. It is believed Schill's army will make for Roſtock or Pomerania.

A letter from Augſburg of May 15th ſays, "a body of Swiſs troops are on their march for the Tyrol." *N. Y. Sp.*

The Syren has arrived at New-York from Bordeaux; in this veſſel Captain Coles, formerly ſecretary to Mr. Jefferſon, and who carried diſpatches to our miniſter in Europe, has returned; he has proceeded to the ſeat of government. *Aurora.*

—o—

The Britiſh army has again changed its commander in chief; the earl of Harrington is to ſucceed ſir David Dundas. Lord Harrington ſerved in America under Howe and Cornwallis.

From the Commonwealth.

SALT WORKS.

Much advantage is expected to the public, from the great and valuable improvements making near the town of Butler. In particular the ſalt works commenced by THOMAS COLLINS, Eſq. deſerve public encouragement. The ſpring of ſaline water, is about a mile and a half N. E. of Butler, and only thirty miles from Pittſburgh. It riſes in bubbles in the channel of Connequineſſing Creek the courſe of which is diverted from the ſpring. A ſmall well has been dug, and two furnaces, each containing 24 kettles of 30 gals. each, have been erected, with ſuitable buildings. The fuel uſed is ſtone coal, procured from inexhauſtible mines in the neighbourhood. The works have been in operation ſince the 16th of June laſt, and the average product of ſalt, has been about five buſhels per day. The whole labour is performed by three men who attend the pumps, fires, and kettles, and one cart and collier ſupplies the fuel. The proprietor is now ſinking a well of diameter and depth competent to ſupply, (when finiſhed) 500 kettles of 30 gallons each—and the water is found to increaſe in ſtrength in proportion to the depth of the well. It is 13 feet in diameter, and as yet only ten feet below the bed of the creek, in a very hard concrete of river gravel and blue ſand. In digging this well on the 18th ult. THE GRINDER OF A MAMMOTH, weight five pounds, ſeven inches in length, was found four feet below the ſurface of the rock among ſeveral fragments of bones much decayed. The quality of the ſalt, ſo far as we are enabled to judge by the ſamples we have ſeen, is greatly ſuperior to the common lake ... We hope the proprietor will meet with the encouragement ſo arduous and expenſive, as well as important an undertaking merits. NUMBERS.

—o—

The following is an account of a moſt ... accident, which lately happened at Southwick, (Maſſ.)

On the 15th July, four young ladies, three of them from 15 to 16, and the other about 11 years of age, viz. Julia Stratton, daughter of Mr John Stratton jun. Mary Langdon, only daughter of Mr. Roſwell Langdon, and Charlotte and Orpha Cannon, daughters of Mr. Clark Cannon, were unfortunately drowned in Congomond pond, in Southwick. The above young ladies had aſſembled at the pond for the purpoſe of picking cherries. Finding the cherries ſcarce, they propoſed to take a boat and puſh off from the ſhore, with a view to gather pond-lillies. They were overheard by Mr. and Mrs. Cannon, who cautioned them againſt ſo imprudent an undertaking. The young ladies, however, ſhortly after proceeded to the boat which lay at the water's edge, entered it, and puſhed off with a ſetting pole about ſix rods from the ſhore, where the water was 8 or 9 feet deep; when, to the aſtoniſhment of the father, who was at work about 60 rods diſtant, he heard the diſtreſſing cries of his beloved children. He inſtantly caſt his eyes upon the pond, and, to his great grief, ſaw them all without the boat, alternatively floating and ſinking. He ran directly to the water, but not being able to ſwim, did not venture beyond his depth. He however, ſwam in his horſe, extended a

Courtesy of Burton Historical Collection

The front page of the first issue, Volume I, No. I, of the *Michigan Essay, or, The Impartial Observer,* Detroit and Michigan's first newspaper, which was printed on the Richard Press. It apparently was the only issue printed. No others are in existence.

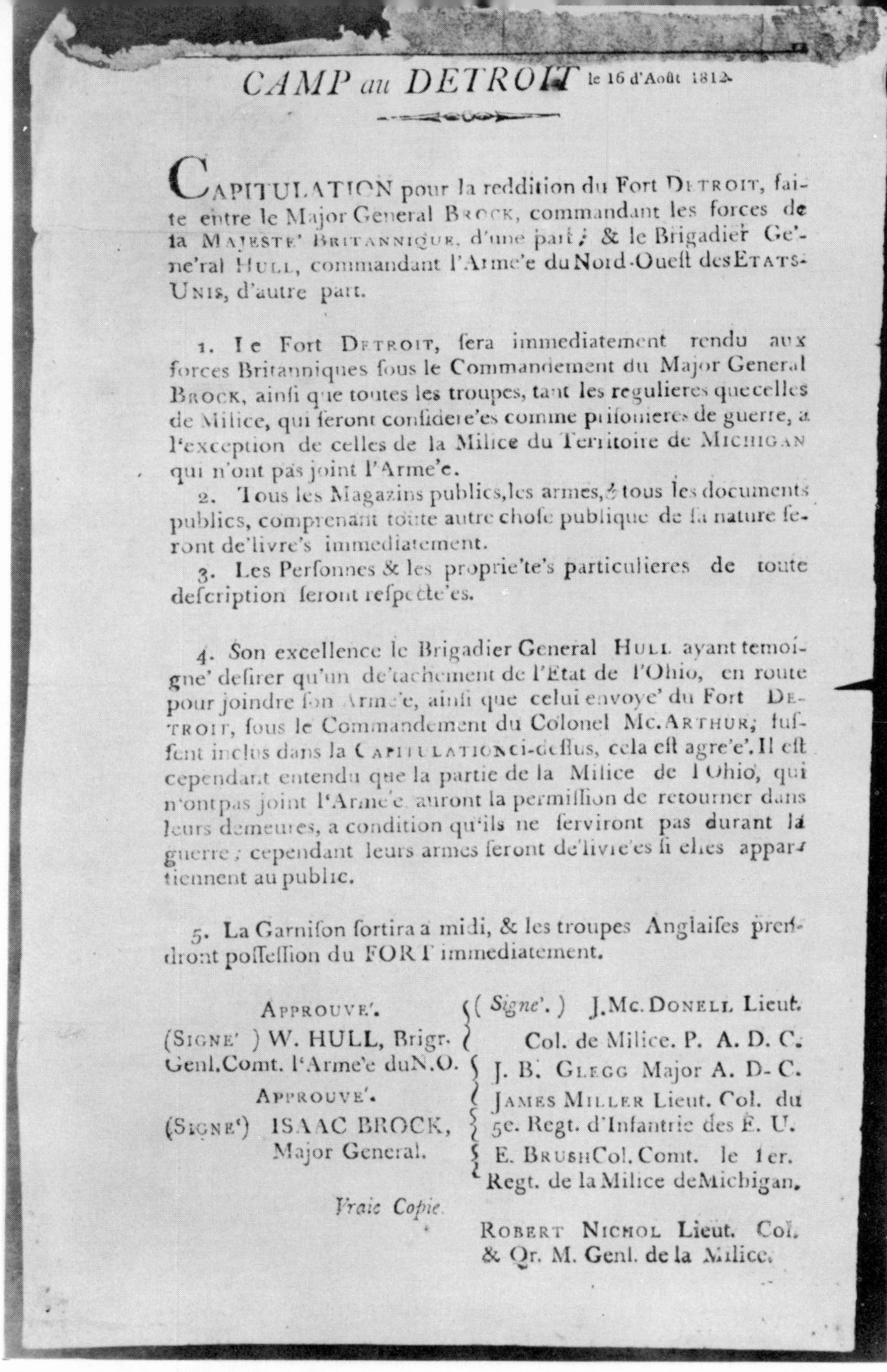

CAMP *au* DETROIT le 16 d'Août 1812.

CAPITULATION pour la reddition du Fort DETROIT, faite entre le Major General BROCK, commandant les forces de la MAJESTE' BRITANNIQUE, d'une part; & le Brigadier Ge'ne'ral HULL, commandant l'Arme'e du Nord-Oueſt des ETATS-UNIS, d'autre part.

1. Le Fort DETROIT, ſera immediatement rendu aux forces Britanniques ſous le Commandement du Major General BROCK, ainſi que toutes les troupes, tant les regulieres que celles de Milice, qui ſeront conſidere'es comme priſonieres de guerre, a l'exception de celles de la Milice du Territoire de MICHIGAN qui n'ont pas joint l'Arme'e.

2. Tous les Magazins publics, les armes, & tous les documents publics, comprenant toute autre choſe publique de ſa nature ſeront de'livre's immediatement.

3. Les Perſonnes & les proprie'te's particulieres de toute deſcription ſeront reſpecte'es.

4. Son excellence le Brigadier General HULL ayant temoigne' deſirer qu'un de'tachement de l'Etat de l'Ohio, en route pour joindre ſon Arme'e, ainſi que celui envoye' du Fort DETROIT, ſous le Commandement du Colonel Mc.ARTHUR, fuſſent inclus dans la CAPITULATION ci-deſſus, cela eſt agre'e'. Il eſt cependant entendu que la partie de la Milice de l'Ohio, qui n'ont pas joint l'Arme'e, auront la permiſſion de retourner dans leurs demeures, a condition qu'ils ne ſerviront pas durant la guerre; cependant leurs armes ſeront de'livre'es ſi elles appartiennent au public.

5. La Garniſon ſortira a midi, & les troupes Anglaiſes prendront poſſeſſion du FORT immediatement.

APPROUVE'.
(SIGNE') W. HULL, Brigr. Genl. Comt. l'Arme'e du N.O.

APPROUVE'.
(SIGNE') ISAAC BROCK, Major General.

(*Signe'.*) J. Mc. DONELL Lieut. Col. de Milice. P. A. D. C.
J. B. GLEGG Major A. D-C.
JAMES MILLER Lieut. Col. du 5e. Regt. d'Infantrie des E. U.
E. BRUSH Col. Comt. le 1er. Regt. de la Milice de Michigan.

Vraie Copie.

ROBERT NICHOL Lieut. Col. & Qr. M. Genl. de la Milice.

Courtesy of Burton Historical Collection

An early imprint of the Richard Press. It is a French version of the surrender terms dictated by British General Isaac Brock to American General William Hull upon the fall of Fort Detroit during the War of 1812.

MACKINAC

If the territory over which Levadoux, Richard and Dilhet were given charge was vaguely defined, that is only because no one knew how extensive it was or where exactly its boundaries lay. Vast, largely unexplored, sometimes even mysterious, it was a veritable empire in itself. The Indians knew it but imperfectly. They occupied portions which, by tradition and ancient warfare, were their tribal hunting preserves; they seldom trespassed beyond their allotted bounds. The French coureurs de bois and the voyageurs had followed its rivers and trails; sometimes they had established remote trading posts, a few families settling down, intermarrying with the Indians. These people farmed indifferently. Their chief living was the fur trade. There were, as at Detroit, a few concentrations of population, and it was with these that the three priests were primarily concerned.

Originally, Detroit was more than a village; it was a geographical organism. The name was derived from the French *la ville de troit*—the city of the straits. Actually, prior to Richard's time, Detroit was the entire district along the river. The name was shared by both sides, and it extended northward from the river's mouth at Lake Erie to at least Lake St. Clair. Above and below the town itself, the farms of the habitants lined the shore. Their frontage was narrow, usually only a few hundred feet in width, and they extended back in the forest almost as far as their owners cared to claim. "Ribbon farms," they were called. Behind whatever fields the farmers cultivated lay unbroken wilderness extending westward into the unknown, beyond the ken of any man, red or white.

Below Detroit—the village—some twenty-five miles, along the River Raisin, was another settlement. That was to be Dilhet's assignment. To the north were other small communities, consisting of a few houses. These were on the Clinton River, at Anchor Bay, at Swan Creek and along the St. Clair and Black Rivers. Many a descendant of those settlers occupies a farm in the same area today and in many regions the French tradition still persists. Still farther north was Mackinac; there were a few families at Sault Ste. Marie and other places to the west in the Upper Peninsula of Michigan. All north of the Raisin was to be the field of Levadoux and Richard.

Upon arriving at Detroit, Levadoux became imbued with a fervor for the United States; his enthusiasm and intense patriotism strongly influenced Richard. From the beginning of their ministry, they were determined to Americanize the northwest frontier. There was purpose in this. At the time Levadoux went to Detroit, the town and all of Michigan had just passed out of British control; however, many of the inhabitants were not ready to shift their allegiance. Some moved into Canada. Others, like one of the trustees of St. Anne's, signed a declaration that he considered himself still a British subject. It was contrary to American law for an alien to be a corporate official, and the authorities notified Levadoux that the trustee would have to be removed. Under pressure, the trustee resigned and a new one was elected. The English, or Tory faction, in the church, then held a rump meeting and restored the first man to his office. At that point the authorities stepped in and citing the trustee and two of his supporters ordered them to appear before the local court under threat of being held in contempt. That ended the matter, but the incident undoubtedly persuaded Levadoux to display his American sentiments and thus bring the authorities to his side, thereby preventing factional splits within his parish.[20]

But Levadoux's patriotism was by no means all contrived. Mostly it was rooted in deep conviction growing out of genuine admiration for the United States. His friendly feelings for Americans and desire to stand well with the authorities was demonstrated, on his arrival, by the *Te Deum* service he conducted. Moreover, his parish now was part of an American diocese, and he wanted no divided allegiance, either political or ecclesiastical. His attitude threatened for a time his influence and popularity with the British element, but, powerful as they were, he refused to knuckle under to them.

"I am a member of the United States," he proudly declared on one occasion. "I would be a wretch to abandon their interests to sustain those of a crown whose yoke they have thrown off. I seek to do my duty honorably and conscientiously."[21]

In February, 1797, Colonel Hamtramck and his staff prepared for a gala celebration of President George Washington's birthday. The observance lasted several days, beginning on the twenty-second with a military review, followed by a ball, and reaching a climax on Sunday, February 26. On the preceding day, a general order was published which stated:

"The preast of the place, having communicated to the Colonel his wish to pay homage in a public manner to the aniversity of the president's Birthday by singing a tedeum in church on the 26th Inst. In the presence of all the

Military Gentlemen the Colonel hopes and wishes every officer to Join the Intended Celebration and Requests all the Gentlemen to meet at his Quarters at 2 Oclock in order to march together to the Church where a place will be made ready for the reception of the Officers."

Resplendent in their uniforms, the officers, led by Colonel Hamtramck and Major Rivard, took their places in St. Anne's. Taking his text from Judges, 13:5—"He will begin the deliverance of Israel from the Philistines"—Levadoux delivered a eulogy in French on President Washington and the government, "as worthy a testimony as any of the loyalty taught by the Catholic Church at the very beginning of the Republic." Father Levadoux concluded the service by singing the *Te Deum*.[22]

Hamtramck and his officers were charmed by Levadoux's patriotic expression and asked for a copy to send the Secretary of War. Levadoux told them he must first obtain his bishop's permission, and a copy was forwarded to Baltimore. Although Carroll replied with fulsome praise of the eulogy and congratulations for its author, it was not published and the only copy, yellowed by age, remains in the archives of the chancery at Baltimore.[23]

This, then, was the atmosphere in which Levadoux and Richard resumed their labors together. For about a year, Richard stayed in or near Detroit, looking after the French Catholic settlements north of the town, while Levadoux attended to St. Anne's. On occasion when Richard was in the village, he assisted Levadoux by performing the duties of *chantre* and *sacristain* in the place of a functionary, Mr. Roucour, who had died. Then, on June 20, 1799, Levadoux felt able to meet an obligation close to his heart; he sent Richard to Mackinac. Finding passage on a government ship, the *Detroit,* Richard sailed north, experiencing a rough voyage, as mariners before and since have done, crossing the mouth of Saginaw Bay. He reached his destination nine days later and was entranced by the beauty of the lovely island, whose citadel, high on a bluff above the Straits of Mackinac separating Michigan's two peninsulas, guarded the passage between Lakes Huron and Michigan. Richard left a chatty and fairly detailed account of his sojourn on the island in a letter to Carroll.

"On the 29th of the same month I did meet there in that place with great many people," he said in his still imperfect English. "It may be said that near a thousand men come there in the Summertime. It is the grand Rendevous of several traders of Lac Michigan, Mississippi, and Lac Superior, etc. There are about 50 houses; I found a great number of Children, I supplied the Ceremonies of Baptism to 30 and better who were above seven years. However it is very sorrowful to see so many poor creatures quite abandoned without instructions. Several of them Know scarcely to do the sing [sign] of the cross. And I was told that there were Good many in the same condition in different places, that they call the hivernement viz. at River St. Joseph, at Wisconsing River, Prairie du Chien, at Green Bay, at St. Mary's Falls, and several rivers of Lac Superior, at Grand Portage, and many for the countries in the North West of lac Superior where the Grand-N.W. Company of Montreal keeps annually seventeen hundred men, almost all of them Canadians. . . ."[24]

He spent two months instructing the children in their catechism, his letter continued, and held evening service in the church, followed by a period of instruction in the basic elements of Christian doctrine. He reported good attendance at these meetings. He described the church as being only forty-five feet in length and twenty-five feet wide, built of cedar poles. While it was very old, he said, it was solidly constructed and would endure for a long time. It was well furnished with ornaments, linen and books, but it lacked a chalice and pyx.

Early in September he paddled across the straits to the Ottawa village on the Lake Michigan shore, some forty-five miles from Mackinac. The chief of the tribe, who had been baptized, had died two years before, and of the thirteen hundred inhabitants of the place, he found only one had received baptism. He noted that the home of a former missionary was marked by a huge cross, standing on a bluff or dune three hundred feet above the lake. He asked the tribal leaders if they wanted a priest to instruct them and their children. Receiving no immediate reply, he suggested that they bring their decision to him at Mackinac. Although he remained on the island until the twenty-fourth, and while many of the Ottawa came to visit him, nothing was said to him about a resident priest.

"To tell you the truth they are so much abandoned to drink spirit, that they do not care much about religion," he said. "When I was at their village they were drinking, and I saw some of them drunk. In the Iland every day some of them were to be seen drunk in the street or in the shore. . . ."[25]

From Mackinac, Richard went to St. Joseph's Island where he stopped briefly, and then proceeded to Sault Ste. Marie. There he was saddened at finding a number of Frenchmen living with Indian women. He expressed regret that he could not legitimatize these unions, feeling himself prevented by the lack of understanding of religion and the significance of the sacrament on the part of these squaws.

"I wished many times in my travell," he declared, "that I could marry at least civilly, that is to say without making sacrament, and consequently without saying words *Ego conjungo vos,* etc. in order to take off the scandal and to legitimate so many innocent children who are born every day from such illawful conjunctions."[26]

Richard was profoundly impressed with the need of the people at Mackinac, the Soo, and other northern settlements, for a priest. Some of the traders urged him to stay. This he was quite willing to do, provided Levadoux could spare him. He wrote Levadoux for permission to stay, and, if granted, asked that the second half of his breviary be sent him, as well as his winter cassock which would be found in the trunk behind his bed. He sent this message by an Indian courier, Oni-g-wi-gan, who was instructed to bring back a reply. But while recognizing the needs of the northern outposts, Levadoux could not spare Richard. Fearing that his colleague might appeal directly to Bishop Carroll for permission to remain, Levadoux peremptorily ordered Richard to return, at the same time speeding off a letter to Carroll pointing out how important Richard's work was in Detroit. The younger priest, he declared, was indispensable because he spoke both English and French; because the people had great confidence in him; and because of the close ties of friendship which bound the two clerics together.

Richard obeyed Levadoux's order to return. Booking passage on the British schooner *Charlotte,* he was back in Detroit on October 21. He expressed the desire that he might soon go back to Mackinac, declaring, among other reasons, that he could perfect his English better at Mackinac than at Detroit where he had less opportunity to practice it.

"There are but very few Roman Catholics amongst the English people of this place," he said, referring to Detroit. "Five or six of them only are used to come to Confession. There is maybe a dozen of our profession, but most part of them are certain perpetual travellers from Ireland some of whom only recollect of hearing their father or mother to be Romans, and know nothing of Catholic Doctrine nor care much of being instructed in it. They are of different trades viz. taylors, tavern keepers, soldiers, etc. You know very well how much it is easy to make such people good Christians! I am very sorry for it, but what is to be done? However I will invite them to meet together at certain days in order to deliver them a clear explanation of our belief. The offers I made by one of them who was to advise them has been unsuccessful. . . ."[27]

Throughout the next year and a half, Levadoux's health declined and Richard's burden increased correspondingly. The months were given over to routine parish duties, highlighted in the summer of 1801 by a visit from Bishop Pierre Denaut, of Quebec, who spent four or five days at Detroit and confirmed 550 persons. He also spent a day or two at River Raisin with Dilhet.

While the three priests were toiling in the Michigan vineyard, events were taking place in far away France that were to profoundly influence their lives. The fury of the French Revolution was spent; order was returning out of chaos. Gradually, church and state were composing their differences and the exiled clergy was beginning to return home. One by one the Sulpicians left America for France; and Richard, Levadoux and Dilhet momentarily expected their recall. Levadoux, because of his health, requested to be relieved of his duties in Detroit. Father Nagot, his superior, instructed him to report at Baltimore; and he left Detroit about mid-April, 1802. The farewells exchanged between him and Richard were made easier by the latter's expectation that he, too, would soon follow. Levadoux spent a year in the seminary at Baltimore, then sailed for France.

The two friends parted at Detroit for the last time. Richard and Levadoux were never to see each other again.

"WE HOPE FOR BETTER THINGS"

Gabriel Richard, gaunt, ascetic in appearance, became a familiar figure in the streets of Detroit in his dusty black soutane and shovel hat. The village lay on the north bank of the river which, at that point, made a sweeping curve that broke its general north-south direction. A stockade, twelve to fourteen feet high, surrounded the town. From the east gate to the west gate was a distance of about fifteen hundred feet; from the shore to the north line of the stockade was about four hundred feet. The village was crisscrossed in checker board fashion by four east-west and five north-south thoroughfares which bore the designation of streets only by courtesy.

"The streets are so narrow as scarcely to admit two carriages to pass each other," said General Wayne in describing Detroit. "The whole place is surrounded with high pickets, with bastions at proper distances, which are enforced with artillery; within the pickets is also a kind of citadel, which serves for barracks, stores, and for part of the troops. You enter the town by one main street, which runs parallel with the river and has a gate at each end, defended by a block house; these gates are shut every night at sunset, and are not opened again until sunrise, in order to protect the citizens and their property from insult or injury by drunken, disorderly, or hostile Indians."

Crowded together on the streets and in yards, without reason or plan, was a conglomeration of buildings—houses, barns, warehouses, taverns and shops. All of the structures were of timber, all of them were tinder dry. To the inhabitants, a spark was more dangerous than a hostile Indian, and rigid laws were in force regarding fire and the condition of chimneys. At the extreme west end of town was the citadel, which Wayne mentioned, a collection of barracks, stables and other buildings used by the military. These faced around an open square. One of the buildings was used as the government store where goods were traded to the Indians.

At the extreme east end of town, just inside what was called the Pontiac Gate, fronting on St. Anne Street, was the church, the venerable St. Anne's. Adjoining it was the rectory, and around both was the burying ground. In 1802, St. Anne's was an unprepossessing looking structure, with plain, weather-beaten exterior and, like all else in town, built entirely of wood. Its exact location was about the center of present-day Jefferson Avenue at its intersection with Griswold Street.

Behind the town meandered a small stream, the Savoyard River, and beyond that, on a slight eminence which commanded an unobstructed view up and down river, as well as of the opposite Canadian shore, stood the fort, a formidable appearing work with its high ramparts and glacis, enclosing a parade ground around which were a score of buildings capable of accommodating a fairly substantial force.

This was Father Richard's Detroit. This, and the adjoining countryside with its ribbon farms, was his parish, given into his custody at the departure of Michael Levadoux. On May 3, 1802, for the first time, he signed the parish register as curé. He was humble in the face of his responsibility; he had inner doubts as to his capacity and fitness. Bishop Carroll sensed this from his letters and wrote him words of encouragement. From these letters Richard derived great peace of mind, and he promised the bishop that he would read them over many times in the future when his spirit needed to be refreshed. But, in one of his letters he added with resoluteness, there was much to be done.

"I received great comfort from several of my parishoners," he said. "I feel my wishes for the salvation of the whole increasing. By their docility and some success, my flock becomes every day dearer to me. Pray the Almighty that I may remove all obstacles I have daily imposed to his benevolent designs, that the Holy Ghost may be diffused upon all flesh."[28]

The success which he mentioned was not a complete one. He was meeting some opposition to reforms he was attempting to enforce. In 1791 Bishop Carroll had presided over a synod which adopted certain canonical forms for the American church to follow. Remote parishes, such as Detroit, were slow in accepting them. One of the practices to which Richard put a stop was that of having young girls offer oblations and otherwise assist at services. He forced a showdown relative to this practice by forbidding one girl to participate at a Christmas service because she was, as he explained, indecently dressed. This caused quite an uproar among the parishioners. Several told him he had done the right thing; but the girl's relatives were affronted and objected strenuously. In order to avoid a recurrence of this situation, Richard informed the trustees that thereafter the custom as it prevailed throughout the United States would be followed; only men or boys would be allowed to serve. The trustees demurred at this edict, but he stood fast. "It gives too young girles an opportunity of displaying an uncommon luxury, which may be offensive to many people, particularly to the protestants, who are not used to have such customs in their churches," he declared. He added that Dilhet had introduced the same reforms at River Raisin, where the congregation agreed that "nobody but men will present the Holy bread, or at most their wives . . . but in no case a girl." He and Dilhet also successfully persuaded the people to follow a more devout pre-Lenten attitude, particularly in foregoing the gay dances which were customarily held at that season.[29]

Dilhet was having more trouble than Richard. For some reason his parishioners resented him. Perhaps he was too strict; perhaps it was the nature of the people, as frontiersmen, to oppose any discipline. Richard referred to Dilhet as "a great Reformer," and expressed the belief that he was too scholarly to suit the taste of the simple River Raisin folk. Whatever the cause, they succeeded in making life miserable for Dilhet in many petty ways. He stood it as long as he could and then suggested to his flock that they raise enough money to pay the traveling expenses of a new priest. He sent his resignation to Bishop Carroll, went to Detroit and moved in with Richard.

The latter was glad enough to have him. Richard was extremely busy. His congregation was growing, and his pastoral duties were becoming correspondingly heavier. In 1802, when Dilhet left the River Raisin, Richard's active congregation consisted of eighty families, and they were spread over a distance of twenty-four miles below the town and seventy-five above it. There was plenty for an assistant to do. There was some discussion about building a chapel at Riviere aux Hurons, that is, at Clinton River, a convenient location for the communities north of town.

Even more important, having Dilhet's services at his disposal, Richard was able to give some attention to Mackinac, which had weighed heavily on his conscience. Despite his desire to return there, he had been unable to do so. No priest had visited the island since he had been there in 1799. Disturbing reports had reached him; the church had been defiled by a young Protestant who, in mockery, had placed a dead dog on the altar. The priest's house was being used for illegal purposes; and of the two trustees, one had died and the other was moving to Montreal. He wanted to have the books, vestments and sacred vessels brought to Detroit for safe-keeping. Dilhet was sent north in the summer of 1804 and remained at Mackinac for six weeks. He baptized a large number of children, performed several marriages, prepared a number of persons, including some Indians, for first communion, and generally reorganized the congregation.

Shortly before Dilhet made this trip, the United States had purchased Louisiana Territory from France through negotiations with Napoleon Bonaparte, who had acquired it from Spain. No one realized better than Richard what a tremendous acquisition it was. He wrote Bishop Carroll, calling attention to its importance, and pointed out that it would soon be necessary for the American bishop to provide new pastors "for this additional part of your immense diocese."

The first years of Richard's Detroit ministry were devoted to an enterprise which, considering conditions and resources, was almost monumental. This was the renovation and enlargement of St. Anne's Church. The church, the latest of several structures which served the parish, had been built about 1755. In the following years it had fallen into a state of disrepair. There is no good description available of its actual appearance or condition, other than that "it was a large building, towering far above the surrounding houses." Before Levadoux's departure, he, Richard and the trustees discussed plans for an entirely new church, evidently to be built outside the stockade. They talked in terms of a stone-constructed building, 106 feet long and 42 wide. But it was found that the output of the only quarry in the vicinity was already contracted for, so that phase of the design was abandoned. Subscription lists were opened. Parishioners who could do so pledged money; others offered materials and labor. Colonel Hamtramck promised £20; Levadoux and Richard one-fifth of the tithe for the year, valued at £40. L. J. Lasselle pledged £30 in merchandise or grain; John Shaw, two thousand bricks; Jean Yax, the labor of his mulatto slave. Others offered lumber, stone, the use of horses, and so forth.

Levadoux left before any actual work was begun, and the task fell upon

Richard. The rebuilding process was carried on for about two years, as far as can be determined. At the end of that time a serviceable and, by somewhat primitive standards, attractive church building was ready for parish use. A steeple had been added, a new roof put on and thirty additional pews installed, suggesting that the congregation was growing. All of this was not easily accomplished. At the time the work was completed in 1802, the parish was five hundred dollars in debt; however, it was estimated that the new pews would be rented for four hundred dollars a year. In addition, pledges were five hundred dollars in arrears. The manner in which the work was conducted was criticized by some of the parishioners. Richard said that fault was found with him because he "meddled" too much in the undertaking; some people said he did not do enough. As for himself, he replied to his critics on both sides, saying in a resigned voice: "I have tried to do for the best." In this instance, as in others, the dissension in the parish ranks seemed, at the moment, much more serious than it actually was. In due time, the rift was forgotten.

While all this was going on, the course of the history of Michigan and the Northwest was shifting to a new direction. In 1802, when the Northwest Territory was broken up by the admission of Ohio to statehood, Michigan became part of Indiana Territory. There was growing dissatisfaction with the governmental arrangement. The capital of Indiana Territory was at Vincennes, a long, difficult journey from Detroit. As a result, Michigan people were unable to send respresentatives to the territorial legislature; from 1803 to 1805 only one territorial court held sessions in Detroit. These circumstances led to growing demands for home rule, with the result that on January 11, 1805, Congress adopted an act, signed by President Jefferson, which established Michigan Territory, effective July 1.

The news of this important event reached Detroit a few weeks after the act was passed and was greeted by general rejoicing. Artillery salutes were fired, grand balls were held, and bumpers were lifted in toasts. President Jefferson proceeded to appoint members of the territorial government—William Hull of Massachusetts, governor; Stanley Griswold, of New Hampshire, secretary; and three judges: Augustus Brevoort Woodward of Washington, D.C.; John Griffin of Virginia; and Frederick Bates of Detroit. The townspeople, with the possible exception of Richard, eagerly awaited their arrival.

To Richard the change in governmental status was rather academic, since he hardly expected to be on hand for the great day when Michigan would assume independent territorial status. He daily anticipated the word which would recall him and start him on his way back to France. The pangs of homesickness which had assailed him in Illinois were no longer so acute, but he continued to regard his tenure at Detroit as temporary. He had proposed to his trustees that a fund be raised to pay transportation costs of his successor. He had communicated with Father Nagot about going back to France and had received a favorable reply. He had written Bishop Carroll that his departure was imminent; he even bade farewell to the members of his congregation, who responded by going to court and obtaining an injunction prohibiting his leaving. But even before this climax, something occurred that changed all of his plans.

Tuesday, June 11, 1805, dawned like most other days in Detroit. Farmers came to town early, for it was one of the regular market days, held twice a week. Everybody was talking and speculating about the big event, three weeks away, when the new territorial government would begin to function. The arrival of Governor Hull and his colleagues, the secretary and judges, was momentarily expected. It was a Catholic feast day, too, and by mid-morning St. Anne's was packed with worshipers. Father Dilhet was the celebrant of the mass, assisted by Father Richard. While this was going on, at the opposite end of the town, John Harvey, or one of his employes, was busy in the stable adjoining Harvey's bakeshop. No one knows exactly what happened, but it is the long accepted story that Harvey, or one of his workmen, knocked a live coal out of his pipe, setting fire to a pile of straw or hay. In a matter of minutes the building was afire and the blaze was spreading to neighboring structures. John Askin, standing on the Canadian shore, happened to glance toward Detroit and saw a huge column of smoke rising, and he rightly concluded that the whole village was doomed.

Fanned by its own momentum, the fire jumped the narrow streets. The houses were turned into flaming furnaces from which the occupants were barely able to escape. Futile efforts were made by soldiers from the fort and citadel to check its progress; a volunteer fire department went into action but found its pump clogged and useless. People ran to the river and sought safety offshore in canoes; others fled into the fields outside the town.

"The celebration of the jubilee was about over," Dilhet recorded, "and the town was filled with people who had gathered from the distant settlements to participate in this great event in a fitting manner by assisting regularly at the instructions, at Holy Mass and the other exercises, and by approaching the Sacrament of Penance. The fire began while I was engaged with Mr. Richard. I was interrupted by a person who came to inform me that three houses had already been burned, and there was little hope of saving the others. I exhorted all those present to help one another, and I went to say Mass with only one server. It was a low Mass, and when it was over we had hardly time to save the church furniture, the vestments, the household effects and provisions in the presbytery which adjoined the church. The flames spread with great rapidity, and soon enveloped both, though they were located on the outskirts of the town. In three hours (from nine o'clock to noon) the town was burned to the ground, and nothing could be seen but live embers, and chimneys which seemed to rise like pyramids. At the time of the fire there was no wind, the smoke and flames rose to a prodigious height and the entire town looked like a huge bonfire. It was the most wonderful, and at the same time the most horrible sight I have ever witnessed. . . ."[30]

Even before Dilhet had finished the mass, Richard was gathering up the sacred vessels which he carried to the common between the north stockade and the fort. There the townspeople gathered with what few belongings they had been able to save. Huddled together in their misery and dejection, they eyed the smouldering ruins. Detroit had vanished. All but two of its three hundred buildings were gone; nothing remained except the blackened chimneys, standing among the ashes.

The flames had not flickered out before Richard was at work, offering comfort, gathering supplies and seeking shelter for the homeless. That frightful moment of disaster had wrought a change in him. It was as though the searing heat had tempered his spirit and soul. Probably he, himself, was not fully aware at the moment of what was happening to him. But as the embers cooled, his heart went out to his stricken people. To give them back some measure of what they had lost, to provide for their welfare, became his consuming mission. There was no more thought of leaving Detroit, of returning to France. The idea had faded from his mind.

His people needed him. He would remain.

Surveying the scene of desolation before him, he murmured words of comfort and hope.

"Speramus meliora; resurget cineribus," he said. "We hope for better things; it will arise from its ashes."

Those words would, in time, be incorporated into the seal of the City of Detroit, a solace and a challenge to the citizens whenever adversity touched them.[31]

Chapter 3

The Citizen

A HOUSE DIVIDED

To the miserable inhabitants of Detroit, rendered homeless by the fire of 1805, it must have seemed like the end of the world. Much of what they owned, almost everything that was familiar to them, had disappeared in smoke and flame. But to Father Richard, the disaster brought new personal obligations. The civil authority was not yet established and the people had no one to turn to except their priest. He wasted no time. Up and down the river, on both the American and Canadian sides, he traveled, arranging quarters for the stricken townsfolk in the homes of the farmers, begging food and blankets and all else that a desolate people required.

"He trotted along the shore with his curious shovel hat held tight on his head and the long skirts of his coat of ancient pattern flapping about his legs," says George B. Catlin in *The Story of Detroit*. "With shouts he called out the Frenchmen and led them down to the shore, and soon he had two small flotillas of canoes and a couple of bateaux ranging up and down the river to bring corn meal, milk, eggs and other easily prepared foods from the farms along the shore."[1]

In the accounts that have been handed down, the only activity of which much is heard was his; no one else assumed responsibility, no one but Richard took over the tasks of leadership.

Gradually, under his direction, the natural ingenuity of the people expressed itself and a semblance of organization appeared. Some families moved into tents on the common, supplied, perhaps, by the military; others erected "bowers" for shelter until something more permanent could be obtained. Fortunately, it was at the beginning of the mild, warm season; there was no serious suffering from the elements. A few of the more enterprising citizens began to talk about rebuilding on their original lots, but there was, unfortunately, a shortage of lumber. Others, more easily discouraged, thought the future was hopeless and that Detroit was not worth restoring. They prepared to move away and seek homes elsewhere.

This was the situation on June 30, when Augustus B. Woodward, the newly appointed chief justice of the Territory, arrived in Detroit to join his judicial colleague, Frederick Bates, who, prior to the fire, had been engaged in business in Detroit. Woodward was shocked by the desolation that he saw everywhere, but he went among the people comforting them as best he could and offering words of encouragement. He suggested to those eager to start rebuilding that they wait the arrival of Governor Hull and the establishment of the new government. His advice was cheerfully accepted, and the people retired to their "bowers" for a few more days.

Governor Hull, his family, and Secretary Griswold appeared on the afternoon of July 1, the date the new territory came into being. Despite the warm welcome he received, he, like Woodward, was horrified by what he saw. According to Dilhet, he "spoke most sympathetically to the people of the loss which they had sustained, and inspired them with comforting hopes for the future."[2] The next day, July 2, he administered the oaths of office to Woodward and Bates, and the civil authority began to function.

Following the fire, Richard had set up an open-air altar, presumably in the orchard of the Macomb farm, which adjoined the westerly limits of the old town. This orchard was a popular place for outdoor meetings and assemblies. It was before this altar that the swearing-in ceremonies took place, a circumstance which won favor with the Catholic populace. Hull delivered a sort of inaugural address which, of necessity, was in English. Naturally, the French understood scarcely a word of it. That was rectified by either Richard or Dilhet who translated it so all could understand. Hull promised that immediate steps would be taken to rebuild the town, but he joined with Woodward in recommending that a plan should first be prepared for enlarging the village: giving it wider streets, larger lots and generally beautifying it. To this proposal the people acquiesced.

Woodward, Hull and Bates had the best of intentions. They went into immediate session to plat a new town which would include not only part of the former site, but a large piece of the adjoining, government-owned common as well. Some of the citizens would not wait, however. They began to build on their original lots. But most of the original property owners were willing to bide their time a little longer, accepting the Governor and Judge's plan. The design was largely conceived by Judge Woodward. He followed closely the layout of Washington, D.C., with which he was familiar. His plan included wide streets, grand avenues, parks, circles and circuses. Somewhat of a visionary, Woodward foresaw the day when Detroit would be a large, important city, and he wanted to prepare for its orderly growth.

"I have ever believed," he said, "that your new metropolis . . . is destined to have no common name among the cities which embellish the continent of North America, and that the melancholy conflagration of 1805 may by a judicious improvement of the calamity, be almost converted into a blessing."[3]

His vision was a great one, but it had a serious flaw. Neither the Governor nor the Judges had authority to give, sell or trade the public lands; only Congress could do that. So the Woodward Plan, as it came to be known, was taken late in 1805 to Washington by its chief author and Hull. Presented to Congress, it was allowed to languish for nearly a year and a half, and it was not until 1807 that the exchange of new lots for the old was authorized. The delay caused hardship and inconvenience and considerable resentment, which was aimed at the local officials, particularly Hull. Although he was a well-intentioned man, Hull was not a strong administrator, and he had a petty side to his nature. He could be jealous and vindictive, timid and stubborn. He quarreled with his fellow officials and with the people, who grew to distrust him. After the first few days in Detroit, he never again possessed the full esteem and confidence of the public.

Woodward proved to be the strong man of the new government. He was a close friend of Thomas Jefferson, and this gave him great prestige with the populace. He was an eccentric; he professed, with some justification, to be a scholar with a particular interest in natural science. He was sincerely devoted to the public welfare, and from the beginning, he and Richard found themselves kindred spirits with broad common interests. They became close friends and worked together effectively.

St. Anne's was having the same difficulties in getting its land allotment that the freeholders were experiencing. For a while after the fire, Richard conducted services in the open air or in a tent. Although such makeshift arrangements were all right during the warm summer months, they obviously could not serve permanently. One of the two buildings which escaped destruction in the fire was an old warehouse belonging to George Meldrum; it was located on the river bank near the foot of Wayne Street. This was rented and, at considerable expense, lumber was purchased and made into rough pews and other necessary fittings. Here, with the fragrance of incense mingling with the odor of raw furs, services were held for the next three years. Richard was without a rectory, and he made such shift as he could, boarding with whatever families had room for him. To add to his burden, Dilhet left in September for Baltimore where he remained for a short time at St. Mary's Seminary, then departed for France, dying there in 1811.

The site for a church, once the Governor and Judges had platted the new town, should have been no problem. Actually, however, it created a controversy which split St. Anne's congregation right down the middle and caused extreme bitterness between Richard and some of his parishioners.

On October 4, 1806, before most of the land allocations had been made, the Governor and Judges offered St. Anne's a new location on what was known as the Little Military Square. The offer, of course, was contingent upon the congregation relinquishing its claim to the original church site which was directly in the middle of what was to be Jefferson Avenue, the contemplated main east-west thoroughfare paralleling the river according to Woodward's plans. The new site which was offered was to the east of the old town, and consisted of a "lot fronting on East and West Avenue two hundred feet wide and running back two hundred feet deep, and bounded on three sides by three other streets." In modern Detroit, this location is between Bates and Randolph streets, fronting on Larned Street and extending back to Cadillac Square. Actually, possession of this land had been vested in St. Anne's parish since 1798 when the military commandant turned it over to the church for burial purposes. No use, however, had been made of it.

Richard and some of his people were satisfied with this arrangement, because if the new town developed as Judge Woodward planned, it would be a choice and valuable property. But many of the parishioners were not willing to accept the new site because the opening of Jefferson Avenue would cut through the churchyard which surrounded old St. Anne's. The habitants were superstitiously fearful of the consequences of their dead being disturbed. It had been contemplated, through a land donation by the Governor and Judges, to make a new cemetery farther north in the vicinity of present Grand Circus Park. Richard's intention was to remove the bodies from the old burying ground and re-inter them in the new one. But he met surprising and violent opposition. When the old graves were being opened, a crowd composed of the objecting faction threw dirt back into the openings as fast as it was removed. Large posts were driven into the ground to block opening of the new Jefferson Avenue, an act inconveniencing the town marshal who had to remove them.

The objectors did not stop with such relatively petty acts of interference and annoyance. A committee took the matter before the Governor and Judges and this, to some extent, made it a political issue. In their petition, they stated:

"Having maturely considered the proposal of the Legislature respecting the relinquishment of the ground held by the inhabitants of this country from the date of the earliest settlement, by their French ancestors as a public Burial and Church Ground Lot, in consideration of other ground delineated by the appellation of the little square near the Fortress of Detroit, we acknowledge the intrinsic value of the ground proposed to us, but owing to the strongest natural ties which spring from sources that imperiously bind our sensibilities as civilised men, must and do by these presents decline any alienation of such soil. . . .

"We appeal to the humanity of our fellow citizens to decide whether it would not evince in the highest degree a want of those humane and charitable qualities which are and ought to be the peculiar characteristic of Christians were we to abandon for the purpose of a common highway the earth in whose bosom reposes the remains of our fathers, our mothers and common kindred. O Sympathy! O Nature! where are thy Godlike Virtues by which the great Author of the Universe has distinguished Man!"[4]

Richard suspected that the real motive behind this opposition was the desire of one faction of the parish to build the church northeast of the town, much nearer their farms.

"The respect for the dead bodies is not in my opinion any more than a pretext that they have used to get those signatures in saying that they don't want to have the bones of their fathers sold," Richard commented. "That is false, for one of the conditions of the sale was that the skeletons were to be removed during the course of the summer. . . . I have the protest in my hand, and it is clear that a large number of persons who signed are what we might call voluntary persons and without property, and that a large number are false signatures."[5]

Nevertheless, for the time being, Richard did not insist on the removal. Fearing that the delay might result in forfeiting the new location which the government had offered, he suggested an alternate site for the church and the use of the Little Military Square either for a school or hospital "in which any poor, infirm or sick person, of whatever denomination, should be admitted." If this was done, an adjoining chapel should be erected and called St. Vincent's.[6]

The controversy continued to rage for about ten years. It was finally settled in 1816 by agreement on the part of St. Anne's to accept the new plot which was originally offered, plus some additional footage. The effect had been to delay for years the construction of a new church. What was worse, such bitter feelings were engendered that some prominent members of the parish were led to abandon their Catholic affiliations.

EXPERIMENT AT SPRING HILL

The dissension which thus split St. Anne's was understandably distressing to Richard. He said little about it publicly; instead he tried to heal the breach, compose the bickering factions, and work along with the local government to create a new and better community. Of course, the church was his chief concern, and his major efforts were directed toward holding his flock together. Without a proper church, lacking the religious facilities and inspiration to which they were accustomed, there was an inclination for the members to become lax in their duties, to drift away. To offset this tendency, Richard instituted a Confraternity of the Blessed Sacrament, through which his loyal parishioners, himself included, pledged to devote one hour of adoration daily before the altar. This was to be an around-the-clock procedure. Each member, through his own devotions, represented the entire parish. Young children as well as elderly persons joined; Richard took the hour from one to two each morning.

Despite such worthy devices, the fortunes of St. Anne's and the effective ministry of Richard were at low ebb. It was at this critical moment that the farmers north of the town chose to make matters more complicated. The habitants who occupied the ribbon farms along what was known as the Côte du Nordest were numerous, prosperous and influential. The Côte du Nordest, or Northeast Shore, included all of the river line from about present-day St. Antoine Street to the lower coast of Lake St. Clair, or to approximately Gaukler's Point. These people felt it would be unwise to rebuild St. Anne's in the town, either on the old or new sites. The proper location, they insisted, was in their part of the parish, some place convenient for them. In taking this position, they disregarded the requirements of the few French families in Detroit proper, and the many more living below the town. Following the fire of 1805, the Northeasters paid no attention to Richard and the rest of the parish and acquiring a large tract of land, ultimately known as the Church Farm, prepared to establish a new church on it. This land, which lay opposite the lower end of Belle Isle, had belonged to François Malcher, a silversmith who prospered by making jewelry and trinkets for the Indians. On his farm he first erected a rude log cabin, then a fairly pretentious house. Apparently, Malcher had no heirs and he let it be known he would deed his property to anyone who would agree to look after him in his old age.

This was the opportunity for which the Northeasters had been waiting. They made arrangements satisfactory to Malcher and took over his farm. Of this transaction, the Reverend George Paré, the archdiocesan historian, says:

"That Father Richard had anything to do with this arrangement is extremely doubtful. It was not in accordance with his plans, and neither he nor the Corporation of St. Anne had any control, but apparently were deliberately excluded.

"Thus provided for, the dwellers on the Northeast shore paid a deaf ear to Father Richard's appeals. They had a farm, a building that could be used as a church, they saw no reason why they should contribute to another, and they could bide their time until Father Richard came around to their views. But he was not so easily compelled, and his determination to resist them seems to be the only explanation of his next move."[7]

This consisted of going in exactly the opposite direction from the Northeasters and acquiring property down river, known as the Spring Hill farm, just east of the present Fort Wayne. Formerly the home of a collector of revenues who had defaulted on it, the farm, well equipped with buildings and other improvements, had reverted to the Federal government. In 1808, Richard leased it from the government for $205 a year and moved his base of operations to it.

Richard's primary motive in moving to Spring Hill was not to spite the Northeasters or to force them into compliance with his plans. Neither did it indicate his abandoning hope of building a new church in the town. In Spring Hill he saw a religious community, including a place of worship and a school primarily intended for the vocational training of Indians. It was the latter purpose, aside from the availability of the farm at moderate terms, which decided him in its favor. Spring Hill was located at a point near the river where there were flowing wells. From prehistoric times this had been a favorite gathering place for Indians. Here they had buried their dead and raised ceremonial mounds. It was also so situated as to provide a natural crossing place between the American and Canadian shores. In Richard's time, Indians were still in the habit of concentrating there. For that reason it was an ideal place from which he could carry on educational and missionary activities. In 1809, the Meldrum warehouse was abandoned, and the Spring Hill farm became, for the time being, the home of St. Anne's parish.

Unfortunately, the rift in the church left Richard without sufficient funds to carry on his work. After discussing his plight with Judge Woodward, he decided to go to Washington and other eastern cities and appeal for help from governmental and private sources. Armed with letters of introduction from Woodward to President Jefferson and other influential government leaders, he set out on an errand which was not to be entirely successful. He had hoped to finish his work in the East and then go to France for a visit, and solicit money there from his family and old friends. Although he made plans for the trip in company with a man named Edward Cole, and even booked passage on the ship *Mentor*, he had to cancel the journey.

In January 1809, he was at the nation's capital, and there he presented a lengthy memorial to Congress in which he not only asked that the Spring Hill farm be given to him outright, but he also requested an appropriation to provide for the education of Indian children.

"Everybody knows," he pointed out, "that Indians will do nothing to feed or cloth their children at the schools. Therefore if the Government wishes to have them civilised, and make them useful members of society . . . it becomes now as a duty on the part of the American white people to come to the assistance of their red brothers."

The results, he went on, would soon be apparent in more peaceful relations with the Indians. "A so Generous act of Benevolence towards them shall certainly prevent a sanguinairy war, which should be totally destructive of the settlements in the Territory of Michigan."[8]

Richard returned to Detroit in July 1809, confident that he would have public assistance. He had been kindly received by Jefferson; leaders of Congress had listened to him sympathetically. But the aid he anticipated was never forthcoming. He did solicit some private donations in New York and elsewhere, but his larger hopes ended in disappointment.

Alas, he had no idea at the time how quickly his project at Spring Hill would collapse completely. He paid no rent in 1809, believing the property was to be deeded to him. Perhaps it was because of his lapse, perhaps because others coveted the farm, but whatever the reason, the government was persuaded to offer it for sale at public auction in 1810. Richard was unable to match the bids, and it was sold for five thousand dollars to Judge James Witherell, one of the Territorial judges who had replaced Judge Bates. It was a disheartening blow to Richard; he was forced to start all over. He obtained a new location, known as the Loranger farm, a short distance above Spring Hill, between the present Twentieth and Twenty-second streets. There he converted an old barn into a combination church-rectory-school, and there he struggled along for the next several years under conditions which would have severely tried the patience of one less dedicated and devoted.

During all this troublesome period, Richard plodded along, taking care of his regular pastoral duties. He was, for more than a decade, the only priest in Michigan. In fact, for most of the early territorial period prior to 1816, he was the only clergyman of any denomination on the scene. In 1800, a young Protestant missionary, the Reverend David Bacon, had been sent out from Connecticut to work among the Indians, but, failing to accomplish much, he departed four years later. Officially, only the Catholic church was recognized in the Territory. In 1807, the Governor and Judges adopted an "Act concerning Religious Societies," to which it is believed Richard contributed both ideas and phraseology. This act mentioned the "Church usually denominated Catholic, Apostolic, and Roman." No recognition was given any Protestant sect, and when a few Presbyterians petitioned for land for a church site they were turned down because they were not recognized and did not qualify under the act. Years later, when they were permitted to incorporate, it was not as a Presbyterian society, but as the First Protestant Society of Detroit, indicating that the Governor and Judges conceded the lawful existence of only two general groups—Catholics and Protestants—and not denominational divisions of the latter.

Thus, through necessity, Richard's ministrations were not confined entirely to those of his own faith. Being a man of sympathetic nature, he undoubtedly comforted and counseled any who came to him. There are records extant indicating that he performed marriage ceremonies for Protestant couples. His work took him from the River Raisin to settlements on lower Lake Huron. He paid occasional visits to Father Marchand, who had the Assumption parish across the river in Sandwich. Commenting on Richard's many activities, Marchand said: ". . . he has only a wretched church building, a dilapidated warehouse serving as a church, no sacristy, no rectory. He lodges wherever he can. . . ." On another occasion, Marchand observed that "his parish is so extensive that I fear that all his projects will come to nothing. His enterprises are vast, and in a country poor and thinly populated. In that whole territory there is not a single individual who might be considered a rich man, or who deserves the title of rich."[9]

Indeed, Richard had nothing but a great faith, a vision of a noble future in an expanding United States, and the strength of character to meet and rise above adversity. But these were powerful weapons.

There were many signs, for those who took the trouble to read them, that the United States was advancing in strength and prosperity. Since the time Richard had been in Detroit, the nation's borders had been pushed back. Explorations as far as the Pacific Ocean, and into the southwest, were opening the way to valid claims to continental limits. In this period of national expansion, the Catholic church in the United States did not remain static either. Continuing immigration from Europe, as well as the beginning of the westward migration from the seaboard states, enlarged and diffused the Catholic population.

To meet the growing needs of the American church, Rome acted upon the recommendation of Bishop Carroll in 1808, and created four new dioceses with sees at Boston, Philadelphia, New York and Bardstown, Kentucky. The latter, the western diocese, included Michigan, and Richard thereafter looked to the little village south of Louisville instead of to Baltimore as his seat of authority. An old friend, Benedict Joseph Flaget, was nominated as bishop of Bardstown, but a feeling of his own inadequacy prompted him to decline the honor. He was, however, prevailed upon to reconsider, and in 1810 he was consecrated in Baltimore. Flaget, as his name suggests, was French and he was also a Sulpician. He had been ordained in 1787 at Issy. Flaget was among the group of émigrés who came to the United States in 1792; he preceded Richard by a few months. He first went west, as has been noted, at the same time Richard did, and served for two years at Vincennes while Richard was in Illinois. He was delayed in assuming the duties of his bishopric, not arriving in Bardstown until June 9, 1811. Thereafter, Richard had a firm friend and stanch supporter in the west.

During this period, and for a considerable time thereafter, the Northeasters posed a continuing problem for Richard and St. Anne's. One of the buildings on the Church Farm had been converted into a chapel; here services occasionally were conducted by Richard. On his visit to the east in 1808-09, he had gone over the situation with Bishop Carroll who wrote to the rebellious faction, urging them to accept Richard's decisions and compose their differences. To this appeal, the Northeasters replied impertinently, but with logic, that since the creation of the new diocese they were no longer required to accept Baltimore as their guide. Although other events intervened to prevent settlement of the controversy, Flaget interested himself in it and patiently tried to bring the opposing factions together. The War of 1812 brought its confusion. At the end of the war the civil authorities became impatient and hinted that unless the claim to the Jefferson Avenue site was given up, the offer of new lands in the town might be withdrawn. This threat made it all the more necessary for all groups to get together and agree on where the church would be located.

Flaget, in 1817, made a final decision. The new St. Anne's, he decreed, was to be established on the Little Military Square tract, and that was the end of the controversy as far as he was concerned. Flaget also reprimanded the people, declaring that "one of the adherents has been insolent enough to raise his hand in threatening violence against your worthy pastor who, for more than twenty years, has watered with the sweat of his brow this ungrateful land, sacrificing his own comfort and tastes that you might not be left without the ministrations of a priest, with no other thing to his reproach than an excess of goodness which I might call weakness." This rebuke was accompanied by the excommunication of seven of the Northeasters, and an interdict laid upon their chapel.[10]

Even these extreme measures did not reconcile the opposing parties immediately. Richard even suggested to Flaget that he transfer him to Ohio or Kentucky, in the belief that if he were gone one cause of the dispute might be removed. Flaget would not consider such action. Instead, the following year—1818—he made his first visitation to Detroit. There he held a series of conferences, ironing out the points of contention. He accepted the professions of repentance of those who had been excommunicated, and he lifted the interdict. Thus peace was finally restored. Richard at long last was in a position to proceed with the building of a new church that would meet the requirements of a growing community.

FOR THESE, MY PEOPLE

Gabriel Richard loved his adopted country and the people who inhabited it. The flaming enthusiasm that his friend and mentor, Levadoux, had for the United States and its principles was left to Richard as a sort of bequest when the elder priest was recalled from Michigan. From the time of the fire of 1805, when his personal fortunes were irrevocably cast with the Territory of Michigan, the United States and the American way of life had no more ardent advocate than Richard.

This feeling, which in many ways was to be the dominant emotion of his private and public life, was not rooted wholly in admiration of political principles, although that was a factor. He became a leader in civic activities and endeavors—beyond those of a strictly religious character—because the needs of his people required it. To serve them in every way, including arousing them politically, became an integral part of his ministry. This was the part of his life for which posterity, without regard for denominational lines, was to esteem him most.

The French habitants of Michigan Territory in the early days of Richard's ministry were politically immature. For nearly a century under the old French and British regimes, they had lived in a semi-feudal society. They held their lands originally by royal patent; they increased their holdings from time to time through private transactions with the Indians. The country was vast, the forests and the waters were generous. They appropriated what they needed from nature and asked for little more.

Because of their reliance on the fur trade, their agriculture remained in a primitive state; aside from the work of a few artisans and silversmiths, there was virtually no economic activity which could be described as industry. As late as 1816, Lewis Cass, who succeeded Hull as territorial governor, offered this observation:

"The Spinning wheel and the loom are unknown in the Country. Long since the territory was ceded to the United States and to a certain extent to the present day, the farmers were in the practice of drawing their manure upon the ice of the river during the winter, that it might be carried away into the Lake in the Spring. The wool of the sheep was thrown away and even now I presume a pound of wool is not manufactured in the Territory by any person of Canadian descent."[11]

In other words, their economy was one of bare subsistence. Politically, they were equally backward. They had lived, prior to 1805, under a military government which, although usually benign, was still a form of despotism. They had always been ruled; they had no clear conception of the rights and duties of a system of self-government which the United States, to a limited extent, offered them.

Richard was aware of the shortcomings of these people, and he was equally aware of the necessity for doing something about them. Migrants were pouring into the Old Northwest, coming mainly from the eastern and southern states. While this migration by-passed Michigan in its early stages, Richard, like other civic leaders who realized the Territory's potential, knew that eventually the Americans would move in, that they would become the majority.

Unless the French became Americanized, he feared they would become an impotent minority, in both religion and politics. He sought, therefore, for their own protection, to stir them, to educate them, so they would not be submerged by the Yankee influx. To this end, he wanted them not only to assume responsibilities as Americans, but to establish cordial working relations with the territorial government which, being largely in the hands of outsiders, could not always be expected to understand or be patient with their ancient way of life. The term was not yet coined, but Gabriel Richard became a public relations counselor for the Michigan habitants.

The concern which he felt for their future, and the goal he outlined, was well expressed by a notice which he caused to be published. It stated:

"Frenchmen of the Territory of Michigan! You ought to begin immediately to give an education to your children. In a little time there will be in the Territory as many *Yankees* as French, and if you do not have your children educated, the situations will all be given to the *Yankees.* No man is capable of serving as a civil and military officer unless he can at least read and write. There are many young people, of from eighteen to twenty years, who have not yet learned to read, but they are not too old to learn. I have known those who have learned to read at the age of forty years."[12]

As for himself, Richard's English improved greatly. He was able to write easily and fluently, and his letters soon lost all trace of the early difficulty which he had in expressing himself. However, in speaking, he never lost his accent, which was a source of amusement to his American friends.

Richard sought to impose a healthy discipline upon the gay, fun-loving French by discouraging their propensity for parties, fiddling and excessive drinking. One member of his parish recalled that he often thundered from the pulpit against the vices of intemperance and tobacco—"les chiquers et les irroques," as he called them. Sometimes his efforts to improve the morals of his people had unexpected results, as when he tried to reform the Yax brothers. According to the recollection of one venerable Detroiter, Richard often visited Peter Yax at his farm on the St. Clair River. Yax had three sons, all proficient fiddlers who were in constant demand to play at dances, thereby adding to the family income. Richard declared there was too much dancing among the young people and suggested that the sons of Yax amuse themselves in some other manner. On a subsequent visit, the priest said:

"Well, Monsieur Yax, not so much dance among the young people, I suppose?"

"No Father, not so much dance, but the young men get the cards and gamble," Yax replied sadly. "They drink whisky and get drunk. They curse and swear. No, not so much dance; oh, no, not so much dance!"[13]

History is silent about how Père Richard handled that.

The habitants had always gotten along with the Indians; they had tolerated the British. But when they rubbed up against the bumptious Americans for the first time, animosity sparked. The first Yankees with whom they had experience were mainly soldiers, and the early military was made up of characters who were not exactly ambassadors of good will. Others, from the east, most often of early Puritan stock, mistrusted the French, looked upon them as an inferior people only a cut above the Indians, and tended to be intolerant of the Roman Catholic religion.

In their sentiments, the French repaid them in kind. As F. Clever Bald, the distinguished historian of early Detroit, points out, language differences imposed a barrier to understanding and cordial relations. Judge Bates noted that the young ladies of the habitant families "had a strong dislike for Americans," and he bemoaned the fact that he "could make but little progress with the French girls." They regarded the Yankees, he said, as "a rough unpolished, brutal set of people," which, in all truth, was sometimes the case. A common term of contempt, used by the habitant with reference to the Americans, was "sacré cochon de Bostonnais," which, freely translated, comes out "Yankee pig." The Americans, on the other hand, found much to complain about and little to admire in the French. Solomon Sibley, one of the first Americans to enter the Territory, characterized them as "exceedingly ignorant and lazy." Provisions were short in Detroit, he suggested, not because the soil was unproductive, but because the French farmers were shiftless. Many Americans suspected the loyalty of the French, and Sibley expressed fear that if French troops should invade the country, the habitants and Indians would join them against the Americans and British. This, then, was the atmosphere of suspicion and dislike which Richard felt it his duty to change.[14]

Father Richard—"Reesh-aur," as the townspeople pronounced his name—set out to accomplish this, as Levadoux had done, by putting himself into the good graces of the civil authorities and accepting whatever civic obligations fell upon him. Among the first of these was acceptance of an appointment on April 20, 1805 to be chaplain of the first regiment of militia, an organization composed almost entirely of Frenchmen. This was, in itself, not a significant matter, especially in view of the fact that every able-bodied man and boy was required to belong to the militia and undergo periodic training. It simply demonstrates that Richard was willing to conform to custom and to serve in what, for him, was the most appropriate capacity. In the same manner, every resident of Detroit was a fireman. Alarms brought out all able-bodied men to form bucket brigades; Father Richard rarely failed, it is said, to be in the ranks.

More important was his habit of lending his prestige and name to enterprises which the habitants formed for their mutual advantage. As early as October 26, 1807 his name appeared on a petition to Congress, asking for a review of land claims and an extension of time under which titles might be certified. Many of the farmers, up and down the river, held their land, as has been stated, by royal grant or by private purchase from the Indians. Following the American occupation of the Territory, it was required that these grants be reviewed and confirmed, and a deadline was set under which this was to be done. Either through neglect or ignorance, many of the French did not comply with the deadline which resulted in their titles being clouded. Moreover, some of them had long been encroaching on public lands in the rear of their farms. Facing the loss of this privilege, they asked that these lands be given to them.

"Most of the inhabitants in the old Settlement on Detroit River," their petition stated, "have claimed by virtue of ancient written titles, only a single piece of ground extending forty arpents [a linear arpent was the equivalent of twelve rods] in depth, by two or three arpents in front and rear. These few arpents have, in a long course of Cultivation, become almost wholly cleared up and worn out; and for many years we have been obliged (as well as our fathers before us) to have recourse to the lands in rear to Supply one of the first necessities of life in this climate, wood for fuel, for building, for fences. These rear lands have also been essential for subsistence of our Cattle. To be now cut off from this resource would throw us into a state of want and suffering, which could not be supported."

A few landholders had valid claim to farms of eighty arpents in depth. The petitioners asked that their farms be extended back that distance, thereby establishing a standard or common boundary.[15]

Richard was not the author of this petition, although his name appeared on the list of signers, and this despite the fact that he was not known to possess, at that time, any property which might be involved. But he knew his signature would carry weight. Moreover, it is more than probable that he carried the petition with him when he went to Washington in 1808 and presented it to Congress. It might be noted that the requested adjustments were made.

It was such problems that made Richard realize that unless the French became familiar with American law and custom and cooperated with the government, they would have constant difficulties. To make things easier for them, Congress was handed another petition, this one quite possibly inspired, if not written, by Richard, asking that the laws of the Territory be published in the French language.

"Sincerely attached to the government of the United States and viewing with appreciation and approbation the care which has been taken for the welfare of their local government," the supplicants declared, "it is knowledge and not good intentions which your petitioners need to make them capable of satisfying their ambition to show themselves worthy citizens of this young and splendid republic. . . . As soon as the Congress of the United States is informed that outside of the garrisons and their neighborhoods, nineteen-twentieths of the inhabitants of this country speak only the French language and that most of them are completely ignorant of the English language, your petitioners flatter themselves that the generosity and policy of the Congress of the United States will willingly bear the expense of authorizing an edition of their new territorial code in the French language as well as several of the more important laws of the Union."[16]

This petition, reasonable and sensible, appealed to Congress, and the request was promptly granted.

For twenty years following the territorial establishment, it was customary for the inhabitants to make known their wants and their complaints to Congress, or to their local officials, through the medium of petitions. And in almost every instance in which the public interest was involved, Richard's name was prominent among the list of signers.

Through considerate activity, Richard earned the respect and friendship of the English-speaking Protestant element of Detroit, thereby helping establish better understanding between them and the French. He initiated the practice of conducting non-denominational religious services for those who were without any formal church organization of their own. Itinerant Protestant preachers did appear in Detroit from time to time, but their visits were infrequent. It may also be assumed that occasional army chaplains attached to the garrison were available. But for the most part, the non-Catholic needs of the community were unfulfilled until Richard stepped into the breach. One of the earliest acts of the territorial government had been to construct a Council House—a stone structure housing government offices and designed as a place where Indian councils could be held. In this building, at the invitation of the town's Protestants, Father Richard regularly conducted services in English on Sunday afternoons. More in the nature of discourses than formal religious services, these meetings were well attended, often by such dignitaries as Governor Hull and his family, and by the judges and other officials.

This activity was regarded dubiously by Father Marchand from across the river, and Richard felt obliged to explain his purpose in a letter to Bishop Carroll in 1807.

"This letter is to have you advise me on a point of my present conduct that seems somewhat irregular on some respect," he said. "About the end of August last, I have been invited by our Governor and some other Gentlemen to try to preach to them in the English language. Although I was sensible of my incapacity, as there is no other English minister of any denomination, I thought it could be of some utility to take possession of the ground. In order to prevent any irreverence towards the Blessed Sacrament, I have found proper to hold our English meetings not in our chapel but in the Council House. As there are many prejudices against our Society particularly among the people of the lower class, or mechanics (N.B. in the whole town there are no more than two English persons of the Roman Cath. Society), I found it would be a great point if I could obtain that they were willing to hear me. For that reason I have chosen for the subject of my Discourses to establish the General Principles of the Christian Religion, that is to say the Principles used in the discovery of truth, the several causes of our errors, the existence of God, the spirituality, immortality of our souls, the Natural Religion, and the several evidences of the Christian religion in General; I have avoided to make any other ceremony but a Discourse or familiar conference. To make an experiment, that plan may take more than a year before I should enter into any discriminating point of the Cath. faith. Every Sunday since the 30th August I have met about twelve o'clock in the Council House for the above purpose. Last Monday, Mr. Marchand, the priest of the British side, advised me to write to you as that matter of preaching seemed to him a little strange and it is to comply with his direction that I now pray you to direct me on this important affair. . . ."[17]

There is no record of the bishop's reply to this letter, but it is known that Richard continued to hold this kind of service at intervals until 1831. The remembrance of them to the present-day among Detroit Protestants adds greatly to the high regard in which the memory of Richard is held by all groups, regardless of sect or belief. As a preacher, he was handicapped by a slight accent. Nevertheless, he was described as eloquent. A few of his listeners thought his discourses were over-long.[18]

Another matter in which Richard interested himself at this period, and which caused him much concern, was the realtionship of the whites with the Indians. It was natural that he should have this feeling for purely humanitarian reasons; but he also sought their conversion and spiritual welfare as part of his pastoral work. Beyond that, he was troubled by the possibility of an Indian uprising, which could be disastrous for the French. That such a danger existed, he knew full well. The supplanting of British supremacy in the Northwest by the United States resulted in disruption of the fur trade upon which the Indians relied almost exclusively for existence. The United States was slow to adopt an enlightened Indian policy; the result, particularly in the north, was a general unrest, which the British exploited. If hostilities exploded, the French, living on their isolated farms, would find it difficult to defend themselves. Their plight was well expressed by the statement: "Every individual house is a frontier."[19]

Richard was particularly distressed by the effects of the liquor traffic which went hand in hand with the fur trade. During his visit to Mackinac in 1799 he had the opportunity of seeing the results at their worst.

"The most part of the trade," he reported at that time, "consists only of liquors. As long as it will be so, there cannot be any hope of making them [Indians] Christians. The traders themselves confess that it would be better for their own profit to not give rum to the Indians, but as the Indians are very much fond of it, every trader says that he must give them rum not to lose all his trade. . . . God knows how many evils will flow from that trade. Some have observed that English rum has destroyed more Indians than ever did the Spanish sword."[20]

He was determined to do what he could to stamp out the liquor traffic, going so far as to threaten to excommunicate any of his parishioners who sold spirits to the Indians.

In the light of Richard's attitude there is something puzzling in the accounts of Joseph Campau, merchant. Campau imported from time to time fairly large quantities of wine for Richard. While Richard was brought up in the vineyard country and must have been accustomed from early youth to the consumption of wine, the amounts which Campau obtained for him seem to exceed what was required either for sacramental or personal table use. Richard certainly did not give it to the Indians; there was some speculation that it was intended for medical use, or that he may have resold it to the public to raise funds for his church.

Producing an even more immediate crisis than the liquor traffic was the government's acquisition of Indian lands without, at least as Richard felt, just compensation. The errors which he believed the government to be making, were described in a letter to Bishop Carroll in 1807.

"The news of this day is that our Indians (who were assembled here from several quarters to make a Treaty and sell a certain Tract of land where many white people have already made Improvements) have plainly refused to sell any parcel whatever, alledging that they have been cheated already too much."

They complained, he continued, that some lands previously sold by them for only half a cent an acre, were being resold by speculators for as much as fifteen dollars an acre.

"The Indians are every day complaining of the Americans in general on that account particularly. . . ."[21]

This letter was forwarded by Carroll to the Secretary of War who placed it in President Jefferson's hands. It prompted immediate action on his part and resulted in instructions intended to add a larger measure of justice to the official Indian policy.

The situation which Richard reported, Jefferson said, "ought absolutely to stop our negotiations for land. Otherwise the Indians will think that these preparations are meant to intimidate them into a sale of their lands, an idea that would be most pernicious and would poison all our professions of friendship to them. The immediate acquisition of the land is of less consequence to us than their friendship and thorough confidence in our justice. . . ."[22]

This conveys a picture of the active and useful life which Richard was leading, a picture brought into sharper focus by Bishop Plessis of Quebec, after a visit to Detroit.

"This ecclesiastic," Plessis noted of Richard in his journal, "is . . . thoroughly estimable on account of his regularity, of the variety of his knowledge, and especially of an activity of which it is difficult to form an idea. He has the talent of doing, almost simultaneously, ten entirely different things. Provided with newspapers, well informed on all political matters, ever ready to argue on religion when the occasion presents itself, and thoroughly learned in theology, he reaps his hay, gathers the fruits of his garden, manages a fishery fronting his lot, teaches mathematics to one young man, reading to another, devotes his time to mental prayer, establishes a printing press, confesses all his people, imports carding and spinning-wheels and looms to teach the women of his parish how to work, leaves not a single act of his parochial register unwritten, mounts an electrical machine, goes on sick calls at a very great distance, writes letters and receives others from all parts, preaches every Sunday and holyday both lengthily and learnedly, enriches his library, spends whole nights without sleep, walks for whole days, loves to converse, receives company, teaches catechism to his young parishioners, supports a girls' school under the management of a few female teachers of his own choosing whom he directs like a religious community, while he gives lessons in plain-song to young boys assembled in a school he had founded, leads a most frugal life, and is in good health, as fresh and able at the age of fifty as one usually is at thirty."[23]

The only criticism of his habits, coming from another source, was that he ate too much meat and not enough vegetables.

Such was the stuff which our pioneers were made of and by which the American frontier was molded!

THE RICHARD PRESS

While on his eastern junket in 1808–09, Richard somewhere acquired an organ and a piano, or harpsichord, which he shipped back to Detroit. These two instruments were welcome gifts to the habitants. A gregarious, socially-inclined people, they loved music and delighted in singing. A piano and an organ, the first of either to be seen in the Territory, were important cultural additions, and the latter, it may be assumed, lent dignity and charm to the services at St. Anne's. Richard was said to have been accomplished on both instruments, and even composed music for them.

But that eastern trip produced something much more significant; something which marked an important advance in the Americanization of the frontier. This was a printing press, known as the Richard Press. Unfortunately, too little is known about it, and about Richard's connection with it. It was purchased—for how much and with what funds are not known—from one G. G. Phinney, of Herkimer, New York. From this fact it may be surmised that the press and the type had been used in that town, although one historian says Richard acquired it in Boston while other accounts say it came from Baltimore. About the time the press arrived in Detroit, there also appeared a journeyman printer, James Miller of Utica, New York. That Richard influenced him to go to Detroit along with the mechanical equipment is more than possible.

There had been a printing press in Detroit during the period of British occupation. It was used exclusively, as far as can be determined, for printing

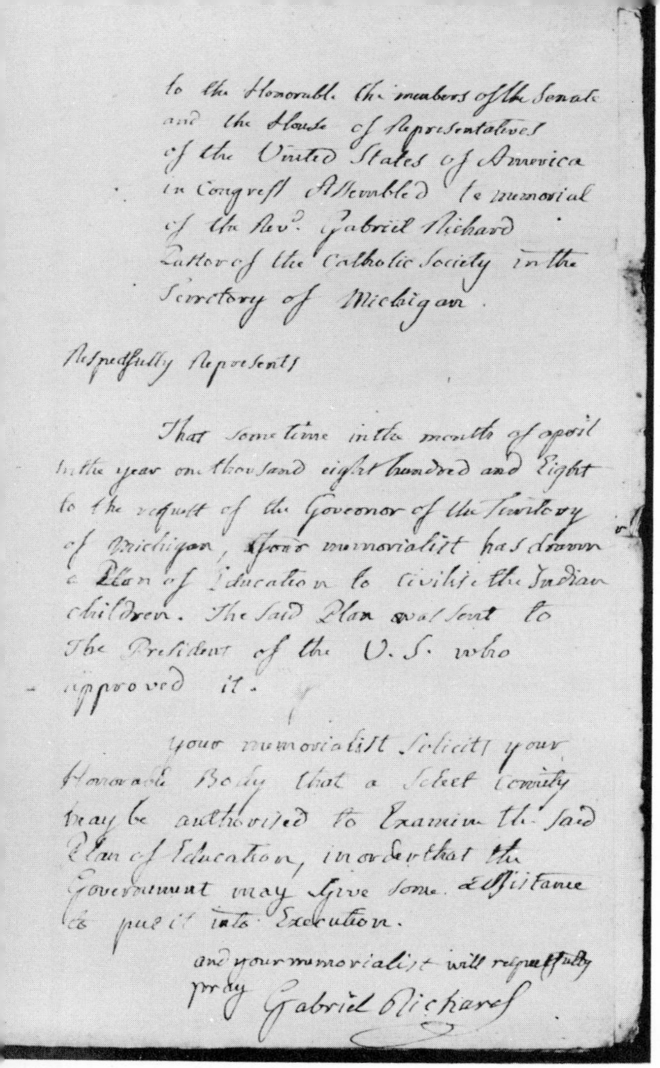

To the Honorable the members of the Senate and the House of Representatives of the United States of America in Congress Assembled the memorial of the Revd. Gabriel Richard Pastor of the Catholic Society in the Territory of Michigan.

Respectfully Represents

That sometime in the month of april in the year one thousand eight hundred and Eight to the request of the Governor of the Territory of Michigan, your memorialist has drawn a Plan of Education to civilise the Indian children. The said Plan was sent to The President of the U.S. who approved it.

your memorialist Solicits your Honorable Body that a Select comity may be authorised to Examine the said Plan of Education, in order that the Government may give some assistance to put it into Execution.

and your memorialist will respectfully pray
Gabriel Richard

Courtesy of Burton Historical Collection

Courtesy of Burton Historical Collection

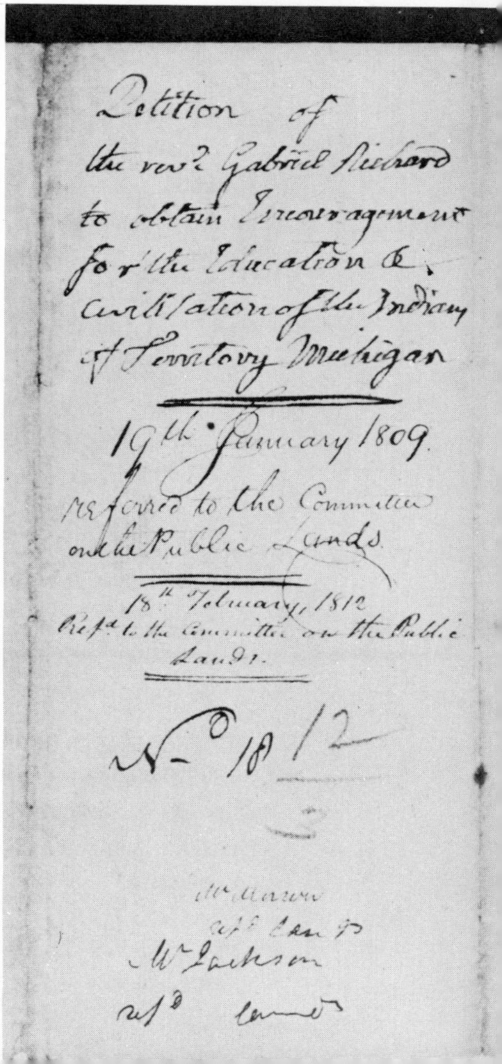

Petition of the revd. Gabriel Richard to obtain Incouragement for the Education & civilisation of the Indians of Territory Michigan

19th January 1809.

referred to the Committee on the Public Lands.

18th February, 1812
Refd. to the Committee on the Public Lands.

No. 1812

Mr Jackson

The preamble to Richard's "Outlines of a Scheme of Education," a petition he presented to Congress in 1809 "for the education & civilization of the Indians" of the Territory of Michigan. This preamble consisted of the foreword shown on the right, followed by the letter above. It specifically requested that a congressional committee examine the merits of his plan for Indian education and the possibility of its execution. Richard's interest in Indian education was life-long.

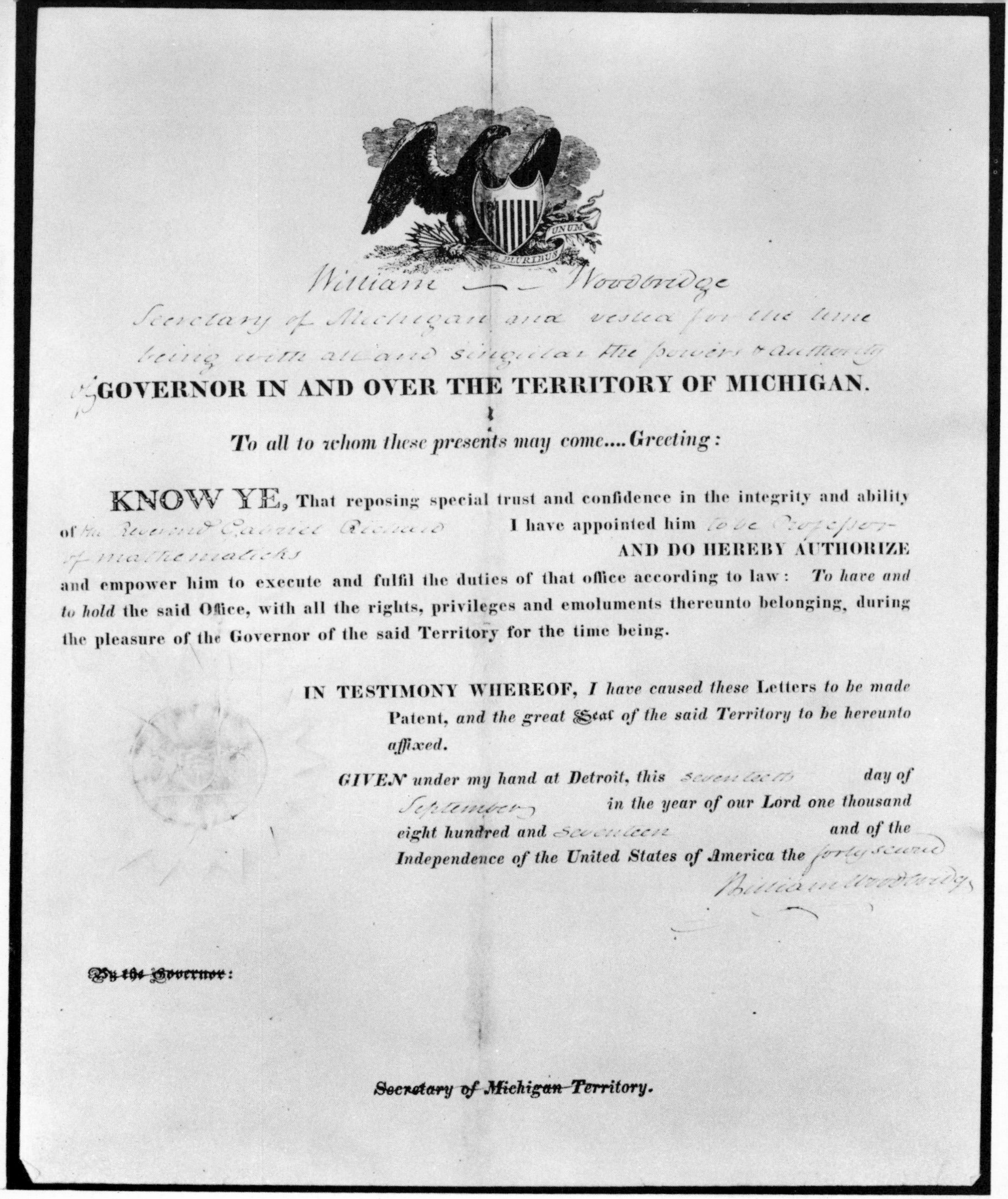

E PLURIBUS UNUM

William Woodbridge

Secretary of Michigan and vested for the time being with all and singular the powers & authority

of GOVERNOR IN AND OVER THE TERRITORY OF MICHIGAN.

To all to whom these presents may come....Greeting:

KNOW YE, That reposing special trust and confidence in the integrity and ability of the Reverend Gabriel Richard I have appointed him to be Professor of mathematicks AND DO HEREBY AUTHORIZE and empower him to execute and fulfil the duties of that office according to law: *To have and to hold* the said Office, with all the rights, privileges and emoluments thereunto belonging, during the pleasure of the Governor of the said Territory for the time being.

IN TESTIMONY WHEREOF, *I have caused these* Letters *to be made* Patent, *and the great* Seal *of the said Territory to be hereunto affixed.*

GIVEN under my hand at Detroit, this seventeenth *day of* September *in the year of our Lord one thousand eight hundred and* seventeen *and of the Independence of the United States of America the* forty second

William Woodbridge

~~By the Governor:~~

~~Secretary of Michigan~~ Territory.

Courtesy of Detroit Chancery Archives

The document appointing Richard to the professorship of Mathematics at the University of Michigania (Michigan). It is dated 1817. In addition, in two other documents, he was designated professor of astronomy and professor of intellectual sciences. This latter appointment also carried the responsibility and rank of the vice-president of the university.

Replica of a plaque commemorating the first building which comprised the University of Michigania (Michigan) in whose founding Gabriel Richard played such an important role. The building was erected in 1817-1818 in Detroit on what is now the west side of Bates Street between Larned and Congress. This replica is now in the lobby of Detroit's City-County Building, which now stands adjacent to the former site of the University of Michigania building. The location of the original plaque is unknown.

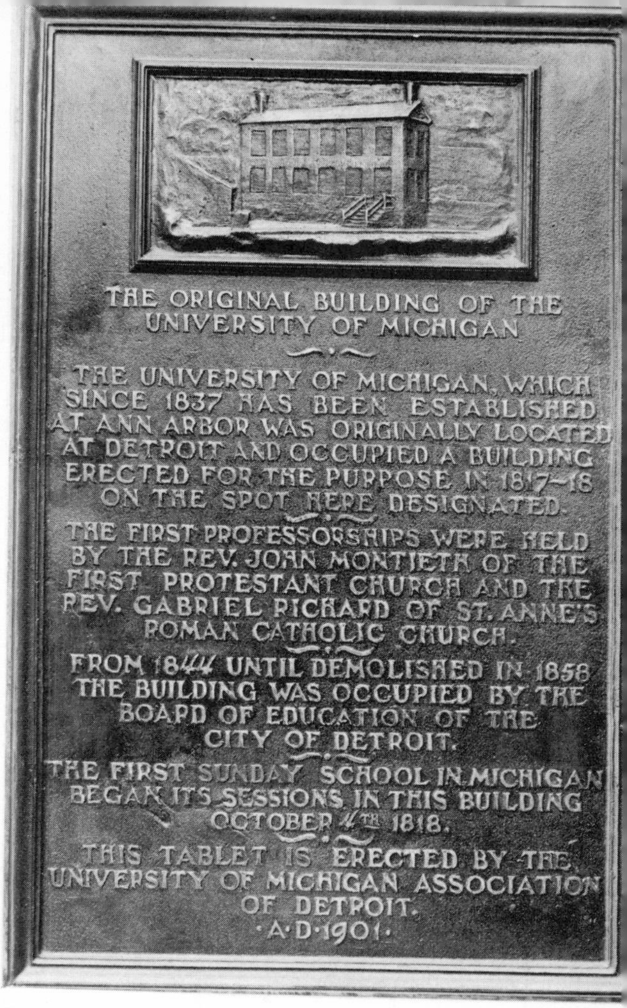

Photograph by Henry Leung

The University of Michigania's (Michigan) first building as seen about 1858 when it was being torn down. Its cornerstone was laid on September 24, 1817. Richard taught classes here for a brief period. After the university was established at Ann Arbor this building was still maintained as a branch, but it was finally abandoned.

Courtesy of Burton Historical Collection

An engraving of St. Anne's Church as it appears in the *Detroit City Directory* for 1837 (now in the Detroit Public Library's Burton Historical Collection). The structure shown here is now on the site of the Greyhound bus terminal, Bates and Larned Streets. It stood until 1886.

business forms. About 1800, it was sold and moved to Niagara. This resulted in a hiatus during which a critical need developed for some vehicle of public information. Richard employed his sacristan, Theophilus Mettez, as a public crier. Taking up his station outside the porch of St. Anne's following Sunday mass, Mettez would cry the news, including such titbits as notices of auction sales, when the next horse races were to be run, and the bargains being offered by local merchants. The Pittsburgh *Commonwealth*, first issued in 1805, devoted considerable space to Detroit news and had the widest circulation of any journal in Michigan Territory.

Richard returned to Detroit in July 1809. The press, type and a large stock of paper must have preceded him, because by August 1 the press was set up and operating. On August 31, Detroit's first home-town newspaper appeared on its streets. *The Michigan Essay; or Impartial Observer* was its name.

Although Richard was the entrepreneur, he was neither editor nor publisher of the paper. These functions were performed by Miller, although the priest obviously was a contributor. The announced intent was to publish every Thursday; the first issue—Volume I, Number 1—consisted of four pages with dimensions of nine-and-a-quarter inches by sixteen inches. Each page had four columns. Despite the fact that relatively few of the French could read, the *Essay* was printed in English, except for one-and-one-half columns written in French, probably by Richard.

The contents consisted of the customary "foreign intelligences," brief items culled from the London *Morning Chronicle*, the Liverpool *Aurora*, the New York *Spectator*, the Pittsburgh *Commonwealth*, the Boston *Mirror*, as well as Baltimore and Dutch papers. The items undoubtedly were merely reprints of dispatches which came into Miller's hands. This supposition is borne out by the fact that the briefs were several months old. But of course, they were new to Detroiters. As was often the early journalistic custom, there was no local news, editors apparently assuming that everything worth knowing circulated through the community by word of mouth faster than it could be put into print. It was information about the outside world for which readers thirsted.

A great part of the *Essay's* first issue consisted of pirated literary selections, including extracts from Young's *Night Thoughts*, and from Ossian. There were three short poems, and essays on such varied subjects as manufactures, politeness, early rising and husbandry. Advertisements were few. One called attention to St. Anne's school; others were in the nature of institutional ads for books, published and to be published by Miller, who also doubled as bookseller and book publisher. One of the ads offered *The Child's Spelling Book; or Michigan Instructor*, "Price 25 cents, single." It was a recent product of the Richard Press. Other books listed for sale included about thirty titles of popular and religious works. These came from other presses. Advertising rates were fifty cents per square for the first insertion; twenty-five cents thereafter. Subscription prices were five dollars per year for Detroit subscribers; four dollars and fifty cents by mail to Upper Canada and Michigan and four dollars elsewhere.

The *Essay* was obviously an experiment and not a successful one. It has been said that three or four issues were published, but that is probably incorrect. No known copies exist other than Volume I, Number 1, which was almost certainly the only one. Yet, it was not a complete failure. It not only established the tradition of journalism in Michigan, but it did more. Paul J. Foik, in his article, *Pioneer Catholic Journalism*, says of Richard and the *Essay*: "The establishment of this periodical was part of his comprehensive scheme for the enlightenment of the people of his own flock and of the Territory at large. As an initial step in such a plan for the uplifting of his fellow citizens, the newspaper was perhaps the best means that he could have employed. We may regard this scheme of Father Richard as one of the determining causes which gave to this country its first Catholic periodical."[24]

If the *Essay*, for whatever cause, failed, the Richard Press did not. It filled a definite local need for commercial items, largely consisting of blank legal and business forms. It turned out a stream of pamphlets and other documents, some of the latter being related to affairs of the territorial government. Miller continued in charge until 1810. He was succeeded by Aaron Coxshaw, who trained Mettez, the sacristan, as Detroit's first printer's apprentice. The latter learned his trade well, and in 1812 became the proprietor of the press, operating it from a farmhouse a short distance below the town.

The chief value of the press was its output of books—a commodity hard to come by on the frontier. All told, there was a total of fifty-two known imprints. *The Child's Spelling Book*, previously mentioned, was the first, dated August 1, 1809. It was followed over the years by a succession of such titles as *The True Principles of a Catholic*, in 1810; collections of prayers and other religious items; school books and reprints of classical works, including a collection of La Fontaine's fables. Many of these books reflect the need as well as the influence of Richard; they were intended for his pastoral use, for the instruction and elevation of the Catholic mind. Most of the published works in the latter category bore French titles and were in French text, but some were in English. As far as can be determined, Richard wrote nothing original for publication, unless it was the spelling book, although, as has been stated, he was the translator of some of the press's items. It is certain that he exercised general supervision over its operation and output.

All of the known imprints appeared between 1809 and 1816. After that date, the press, as far as is known, ceased to operate. In 1817, the *Detroit Gazette,* an English language paper, was established, and for the next several years it adequately met the Territory's journalistic needs, its shop filling all local job requirements. What became of the Richard printing press remains a mystery, although its type was preserved, if not used, until 1843, when seven hundred pounds of it were sold to two local printers who in turn disposed of it to a type foundry at Buffalo which probably melted it down.

One of the most interesting uses to which the Richard Press was put was the production of material reflecting Richard's interest in civic affairs. On September 26, 1809, a broadside was published containing a report of a grand jury severely criticizing Governor Hull. The grand jury had a dual function; it not only issued true bills, it also acted as a public forum in which governmental matters relating to the needs of the people were discussed. Under the system known as the Governor and Judges, the grand jury took the place of a representative body, although it had no power to enforce any of its recommendations. Governor Hull had become increasingly unpopular, and the broadside described a number of alleged instances of official misconduct and abuse of office. It was followed three weeks later by a reply from Hull, printed by the press in French, defending his actions.

In October 1809, perhaps as the result of the grand jury report, a committee of citizens met in the tavern of Richard Smyth and adopted a resolution calling upon Congress to abolish the Governor and Judges in favor of a representative form of government. This, too, came off the Richard Press in broadside form, and, in addition to being sent to members of the House and Senate in Washington, it was distributed in Michigan, printed both in English and French.

One of the last productions of the press was a book of one hundred and thirty-eight pages, handsomely bound, and published in 1816, containing a compilation and digest of the territorial acts. Known as the *Cass Code,* this work was long regarded as the manual of jurisprudence upon which the basic framework of Michigan law was erected. It represented a prime example of the usefulness of the Richard Press as a civilizing influence on the western frontier.

THE DRUMS OF WAR

The War of 1812 broke with devastating fury across the Old Northwest. The forests echoed to the shrill of the war cry; the clearings were made hideous by the red flames that consumed the cabins of the settlers. Michigan Territory came to know the brutality of armies, the horror of massacre, the bitter taste of defeat. It was another of those "times that try men's souls." It offered a test of Gabriel Richard's loyalty to the United States, and he met it without faltering. Of all the leading citizens of Michigan, he emerged from that conflict with his reputation spotless, his prestige undimmed.

Speaking at a later time, William Woodbridge, one of Michigan's foremost statesmen during its territorial and early statehood period, described in eloquent words the conduct of the priest during the war.

"He is zealously attached to this nation," Woodbridge declared. "I know of but one instance in which he ever occupied himself with the political concerns of the Country. It was when the enemy were in possession. It was when destruction stared this people in the face, when the Tomahawk was over every man's head. It was when every persuasion was at the same time used to alienate the affections of this people from the nation. It was then that Mons. Richard came forward zealously, boldly and with devotedness to the cause, using that powerful influence which he had acquired over the minds of his people and kept them fast in their faith. Not one within his influence ceased for a moment to remain true and faithful to the United States. . . ."[25]

Those words were truly spoken. Not only did Richard, even when suffering persecution, remain steadfastly loyal to his country, but he also provided an example which the habitants followed. All the fears that the French might go over to the enemy, or at best remain neutral, proved groundless. Rosters of the territorial militia reveal that it was largely composed of French serving as officers and enlisted men. The Detroit River area saw a considerable amount of fighting; it suffered hardships more severe than almost any other part of the United States. Yet there is not a single known incident in that region of French defection to the British or Indian side, although there were some at Mackinac and elsewhere where Richard's influence did not reach. In those perilous times, the United States boasted no better citizens than the Frenchmen of Michigan. History may well accord to Gabriel Richard the credit for Michigan remaining a part of the United States instead of being absorbed into British Canada.

The story of Richard requires no detailed account of the course and events of the War of 1812. To the eastern United States "Mr. Madison's war" meant one thing; to the west it was something else—a matter of survival as much as anything. Of what Richard thought, how he reacted, what he did, little is known from his own writings or statements. He was too preoccupied with events to keep any record of them. Certainly he did not consider himself as one cast in the hero's role. Most of what is known of his activities comes from what others said; unfortunately, these accounts are sparse and lacking in detail.

As far as the Northwest was concerned, the War of 1812 was inevitable. Those who took the trouble to inform themselves knew it was coming far in advance. The intransigence of the British, who never gave up hope of regaining the country, was one factor. From Fort Malden, below Detroit, their agents wooed the Indians and won them to the British cause. Throughout the western war, the Indian alliance proved to be Britain's sharpest sword.

On the other hand, American Indian policy played into British hands by alienating the tribes in the west. This policy was weak, short-sighted and inhumane. While an occasional voice was raised in Washington on behalf of justice for the savages, the Americans' chief interest was to acquire tribal hunting lands as cheaply as possible. This led the Indians to commit atrocities upon the settlers; the latter thirsted for revenge and hated the English for their suspected part in encouraging the depredations which kept the frontier aflame for years.

For a decade prior to the actual outbreak of the war, Detroit lived in constant dread and regular anticipation of an Indian attack. Governor Hull pleaded with Washington for protection.

"You cannot be insensible to our situation here," he told the Secretary of War in 1807. "In the neighborhood of a British Garrison, and settlements, and accessible to vast bodies of Indians, on whose friendship and fidelity, it is impossible to make any certain calculations, separated by an extensive wilderness from any settlements, which could reasonably afford us aid. We have only to depend on our own exertions for safety." He added that all reports coming in from the Indian country indicated "that their intentions are hostile to the U. States, and they are meditating to strike upon the Americans somewhere."[26]

It has been observed that Richard in 1809 warned the government that it should adopt measures to civilize the Indians in order to avert "a sanguinairy war." Two years earlier he had warned that "they shew some disposition to go to war." Richard was at the time enlisted in George McDougall's company of infantry, ready to bear arms for the defense of the country.

Despite these and many more danger signals, the outbreak of hostilities in midsummer of 1812 found the United States woefully unprepared to defend its northwestern frontier. A brigade of Ohio militia was hastily organized; these, with a regiment of regulars, were marched to Detroit where they were augmented by the local militia. The entire force, numbering between twenty-five hundred and three thousand men, was placed under the command of the governor, General William Hull. In July, Hull invaded Canada where he was opposed by an inferior British force. But having crossed the Detroit River, he refused to attack, giving the enemy opportunity to bring up reinforcements. While Hull was wavering indecisively in Canada, he received the shocking report that Fort Dearborn, on the present site of Chicago, had surrendered and its garrison was massacred. News also reached him that Mackinac had fallen. The loss of the latter was a real disaster because it freed the warlike northern Chippewa to join the alliance of Wyandots, Pottawatomies and Shawnees under Tecumseh on the Detroit front. Frightened half to death at the prospect of a savage horde being thrown against him, Hull evacuated Canada and sought safety in the fort and behind the stockade of Detroit. Then, on August 16, without firing a shot, he surrendered his entire army and all of Michigan Territory to the able and daring General Sir Isaac Brock. It is significant that of the entire American force, only a small detachment of Ohio volunteers under Colonel Lewis Cass and the Detroit militia regiment, composed almost wholly of French, showed a willingness to fight. But Hull allowed them no opportunity; they were included in the capitulation, the terms of which Brock dictated and had struck off in broadsides by the Richard Press.

The American army was transported to Canada. Its officers, including General Hull, were taken to Montreal; the rank and file were paroled and sent to their homes in Ohio. The Michigan militia was disarmed and the men paroled and permitted to return to their farms. General Brock left immeditely after the fall of Detroit for the Niagara frontier. He was succeeded in command by his senior colonel, Henry Procter, a violent, brutal man, who felt his position so insecure that he resorted to the worst kind of repressive measures against the Michiganders. There followed a reign of terror and hardship under which the habitants, plundered and threatened by Indians, oppressed by the British, lived in constant fear of their lives and property.

Not even Richard was immune from indignities at the hands of the

Indians. One band, according to Silas Farmer, stole the pipes of his organ and used them as horns, "making the woods ring with their shouts and tooting." Unable to stand the noise any longer, one citizen told the Indians they were blowing upon the flute of the Great Spirit and that the sound might displease him. Before the day was over, every scattered part had been returned from whence it had been stolen.[27]

What Richard's activities were at the beginning of hostilities is not entirely clear. There is evidence that he operated a hospital in Detroit. At least a few days after Hull's surrender, he received a voucher from James Abbott, the postmaster, for ten dollars "for one month's rent of an Hospital," to be paid by the United States government whenever it was in a position to do so.

Immediately after the capitulation Richard apparently resolved to maintain a strictly aloof attitude, respectful but not friendly, to the British invader. The day after Hull's surrender, he and Father Marchand, who was intensely pro-British, called on Procter to pay their respects.

"He was received," Marchand reported, "with politeness, but I am uncertain as to the outcome. Richard has always shown himself extremely republican, and even anti-British, a sentiment from which, as I have often told him, he might well refrain."[28]

Marchand had reason to be apprehensive about his colleague's conduct. When Richard observed the Indians making free in the town—plundering the homes of the citizens, waving bloody scalps in the streets and offering prisoners for ransom—completely unrestrained by Procter or other British authority, he could remain quiet no longer. The people themselves were driven to the brink of rebellion; and Procter, as he became more apprehensive, became more of a tyrant. Richard championed the people; he was utterly disgusted by the savage repression. British military officials began to view him with suspicion as a troublemaker. One officer remarked to Marchand, "We know that gentleman. His principles are too much at variance with ours."

Marchand became increasingly worried as he saw his friend drifting into danger. "All this," he said, "will prove dangerous for him. He loves to talk politics, and if things are not conducted according to his ideas, he is neither slow nor gentle in expressing his opinion."[29]

In late January 1813, an American relief column of Kentuckians under the command of the incompetent General James Winchester was surprised and completely defeated at River Raisin. The day after this debacle, the Indians ran wild and massacred about three hundred American prisoners while the British looked passively on. The lives of others were spared; they were paraded through the streets of Detroit, and Richard joined other citizens in ransoming them. Civilian indignation became so intense that Procter declared martial law and ordered thirty leading citizens of Detroit into exile. Although Richard, as Paré points out, was a marked man, he was permitted for some unexplained reason to remain behind. But no threats quieted his voice, and his contempt for Procter and all his evil works was so strongly and openly expressed that the British commander at last felt compelled to take measures. He insisted that Richard take an oath of allegiance to the crown, but Richard refused, stating: "I have taken one oath to support the Constitution of the United States and I cannot take another. Do with me as you please."[30] The words have a somewhat apocryphal ring, but at any rate Richard was placed under arrest and taken across the river to Sandwich as a prisoner.

There is some confusion about Richard's status as a prisoner. It has been said that he was held in the jail at Fort Malden; there is other evidence that he was placed in the custody of Father Marchand and subjected to what amounted to house arrest. The latter is likely more correct, although he may have been detained for a short time at Malden. Whatever the circumstances of his detention, his imprisonment lasted about three weeks.

On the night of June 16, Procter strode into the Assumption rectory with Jacques Baby, an influential Canadian. He offered Richard a choice of exile, or of signing a bond to keep his opinions to himself. Paré describes the scene in the following words:

"Thinking only of the welfare of his people, Father Richard signed while the candle light flicked on Procter's red face set in its half circle of beard, and on Baby and Father Marchand, waiting their turn to sign as witnesses. Father Richard was now free to return to Detroit. . . ."[31]

What persuaded Procter to release his prisoner makes a dramatic story. Richard was held in high esteem by many of the Indians. It has been related that when Tecumseh, the leader of the Indian confederation, and a chieftain of humane and chivalrous instincts, heard about Richard's arrest, he went directly to Procter and demanded that he be set free. Unless this was done instantly, he threatened to gather his warriors and return to his tribal lands on the Wabash, leaving the British to conduct the war as best they could. Procter feared his red ally almost as much as he did the Americans. Moreover, he was under orders not to interfere with the Indians. He had no choice except to bow to Tecumseh's ultimatum.[32]

The accuracy of this account has been challenged, but there may be an element of truth in it. It may explain the reason Richard was released from the

Fort Malden jail, if he actually was held there, and turned over to Father Marchand's custody.

That was about the end of the trouble with Procter. By the summer of 1813, the American forces were gathering for the relief of Michigan; in September, Oliver Hazard Perry's flotilla defeated the British fleet at the memorable Battle of Lake Erie. This opened the way for General William Henry Harrison's invasion of Canada. Procter evacuated Detroit and fled eastward with his army. In October, he was overtaken at the Thames River and his force destroyed. A coward, Procter ignominiously fled the field before the final issue was determined; Tecumseh remained and died.

Now there was peace along the border, but the people of Michigan were in no condition to enjoy it. As war's aftermath, famine's hand hovered over the land. During the period of fighting and British occupation, farmers had been unable to put in any crops. Foraging soldiers—American as well as British—and Indians had stripped the countryside of food and clothing. The inhabitants had nowhere to turn for relief except to the government. Unfortunately, hostilities had not ended on other fronts in the United States, and the supply of armies took precedence over relief for civilians.

Lewis Cass was named territorial governor on October 29, 1813, succeeding Hull; for the next eighteen years his was to be the dominant personality in Michigan. He was all that Hull was not: a decisive, vigorous man; a capable administrator possessed of the knack of bringing together all factions to advance the public interest. He was well aware of the plight of the people, and he begged for Federal assistance. Even the troops left in the garrison were on starvation rations. Fishing details were organized among the soldiers so they would have something to eat. Because of official duties, Cass was absent from the Territory during most of 1814 and early 1815, the time of the worst distress. It fell upon others, principally Judge Woodward and Father Richard, to organize some kind of emergency relief.

"The desolation of this territory is beyond all conception," Woodward reported to the Secretary of War. "No kind of flour or meal to be procured and nothing for the subsistence of cattle. No animals for slaughter and more than half the population destitute of any for domestic or agricultural purposes. The fencing of their farms entirely destroyed by the incursions of the enemy and for fuel for the military. Their houses left without glass and in many instances even the flooring burnt. Their clothing plundered from them by the Indians.

"It is a literal fact, and it will scarcely be deemed permissible to shock the feelings of human nature so much as to state it, that the inhabitants of the River Raisin have been obliged to resort to chopp'd hay, boiled, for subsistence. Many possessing neither firmness of mind or body sufficient to sustain the calamities with which they have been assailed have sunk into that asylum where the wicked cease to trouble, and the weary are at rest.

"I would humbly suggest to government to allow a supply of provisions to the amount of a thousand dollars to be purchased at Erie in Pennsylvania and transmitted to this place for the relief of the Territory generally; to be distributed by the commandant on the certificate of the Roman Catholic Clergyman, a gentleman of the firmest patriotism, and of unquestionable and unquestioned purity and virtue. . . .

"This country will be destitute of seed-wheat this season. I suppose five hundred bushels would supply it. In affording relief it might be well not to overlook that object. They will never again give a similar trouble; and while objects of splendid charity, such as the relief of Venezuela, and the western islands of Europe, have not been unattended to, shall it be said that the more humble and perhaps more immediate duty of relieving these inhabitants has been neglected? I should suppose if there is, as there usually is, a contingent fund at the disposal of the President a little of it might be applied in this way."[33]

Richard added his voice to those of Cass and Woodward. To the commandant at the fort, he sent an urgent plea for assistance for Francis Pepin, "the most distressed person existing in the territory . . . afflicted with a palsy, and Dysnry." The following day he sent this appeal: "Since you are a friend of humanity, see this poor woman burdened with a family, who for eight has had no food but corn soaked in water. To accord her a ration is to render her a great service."[34] He also extended his welfare ministrations to the sick soldiers of the garrison.

At last help came from Washington. Fifteen hundred dollars was earmarked for the people along the River Raisin, but Cass, deciding others were suffering just as much, spread the money around where it was needed.

The regulations covering the distribution of these and other funds stated: "In order that the public bounty may not be misapplied the Governor has determined that a certificate shall be given by the commanding officer of the company in whose bounds the applicant resides, stating his infirmity or inability to support himself which certificate shall, if the person be of the roman Catholick religion be countersigned by the Revd. Mr. Richard and a Justice of the Peace, if the person be not of the Roman Catholick Religion, it shall be countersigned by two Justices of the Peace."[35]

"In extending it [relief] to the people of the Territory," Cass said, "I consulted with the Catholic Rector whose ecclesiastical Jurisdiction comprehended the whole country, and whose character as well as office gives to his representations upon this subject great weight. To him I have committed the task of distribution . . . the resources of this country are totally inadequate to support the number of indigent and helpless people in it. I am told by the Catholick priest that in the immediate vicinity of this small place, there are not less than forty widows with families. They are in a state of actual want, and unless the arm of the General Government is extended for their relief, their sufferings must be extreme."[36]

In time, seed for the 1815 crop was shipped in, along with sufficient cattle to restock the farms. The distribution of all was supervised by Richard, who became a real, if unofficial, relief administrator. Through his efforts, the people were tided over until the 1815 crop was harvested, and peacetime commerce was again able to provide the items of food, clothing and other materials which were so badly needed.

Richard resolved that the bounty of the government and the sympathetic assistance of Cass should not be taken for granted by the people. He sent out a call for a meeting to be held January 14, 1816—a sort of general thanksgiving observance. There he offered, and his parishioners adopted, a resolution expressing their gratitude for what they had been given in the trying months just past. The resolution asked that Governor Cass, "who is himself entitled to the Gratitude of the Inhabitants, be respectfully requested on behalf of the said inhabitants of the said territory Michigan to express to the President of the U.S. the high sense they entertain of the innumerable favors received from the Bounty of the Government during his administration, and especially in procuring provisions and seed wheat to the poor, in the said territory. Resolved 2/y, by the said inhabitants of Detroit and its vicinity that a copy of this Resolution shall be forwarded to the President of the U.S. as a token of their approbation and as a merited tribute of their acknowledgement of his truly paternal benevolence, and as a perpetual testimony of their attachment to a Government always just and generous."[37]

The trying times were over. The shoots of loyalty which Richard had cultivated in the hearts and minds of his people had flowered. Americans and French settled down, side by side, to enjoy the blessings of peace, and to prepare for a dawning era of growth and prosperity.

Due in large part to Gabriel Richard, there were no longer any Frenchmen in Michigan Territory. Now, there were only Americans.

Chapter 4

The Educator

"SUFFER THE LITTLE CHILDREN..."

ONE HAD only to scratch Gabriel Richard, priest, very lightly to find Gabriel Richard, schoolmaster.

His background, training, and expressed interest, all indicate that he regarded education and the development of schools as an integral part of his ministry. From the time he left the seminary, Richard considered himself destined for a career within the church as a scholar and educator, instead of as a priest primarily devoted to pastoral work or the missionary life. The vocation of seminary professor had strong appeal for him; his early plans envisioned a continuance of that role, even after he was forced to leave France and go to the United States. He never abandoned hope of finding that niche in life. No matter where he set his feet, no matter how raw the wilderness or crude his surroundings, he always saw, just ahead, a school or a seminary. The realization of one, or the other, or both, was part of the task to which he was dedicated. The history of education in the early stages of territorial development is virtually his personal history.

He was admirably equipped for the role of educator, possessing all the attributes of a scholar, plus a quick, eager and penetrating mind. One of his colleagues said that he spoke and wrote seven languages; in all probability at least one of them was an Indian tongue. The breadth of his interests is revealed, as much as anywhere, in his library, a collection which at one time must have been fairly extensive. It is easy to believe that in his day it was without equal in Michigan. He apparently was not a particularly creative scholar; what he wrote himself consisted mainly of philosophical analysis and comment on the works of others. Yet, these were often acute and, as related to his time, occasionally profound. He carefully preserved much of this material, some of it dating back to his own seminary days. When Theophilus Mettez learned the bookbinder's art, Richard kept him well occupied binding his treatises and commentaries, some printed, some in manuscript form. He wanted to save these against the day when they would be used again as the basis of discourses and lectures in his own seminary. The greater part of this material, naturally, was theological. Some of it was related to such fields as philosophy, rhetoric and physics. There were treatises on divine attributes, human behavior and canonical law.

His library contained, in addition, standard classical works with a range which extended from theology and philosophy to science, law, history and literature—and education. Among his books was a copy of Blackstone's *Commentaries*. More curiously, there was a treatise in his own hand on legerdemain in which was described the use of disappearing ink, how to make a bouquet of flowers grow magically out of an urn, how to make a card change color, along with some notes on horoscopes.[1] What use he made of these curiosa is not known. It is pleasant to speculate that he practiced the arts of bafflement and exhibited them to the delight of the small fry, white and Indian. In one of his lists of supplies there is the intriguing requisition for "a case of viper's bones."

There were occasions when Richard's educational projects appeared grandiose and impracticable. There was, for example, his plan for a seminary in the Illinois country. Obviously, it could not be a success both from the standpoint of the small population from which students would be drawn and from the generally low level of educational background which existed on the frontier. At the time, Richard was new in the country; he may have been disappointed that he was not able to stay in Baltimore or Georgetown as a mathematics instructor. He was trained for the task; and when he reached the Illinois country, and later in Michigan, he did not want that training to be wasted. Accordingly, he may have felt the urge to utilize it without first weighing how effective it could be.

In Detroit, his opportunities were somewhat better. There existed among the general population a small element of sufficient wealth and culture to give education real meaning. Some of the people, principally the English and Americans, sent their children to eastern schools and academies. Others used facilities closer at hand. There had been itinerant schoolmasters and private schools in Detroit long before Richard's arrival; there would be others during most of his residence there. But such instruction was for the fortunate few, and at best, it was somewhat haphazard and uncertain. There was no general system of schools for the sons and daughters of the poor, or even for those in moderate circumstances. The French, exhibiting little interest in learning, probably would not have taken advantage of them in any case.

In Michigan, as in Illinois, Richard's first thought was for a seminary. His letter to Bishop Carroll, following United States acquisition of Louisiana, has been referred to. In pointing out to Carroll the extent of the addition to the latter's diocese in 1803, and the eventual need of new parishes and priests to serve them, Richard definitely was thinking of a seminary in the west. It was this idea which prompted him and Dilhet "to look for young children in my parish that could be brought up to be priests." He and Dilhet went ahead with their seminary plan, and in October 1804 Dilhet opened a "college or clergy school" with an enrollment of nine boys. This enterprise was to have been partially supported by the grant of a township, given by Congress, and partly through the efforts of Richard. Similar grants were made by the government in later years for the support of public schools, particularly in 1826, when the Territory's educational establishment was more matured. The course of study in Dilhet's "college" included Latin, geography, history, sacred music and mental prayer. The school did not flourish; and within a year, it was abandoned, due, as Richard explained, to "the scarcity of Scholars."

Now the more practical side of Richard's mind asserted itself. He realized that children must first be given an elementary education before they could successfully cope with the advanced work of a seminary. Lower schools, then, became his immediate objective.

The fire of 1805 seems to have ignited in Richard a new determination to get his school plans under way. If conditions following that disaster were not exactly propitious for such an undertaking, the challenge was that much greater. Schools were opened shortly thereafter, both for boys and girls. Unfortunately, not much is known about them; the information which has come down is incomplete and often confusing. The first accomplishments are described by Paré who says there was most likely a boys' school in existence in 1806; four schools are mentioned for 1808, although there is no proof that all of them were sponsored by Richard. An account of 1808, which Paré accepts with some reservations, takes note of an academy for young men under the direction of Richard, with assistance of a M. Salliere, "a young professor of literature, chemistry, and astronomy, whom Father Richard had brought from France. . . ."

It was to obtain support for these efforts, the last mentioned in particular, that on October 3, 1806 Richard petitioned the Governor and Judges in the following terms:

"Gabriel Richard prays that for the purpose of erecting a College in which will be taught the languages ancient and modern, and several sciences and enabling him to render the education partly Gratuitous, the Corner lot on the military square of the section number 3 and the whole same section or a part thereof according to the will and benevolence of the Legislature be given." This request was supplemented by another submitted by two instructress in a girls' school sponsored by the priest, in which the authorities were asked to donate still another lot "for the purpose of erecting a young ladies school."[2]

The term "college" which Richard used in his petition meant academy or high school, being used in the sense familiar to him, that is, the college he had attended in Saintes.

It would be doing a disservice to his memory to assume that in this early period he alone was interested in schools and some form of public education. Others were also concerned, among them Governor Hull, and principally Judge Woodward. After the War of 1812, Governor Lewis Cass and Territorial Secretary William Woodbridge were also champions of schools, and they became strong allies of Richard. All of these men had good backgrounds. Hull was a graduate of Yale College; Woodward of Columbia College; while Cass received a sound classical education at the Phillips Exeter Academy in New Hampshire.

Thus, it is not surprising that soon after Richard had submitted his petition for school land, Woodward offered a resolution to the Governor and Judges, pointing out that "it is expedient to provide by law for the establishment of one or more seminaries of learning in the Territory of Michigan." Hull rarely agreed with Woodward on any subject, but referring to this resolution, he commented that "nothing can be more laudable; nothing more useful; it will advance the future prosperity of the country and the happiness of millions yet unborn—To effectuate so important a measure every means in our power ought to be exerted, and our labours ought never to cease untill the object is accomplished."[3]

Reference has been made to some women who assisted Richard in conducting his schools. Actually there were four of them—Elizabeth Williams, Angelique Campeau, Elizabeth Lyons and Monique Labadie. They were all from good families and presumably had better than average educations. They formed a sort of sisterhood which Richard contemplated formalizing into a religious order. In his plans for it, Richard often referred to it as the Monastery of St. Mary. Although it did not materialize, Miss Williams and Miss Lyons did eventually enter religious houses; Miss Labadie married; and Miss Campeau continued to serve the parish and diocese, her status unchanged, until her death in 1838.

These four teachers, whom Richard called "sisters," accomplished so much teaching children and particularly girls, that the priest in his will of 1806 bequeathed "two hundred and fifty dollars to the new school founded by Angelique Campeau and (or) by Elizabeth Williams, together with my tables, chairs, my clock, six maps, bed, cathecisms, Instructions de Jeunes Gens, Alphabets."[4]

The support which Richard received from the Governor and Judges was more of the moral than the material variety, but evidently it inspired him to present a more comprehensive plan for territorial schools. It should be noted that while he later outlined a parochial school system, his first thoughts were for general public education.

This plan, dated October 1808, called attention to the fact that a building for an academy was then being constructed on the Canadian side of the Detroit River. It would be shameful, he declared, if the American citizens failed to do as much on their side of the border, and he called upon the legislature (Governor and Judges) to help match the Canadian effort.

Attention was called to what he had accomplished and sought to accomplish. In Detroit, there were two English schools, plus four others for boys, and two for girls at various localities outside of Detroit, three of which were conducted by young men who had been trained by Dilhet in the short-lived seminary.

"At Spring Hill," Richard continued, "under the direction of Angelique Campeau and Elisabeth Lyons, as early as the ninth of September last, the number of the scholars has been augmented by four young Indians headed by an old matron their grandmother of the Pottawatomies tribe, five or six more are expected to arrive at every moment.

"In Detroit in the house lately the property of Captain Elliott, purchased by the subscriber for the very purpose of establishing one Academy for young ladies, under the direction of Miss Elisabeth Williams there are better than thirty young girls who are taught as at Spring Hill, reading, writing, arithmetic, knitting, sewing, spinning, & in these two schools there are already nearly three dozens of spinning wheels, and one loom, on which four pieces of Linen or woolen cloth have been made this last spring or summer.

"To encourage the young students by the allurement of pleasure and amusements, the undersigned had these three months past sent orders to New

York for a spinning machine of about one hundred spindles, an airpump, and Electrical Apparatus &. as they could not be found he is to receive these falls but an Electrical machine, a number of cards, and few colours for dying the stuff already made or to be made in his Academy.

"It would be very necessary to have in Detroit a Public building for a similar Academy in which the high branches of Mathematics, most important languages, Geography, History, Natural and moral Philosophy should be taught to young Gentlemen of our country and in which should be kept the machines, the most necessary for the improvement of the Useful Arts, for making the most necessary physical experiments and framing a Beginning of public Library. . . ."[5]

Some time earlier, the Governor and Judges had authorized a series of lotteries to provide revenue for public undertakings for which the Federal government made no appropriations. Richard suggested that the proceeds from at least one lottery be devoted to the maintenance and management of the schools he had described. The lotteries were never held, so no means were forthcoming from that source.

Meanwhile, the Spring Hill school, as he described it, was in operation, and the enrollment of Indian children entitled him to some financial assistance from the government. On April 30, 1808, the Secretary of War instructed Governor Hull "to inform Mr. Richard that, as soon as his proposed establishment shall be in operation, from 2 to 400$ a year, will be advanced . . . towards the Expense of educating Indian Children. . . ."[6]

BROTHERS ALL—INDIAN EDUCATION

Providing funds for educating Indians was part of a broad policy, very dear to the heart of President Jefferson. It would be, he hoped, the means whereby the tribes would be put through the civilizing process and transformed from nomadic hunters into sedentary farmers. This policy was based in part upon what Jefferson considered to be lofty humanitarian principles; in part it was a means of rationalizing the grab of Indian lands at a tiny fraction of their real worth. Whether acquisition of Indian lands was good or bad from the national standpoint, it was definitely not good for the Indians; and it contributed to the frightful incidents which marked the War of 1812 in the west. Richard, as a representative of a highly civilized European society, subscribed to Jefferson's plan and became an instrument by which it was implemented. His concern was not with obtaining vast tracts of hunting domain. On the contrary, as has been seen, he objected vigorously when he felt the Indians were being victimized by the government. His chief interest was in winning infidel souls. To his way of thinking, the most logical manner in which this could be accomplished was through the civilizing process. In his mind, the two things went hand in hand.

This was the germ of the idea behind his Spring Hill farm. This enterprise was to be both church and school, and the latter was to provide him opportunity to conduct some very interesting educational experiments. First, and most important, the Spring Hill community would enable him to educate Indian and white children together, a process which, he felt, would create understanding and break down the barriers between the two races.

He described this plan to the President when he first sought to obtain Spring Hill; it was his justification for asking that the property be given to him. After reading Richard's letter, written sometime early in 1808, Jefferson passed it on to his Secretary of War with the comment that "the writer appears to have that sincere enthusiasm for his undertaking which will ensure success. The education of the common people around Detroit is a most desirable object, and the proposition of extending their views to the teaching the Indian boys & girls to read & write, agriculture & mechanic trades to the former, spinning & weaving to the latter, may perhaps be acceded to by us advantageously. . . ."[7]

Encouraged by Jefferson's favorable reaction, Richard petitioned Congress for an outright grant of Spring Hill during his visit to Washington early in 1809. He went further, and in the name of the Wyandots who, he claimed, had given him authority to represent them, he requested that a farm allotment be given to the head of each family of the tribe, and to each youth "who shall be placed and will have remained Eight years and been Educated in the above mentioned Seminary." These farms were to be cut out of a tract between the Huron and Ecorse rivers, then occupied by the Wyandots. The parts not subdivided, he suggested, might be kept as a reserve for the endowment of the school. Parts of the reserve "could be used and cultivated, as praemiums, by Such Indian children who shall have made more progress in the said Seminary." The management of the entire enterprise, he urged, should be under the local Catholic priest.[8]

Undoubtedly, the subject matter of this petition had been discussed with the President before it was presented to Congress; in fact, the whole idea strongly suggests that the course Richard followed was laid out for him by the President. The petition was received and referred to the House committee on public lands, and there, due to other more pressing considerations, it languished.

With this appeal to Congress, Richard also undertook to submit, with the prior approval of the President, and at the request of Governor Hull, a comprehensive prospectus for a system of education especially adapted for use in Michigan Territory. The tone of much of this outline has a surprisingly modern sound.

He first proposed establishing several free primary schools at distances of from five to six miles from each other. He conceded the difficulty of staffing such schools because of the shortage of trained teachers. "In fact," he declared, "the worst trade in the territory of Michigan is to be a school-master." For this reason, government subsidy would be necessary because qualified instructors could not exist on the contributions which parents of the pupils would be able to make. This incapacity, he continued, was the result of a lack of industrial enterprise among Michigan's inhabitants. To remedy this, he recommended "that the theory and practice of Agriculture and of the most useful arts and Trades, as carpenter, black-smith, shoemaker, weaver &c. may become a part of the System of Education of the youth. . . ."

Richard then proceeded to lay out a curriculum for boys and girls which included reading, writing, "ortography," arithmetic, geography, "use of the Globes," grammar, history, natural philosophy, and composition, while advanced students would be taught languages and higher mathematics.

"The young ladies," he explained, "shall be instructed in the different branches of needlework, sewing, knitting, spinning, &c. the husbandry shall not be omitted, nor such of the fine arts as music drawing & which may contribute to the youth an innocent amusement."

Recreation would have an important place in Richard's program. "Children," he declared, "must be lead to science and virtue by a flowery road. The hope of pleasure shall be the best allurement to study. It is a great & very useful art to surround the most important truths with a circle of agreable Ideas. The Thorns of the most severe virtue, are charming when they are conveniently twisted with the flowers of pleasure. The wise Nature leads man to the food of his body by attraction of pleasure. As the truth and knowledge are the food of our mind, a wise instructor must surround it with the honey of amusement and pleasure."

He then went on in his comprehensive prospectus, to discuss what should be done for the children of Indians who, he contemplated, would be admitted to his school on an equal footing with the whites. This, of course, was the crux of his civilizing process. Indian pupils would be exposed to the basic academic subjects, but the major emphasis would be on vocational studies, including "hoeing, gardening, plowhing &c."

"Let them," he suggested, "make their own bred, raise hemp & flax, let them make their own cloths, let them learn to build their own houses, let them take care of the sheep which will supply the wool to cloth them. let the Girls spin that wool, and moove the shuttle, let them meelk the cows, raise large quantity of chicken &c. &c."

Those who proved to be proficient scholars should be rewarded with tools and household implements to be given them "at appointed times in the middle of many spectators under the shade of trees planted by themselves, at the sound of the greeting and martial music executed by their companions of the school. &c. Such public exhibitions should certainly excite the ambition of the children and draw the attention of their parents.—Let it be a rule that at the end of their education, one cow, a pair of oxen or a horse, and a farm of so many acres of land more or less in proportion of the progress made by each, be given as rewards."

The net result, he concluded, would be that the Indians would realize "they are all Brothers, and believe to be one and same people and one family."[9]

Unfortunately for Richard, Thomas Jefferson was no longer President after March 4, 1809. He was succeeded by James Madison who, at the moment, was more concerned with allaying the dangers of a British-Indian war and matters of foreign policy than he was with Indian education. A new Congress was in Washington and Richard's school prospectus ended up in some departmental pigeonhole. His reliance upon Jefferson's promises of financial aid for Spring Hill brought him only disappointment. The government's failure to carry out this program weighed on Jefferson's conscience, and from his retirement at Monticello, he called Madison's attention to the assurance that had been given Richard.[10]

Nevertheless, Spring Hill was not entirely neglected by the government. In a progress report to Madison, made just before he lost the property, Richard said he had five or six persons employed at the farm as instructors and several pupils whose exact number he did not specify. Under the arrangement worked out with Jefferson, the Indian children were being taught useful trades by a weaver, a printer and bookbinder, a mason and a carpenter. He needed more buildings, he said, and he recommended that the government add a black-smith and a shoemaker to his staff. The carpenter, weaver and other artisans, whose continued services he hoped for, were regular government employes of the Indian Department, assigned in accordance with treaties. They were attached to the school as a matter of convenience, as the place where they could work most effectively.

Of course, Richard needed money, too. He asked that the Richard Press be given the contract for government printing; he also requested an additional allowance to buy clothing for the Indian children who came to him—most of them, he observed, "almost naked, dirt & worms Excepted."

The loss of Spring Hill seriously dampened Richard's educational plans. The Loranger farm to which he was forced to move lacked facilities; the government also, about that time, seems to have withdrawn much of its support. Then the War of 1812 gave him another setback. It was at least five years after the loss of Spring Hill before he was again able to give serious attention to his schools. Even then, he had nothing as elaborate as he had earlier contemplated. After the war, with new territorial leaders and with many new Yankee settlers moving into the Territory, more attention began to be given to a publicly supported system of schools. The attainment of that goal required many more years of planning, debate and legislation; Richard did not live to see it completely realized. But during that period he struggled along in his humble way, doing what he could. The records are meager; however, he always managed to have a few pupils under his supervision, and to that extent he helped to bridge the gap to a public system of schools.

Even in the face of his deepest disappointment, he did not lose hope. In 1811, when his Spring Hill program was at low ebb, he was still able to write to a sympathetic Jefferson with words of resolution.

"I have not given up & will not give up the design of Instructing Indian children. I am certain that with constancy we shall succeed."[11]

He concluded his letter with an appropriate quotation from Virgil which the Sage of Monticello had no trouble translating.

Richard won the complete confidence of the Indians by his compassionate and humane attitude. An example of his influence, and the respect in which the Indians held him, is related in an account of an appeal made to him by the Indian Pokagon, who asked Richard to send a missionary to the band of Pottawatomies of which Pokagon was chief. To prove to Richard that he was a good Christian, Pokagon fell to his knees and recited the Lord's Prayer, an Ave Maria, the Apostles' Creed and the Ten Commandments. Richard, it was said, was deeply touched by this demonstration of piety.

Only once was Richard in danger from the Indians. That, if the account can be believed, occurred when sickness swept through a band camped near Spring Hill farm. A council was held, and it was decided the "black robe" was the cause. It was decreed that Richard be tomahawked. Before the sentence could be carried out, wiser members of the tribe prevailed and the Indians sought elsewhere to place the blame.[12]

Gabriel Richard was an idealist, but practical things are frequently instituted upon the designs of dreamers. That was true in his case, particularly in the field of instruction of the Indians. Out of his early efforts came a government policy which was followed well into the twentieth century.

"When the War Department sought to formulate a plan of education that would measure up to the needs of the Indian, it took over a system presented by Father Richard to the United States Congress a decade before." So says one authority on the subject. "The Government had at last caught up with the man who failed because he was ahead of his time. The circular of 1819 states explicitly that those who expected government aid must include in the course of study, in addition to reading, writing and arithmetic, practical knowledge in agriculture and the mechanical arts for the boys, while spinning, weaving, and sewing must be taught to the girls. This plan adopted by the government became the basis of all later training in the Indian schools throughout the United States. Deservedly then might Father Richard bear the title, 'Father of Modern Indian Education.' "[13]

UNIVERSITY—THE GRAND DESIGN

Whenever Gabriel Richard discovered a path which led into the broad fields of education, he followed it, and if his course provided opportunity to aid or comfort the unfortunate, so much the better.

For some reason, there were many deaf-mutes in Detroit and their condition touched his heart. He resolved to help them. In France, Abbé Sicard had successfully experimented in educating this class of unfortunates; by 1817 his work was well known in the United States. Richard was familiar with what Sicard was doing, and in 1824 he sent Elizabeth Lyons to New York to study this special system of instruction. Richard accompanied her, but did not remain in New York, moving on to Montreal to transact other business.

How much Miss Lyons, by that time a nun of the Ursuline order, was able to accomplish for the deaf-mutes in Detroit is not known, but it can be assumed that she did apply the techniques she acquired in New York.

"God knows," Richard wrote, "how many projects great and small go through my head of schools and missions for the Indians, for the deaf and dumb, for poor children, etc., but means are lacking in a new country, where everything must be created out of nothing. My spirit, my imagination, and still more my heart is full of plans, designs, projects, and conceptions which I should call extravagant, and which always remain sterile; they abort or they die at birth. If wishes alone gave one a right to great reward I could expect something. . . ."[14]

Successful or not, he never ceased trying, and of all his efforts, none was more spectacular or contributed so much to his fame as that which resulted in the founding of the University of Michigan. This occurred in 1817; what magic qualities that year possessed which were productive of this high enterprise are most difficult to define. Michigan Territory had barely recovered from the devastating effects of war. The great wave of migration had begun but was still several years away from its crest. To all outward appearances, the face of the frontier had changed but little from the day when Richard first arrived. The entire white population of Michigan could be counted in the few thousands, and a substantial part of that number was still non-English speaking. Untamed Indians continued to roam the woods—their woods, because no more of their lands had been acquired by the government since 1807.

All things added together, it would have been difficult to select any region which offered so little promise for starting a major seat of higher learning.

The answer, if there has to be one, must be found in the energy and determination of a small brotherhood of leaders—men of vision with complete confidence in their hopes, men dedicated to the task of transforming the wilderness into a dynamic America. Already, in 1817, there were those in Michigan who were confidently looking forward to the day—they would not admit to its being far off—when Michigan, like Ohio and Indiana, would be granted statehood and received into full membership in the Union.

Far too much time has been wasted, too much ink splashed, in efforts to prove that this man, or that one, was the prime instigator of the university plan. Candid opinion, based upon careful consideration of the parts played by several, must lead to the conclusion that what was attempted, and what was done, was the result of joint enterprise. It has been said that the university idea suddenly burst, unexpected, upon a surprised and bewildered public—a sort of spontaneous combustion. Nothing is further from the truth. The university, as Professor Andrew Ten Brook accurately observed, "did not spring up without antecedent facts in the public mind to give rise to it."

These facts were planted in the public mind by a group of enthusiastic leaders—such men as Lewis Cass, William Woodbridge, Augustus B. Woodward and Gabriel Richard. In pairs, and as a group, they must have discussed the plan; they were all stalwart advocates of public education, realizing that only through such a route could ultimate political maturity be achieved. Then, in 1816, this band got a new recruit, the Reverend John Monteith, Michigan's first established Protestant clergyman.

Monteith was a native of Gettysburg, Pennsylvania, and shortly before he went out to Michigan he had graduated from Princeton College. He was called by the First Protestant Society, actually a Presbyterian group, to be their minister and, as seems likely, to conduct a school. Certainly his interest in education was equal to that of any of the members of the group into which he fitted so easily.

From the time of Monteith's arrival, he and Richard were in rapport. The Protestants had no church in which to assemble, but that was easily remedied. Father Richard made available to them a structure, possibly the old Meldrum warehouse, which belonged to St. Anne's parish. It was a friendly gesture, graciously accepted, and was typical of the good relations Richard constantly strove to establish.

Here were two men, poles apart as far as background was concerned. But the priest, steeped in the dogma of an ancient faith, and the young theologian, bound to the stern Calvinistic tradition, found a firm basis for friendship. It must have been amusing—and rather touching—to see the fifty-year-old priest, who spoke with a decided accent, and the minister, still in his twenties, with his eastern twang, earnestly conversing together.

Richard, as polite protocol indicated, called upon the newcomer at his lodgings at Colonel Hunt's. "We have a free and pleasant conversation," notes Monteith, the diarist. "He says there is much work for me to do and wishes me success. He stays to tea. I request him to ask a blessing. He answers that he is not accustomed to our mode, that he performs such services in Latin and if acceptable he would do it in that way. I replied that it would not be understood by the family. He therefore declines." A little later, Monteith repaid the call and came away with a gift copy of Thomas à Kempis' *The Imitation of Christ,* a favorite book of Richard's. "The conversation agreeable," Monteith discloses. At a still later date he records: "Visit Priest Richard who is out of health. I think he loves to have me visit him." He needed have no doubts about that![15]

During these friendly meetings and discussions, it was inevitable that the subject of education should have come up. It can be easily imagined that Richard told about his Spring Hill experiment and about the hopes and plans he had for a general school system and for the instruction of Indians. Monteith would have listened understandingly; fresh from college himself, he would have contributed some ideas and suggestions of his own. He must have been familiar with what other leaders in the field in various parts of the country were thinking and saying on the subject. Nor was all of this interchange of thoughts limited to Richard and Monteith. At times Cass and Woodward, both of whom as young men had taught school, must have had things to say on the subject, as did other leading citizens.

At some time during 1817, the idea of a territorial university must have taken form and its objective become clearly understood. On June 20, Monteith recorded in his journal that "Judge Woodward invites me to an interview on the subject of a University." The minister did not specify that this was a private conversation; it is reasonable to think that other interested parties also received Woodward's invitation. In all probability, the purpose of the meeting was to provide Woodward with the opportunity of making a progress report. For to him, as chief justice and the acknowledged legal authority, had been assigned the task of drafting the university idea into legislation. There has been a rather general but erroneous impression that the university act, as Woodward wrote it, sprang complete from his mind and pen and startled all who read it. While absolute proof of the fact may be lacking, there can be little doubt that Cass, Woodbridge, Richard and Monteith were fully informed of what Woodward was doing; it is expecting too much to believe that he dashed off a completed piece of legislation without prior discussion with other interested parties, which, in all likelihood, resulted in some revision and modification before the final text was ready. The university act was adopted on August 26, 1817. On that date Governor Cass was absent from the Territory. He was such a strong and positive-minded executive, with affairs of the Territory so closely under his supervision, that it is impossible to believe he had no prior notice of what was being done, or that it lacked his full approval.

Thus, this product of a meeting of many minds was penned by Woodward into the act which, approved by the other two judges and Woodbridge, the acting governor, established the Catholepistemiad or University of Michigania, and enacted an education concept so far in advance of its time that seventy-five years later President James B. Angell of the University of Michigan had to say of it: "In the development of our strictly university work, we have yet hardly been able to realize the ideal of the eccentric but gifted man who framed the Catholepistemiad, or University of Michigania."[16]

The "eccentric but gifted man," of course, was Woodward, who undoubtedly did the project a disservice by resorting to language in the act so contrived and artificial that it was understood by hardly anyone. The good intent of the act foundered in waves of outlandish verbiage.

Although trained as a lawyer, Woodward aspired to recognition as a scientist, and in this he was encouraged by Thomas Jefferson, with whom he enjoyed an intimate personal relationship. One of Woodward's cherished dreams was to classify into appropriate and related categories all fields and branches of human knowledge. The chief feature of his effort, which he seriously embarked upon some time prior to 1816, was a nomenclature of his devising, based upon Greek roots, intended to provide all knowledge with a universal terminology. During the War of 1812, he was one of those expelled from Michigan by Procter. He went east and spent about two years in New York, Washington and Philadelphia. This recess from his official duties gave him the opportunity to complete, and have published in 1816, his monumental *A System of Universal Science.*

The chief categories of knowledge in this remarkable work were given the designation of *epistemia* which, by his translation, meant science. Grouped together into one combined body, they were called *encatholepistemia* or universal science. This nomenclature, applied to the various *epistemia* and their subdivisions, was quite understandably fresh in Woodward's mind when he began to write his act for the establishment of a university. It offered him a chance to apply what he had propounded in his book. The result was that in writing the prospectus of the university organization, which, by the way, was incorporated into the law, he relied upon this system; that is, for the various departments he adapted the terminology which he had invented. In designating a name for the whole university enterprise, he fell back on the root word *encathol* and created the term *encatholepistemiad,* by which he intended to imply that the university would be universal inasmuch as it would encompass all branches of learning.

To demonstrate how the system worked, he proposed thirteen *didaxiim* or university departments. A list of these not only reveals the strangeness of Woodward's neo-scientific language but, more important, the remarkable academic scope intended for the university. In brief, the *didaxiim* were:

1. *Catholepistemia,* or universal science
2. *Anthropoglossica,* covering literature, grammar, speech
3. *Mathematica,* all branches of mathematics
4. *Physiognostica,* natural science
5. *Physiosophica,* philosophy
6. *Astronomica,* astronomy
7. *Chymia,* chemistry
8. *Iätrica,* medicine
9. *Oeconomica,* vocational and fine arts
10. *Ethica,* law and political science
11. *Polemitactica,* military science
12. *Diëgetica,* history
13. *Ennœica,* a group of subjects including theology.

The list certainly was all-inclusive, establishing standards of curriculum which many modern institutions of higher learning cannot duplicate. But the people in Michigan paid no attention to that. Woodward's strange and unfamiliar terminology was greeted with a derision which has persisted down to modern times. One man, who later became governor of Michigan, called the Catholepistemiad "unchristian"; a future chief justice of the supreme court described it as "a piece of language run wild." The town wits ridiculed it, and even Governor Cass, before much time had passed, could not remember the name Woodward gave the university and referred to it as the "Cathola-what-you-may-call-it."

LAMP IN THE WILDERNESS

People who saw the university act as a collection of outlandish, unpronounceable words, overlooked some important things. First, they ignored the fact that Woodward set down in parallel columns a perfectly clear and understandable statement of what each of his *didaxiim* stood for. But even more important was the manner in which the general purpose and intent of the act was overlooked. Had Woodward's critics read further, and read carefully, they would have discovered in the law a complete framework for a system of public education. The administration of the university was to be in the hands of the *didactors*—those who taught, or headed, the various *didaxiim* or departments. In other words, the faculty was to run the university. Each professor was to receive the munificient sum of $12.50 for each subject he taught. Whoever held the chair of universal science was to be the president; the *didactor* of *ennœica,* or religion and morality, was to be vice-president. As part of the whole university, there was to be a collection of colleges, academies, schools, libraries, museums, botanical gardens and "other useful literary and scientific institutions consonant with the laws of the United States and of Michigan." (It is interesting to note that through its extension service, reaching into every community in Michigan, and through its comparatively new policy of establishing branch colleges, the modern University of Michigan is assuming a character very similar to that which its 1817 founders envisioned.)

Without any form of existence other than a law and a table of organization, the Catholepistemiad could not immediately begin to function, and even if there had been students there was no available faculty. But to put the breath of life into the university, all the *didaxiim* were divided between Monteith and Richard; the former took seven chairs, Richard six. Monteith became president, and on September 17, 1817, Secretary Woodbridge, acting for the still absent Governor Cass, issued a certificate of appointment naming Richard "Professor of Intellectual sciences in & of the University of Michigania," thereby automatically conferring upon him the title and additional duties of vice-president.

The act did not neglect to provide financial support for the new institution. A schedule of fees was drawn; an additional fifteen per cent was added to the current tax rate; and four lotteries were authorized to furnish immediate funds. Private donations also were made, an indication that the general public saw some hope and merit in the university. With money at hand, contracts were let for construction of a building on Bates Street, between present-day Congress and Larned, close by the site which had been reserved for St. Anne's Church.

The Act of Appropriation was adopted by the Governor and Judges on August 26, 1817. This was a formality, a legislative recognition of the validity of Judge Woodward's act. It conformed to the federal requirement that territorial acts be based upon the laws of some of the states. In this case, the Governor and Judges found precedent for Woodward's university law in existing statutes of Kentucky and New York.

On September 24, the cornerstone was officially laid; about a year later, although not yet completed, about three thousand dollars had been spent on the structure. The building was of two stories with ground dimensions of about twenty-four by fifty feet. It was long one of Detroit's landmarks, standing until 1858 when it was demolished to make room for a new commercial building.

One of the first things Monteith and Richard did was to draft an order creating elementary school systems in Monroe and Mackinac with specified curricula consisting of reading, arithmetic, grammar and elocution. This, undoubtedly, was Richard's contribution because he had been as much concerned for the need of schools in the outlying districts as in Detroit. Understanding the pattern previously established in France, the term "university" meant to him a territory-wide system which included elementary schools.

Monteith and Richard also authorized the opening of a classical academy in Detroit, offering courses in "French, Latin and Greek antiquities, English grammar, and Ornamental Accomplishments." Many of the leading families of Detroit, including Governor Cass, immediately enrolled their children.

On August 10, 1818, Monteith and Richard opened an elementary school, located on the first floor of the new university building. The classical academy was temporarily housed in other quarters until the second floor of the university building was completed. During its first year of operation the elementary school had an enrollment of 180, and the classical academy, a continuation of Richard's own institution, had somewhat fewer. Outside instructors were appointed for both schools.

As far as can be determined, neither Monteith nor Richard ever taught any university classes and there is no evidence that any courses were offered beyond the academy level. Monteith did perform, as president, a few administrative duties, such as handling and supervising accounts, until 1821, when he left Detroit. Richard, as vice-president, then took over. Certainly his responsibilities were not heavy and he had little to do. In fact, there was a growing public awareness that the Catholepistemiad was too elaborate for the needs of the Territory. In 1821 the original act was amended. Control was placed in the hands of a twenty-one man board of trustees, and the name was changed to the University of Michigan. This arrangement continued, with the actual operation of the university in a virtual state of suspended animation until 1837. In that year, Michigan having become a state, the university was transferred to Ann Arbor and began to function as such in the modern sense. But during this period of moribundity, when the Catholepistemiad and its successor, the University of Michigan, were little more than laws on the statute books, Richard continued to be actively associated with the enterprise. Following the 1821 reorganization, he served as a member of the board of trustees.

Actually, the university was more than simply a law on the books during these fallow years. It was a starting point; the expression of an ideal and a preparation for the day when its facilities would be needed. Too much stress has been placed on its failure to immediately achieve the status of an institution of higher learning. It was never intended to equal in form, or function, its modern counterpart; however, it still remains its legal and traditional ancestor.

What Monteith, Richard, Woodward and the rest had in mind was legal recognition for a basic educational system. It may be somewhat over-simplifying, but it comes closest to reality to describe the Catholepistemiad as a territorial department of public instruction based on a fundamental law which could be applied whenever the occasion required, or whenever circumstances and conditions warranted as the Territory developed.

To that extent it was neither ridiculous nor a failure. Thomas M. Cooley, a later justice of the Supreme Court of Michigan, and a man of vast erudition, recognized the Act of 1817 for what it was. "The plan was crude and pedantic," he said, "but its author had grasped certain principles which were of the very highest importance, and which from this time became incorporated in the polity of the Territory, and subsequently of the State also."[17] If it did nothing more, it conditioned the public mind to an awareness of the need for a broad system of publicly supported universal education. In time it helped put Michigan in the forefront as a successful innovator and advanced practitioner of public education.

But what, one may ask, did Gabriel Richard specifically contribute to the university idea? The language was Woodward's; Woodward, Cass, Woodbridge, and Judges Witherell and Griffin made it into law. And strangely, most of the credit for being the founder of the present University of Michigan went to Monteith. To find Richard's true place in the picture, it is necessary to look into some of the ideas then prevalent regarding a broad scheme of education; only then will his real influence be found.

The genesis of the university was, according to many historians, the University of France which Napoleon Bonaparte instituted in the first years of the nineteenth century. As Professor Burke A. Hinsdale, of the University of Michigan, wrote, Napoleon's university "was not, in fact, a university at all, but rather a highly centralized organization of state instruction, having its center in Paris."[18] Richard was fully aware of what Napoleon had done; his library contained the literature about the French plan. Because of his background, his familiarity with French education, he undoubtedly could foresee how Napoleon's project could be adapted for use elsewhere.

Woodward also was familiar with the University of France, as was Jefferson. These two men together discussed and corresponded about a plan for a national university of the United States. Jefferson, at the time Woodward was writing his *A System of Universal Science,* was preparing a prospectus for a university in Kentucky as well as perfecting his cherished University of Virginia. Therefore, with Richard and Woodward thinking along the same lines, and in almost constant association, it is impossible to believe that their conversations did not lead to a meeting of the minds out of which came the idea of a "centralized organization of state instruction" such as Hinsdale described, adapted to the immediate and future needs of Michigan. Credit Richard, then, with some of the philosophical spadework which, through Woodward's exotic manner of expression, gave Michigan the basis for a department of public instruction.

Woodward, the legalist and scientific dilettante, contributed the legal form and the language of the act. Monteith represented the viewpoint and aspirations of the Protestant element which had sent him to Detroit. But Richard alone of the group was the only true pedagog with training and experience in the field of education. Better than the others, he was aware of the Territory's great need for educational facilities. Monteith's association with the university was brief; he left Detroit in 1821 and never, thereafter, apparently displayed the least concern over the fate of the institution. Woodward, after its founding, had no further official connection with the university. Only Richard preserved and kept alive the ideal.

While the organization of the Catholepistemiad, or University of Michigania, was proceeding in Detroit, Governor Cass, as has been noted, was absent from the Territory. With General Duncan McArthur, of Ohio, he was negotiating a land cession treaty at Fort Meigs (Toledo) with representatives of the Ottawa, Chippewa and Pottawatomie tribes. When the terms of agreement were finally reached, an article was included in which the Indians gave six sections of land for equal sharing to the Church of St. Anne at Detroit and to "the College at Detroit." This land was part of a tract which, by earlier treaty, had been reserved specifically for the Indians' use. It was located along the River Raisin in southern Michigan.

It was a gift, freely given. But what prompted it? It has been suggested that the government insisted as a condition of the treaty that land be set aside for education purposes. But this explanation will not hold up. Otherwise, how can the donation to the church be explained? It also has been claimed that Cass persuaded the chiefs to make the donation. He may, it is true, have exerted some influence, but it is doubtful that his influence was that great.

The terms of the gift stated that it was the result of the Indians being "attached to the Catholic religion, and believing they may wish some of their children hereafter educated."[19] This strongly suggests the influence of Richard and the gratitude of the Indians for his efforts in their behalf. That they thought well of him was indicated at the time of his imprisonment during the War of 1812 when Tecumseh came to his aid. The tribesmen dealing with Cass and McArthur may well have remembered the school at Spring Hill; it is even possible some of them may have attended that school or some other one under Richard's supervision. Certainly, the donation was more of an expression of good will to a beloved priest than to the government. Eventually when the land was sold, the proceeds were used for the university at Ann Arbor; this represented the first substantial endowment given that institution. It was important, as Cooley says, because it was made after the Indians had given up the greater part of their tribal lands; it came out of a relatively small domain which had been retained by them. It was, moreover, "fully equal in positive value and prospectively superior to the gifts for like purposes which made John Harvard and Elihu Yale immortal. . . ."[20]

The exact meaning of "the College at Detroit" has always been the subject of speculation. Paré expressed belief that it may have referred to Richard's plans for a Catholic school or academy, something which could quite properly have been established under provisions of the Act of 1817. It has been stated that Richard told the Indians that the school for which they gave their land would be called "the College at Detroit," and, anticipating the donation, he requested Monteith to authorize the school under the new law. It was to be named the First College of Michigania. Monteith, as president, acquiesced, adding that "the president and professors of the University of Michigania shall be the president and professors of the said college. The University shall appoint one or more persons, not exceeding thirteen, to be trustees and visitors of the said college." Monteith may have been prompted further to issue the "College" decree in order legally to qualify the university to take title to the grant of 1804 for "the seminary of learning at Detroit" as well as to the Fort Meigs treaty donation.

Thus, there is established a direct link between Gabriel Richard and the university—not the rather vague and ill-defined establishment of 1817, but the great institution of learning which stands today, recognized as its legal descendant.

The proud title of "Father of Michigan's Educational System" was given to one who followed Gabriel Richard. But even if Richard does not completely merit that designation, he is still gratefully remembered as a pioneer who helped light the lamp of knowledge in a wilderness where, prior to his coming, there had been naught but darkness.

Courtesy of Burton Historical Collection

St. Anne's Church just before it was torn down in 1886. Services were held here from 1818 on. The preceding church was destroyed by the fire of 1805.

Interior of St. Anne's sometime between 1871 and 1875. Shown in a frontal view is the main altar. On the right is Father E. Anciaux, pastor during this period. Using two separate photographs, one of Father Anciaux and one of the interior, the unknown photographer superimposed Father Anciaux on this altar picture.

Courtesy of Burton Historical Collection

Courtesy of Detroit Institute of Arts

Silver gilted chalice made by Victor Rouquette of Detroit in 1819 for St. Anne's Church. Father Richard used it in his daily mass after this date until his death in 1832. It is presently in the possession of the archdiocese of Detroit.

Courtesy of the *Detroit Times*

Gabriel Richard's tomb in the crypt under the nave of the present St. Anne's Church, located at Ste. Anne and Howard Streets. Above is Rev. Fr. John Glavin, C.S.B., pastor of St. Anne's in 1946 just before restoration work on Richard's tomb was undertaken. Below is a 1958 picture of the renovated tombstone. Richard was originally buried in the crypt at old St. Anne's, at Bates and Larned Streets.

Photograph by Henry Leung

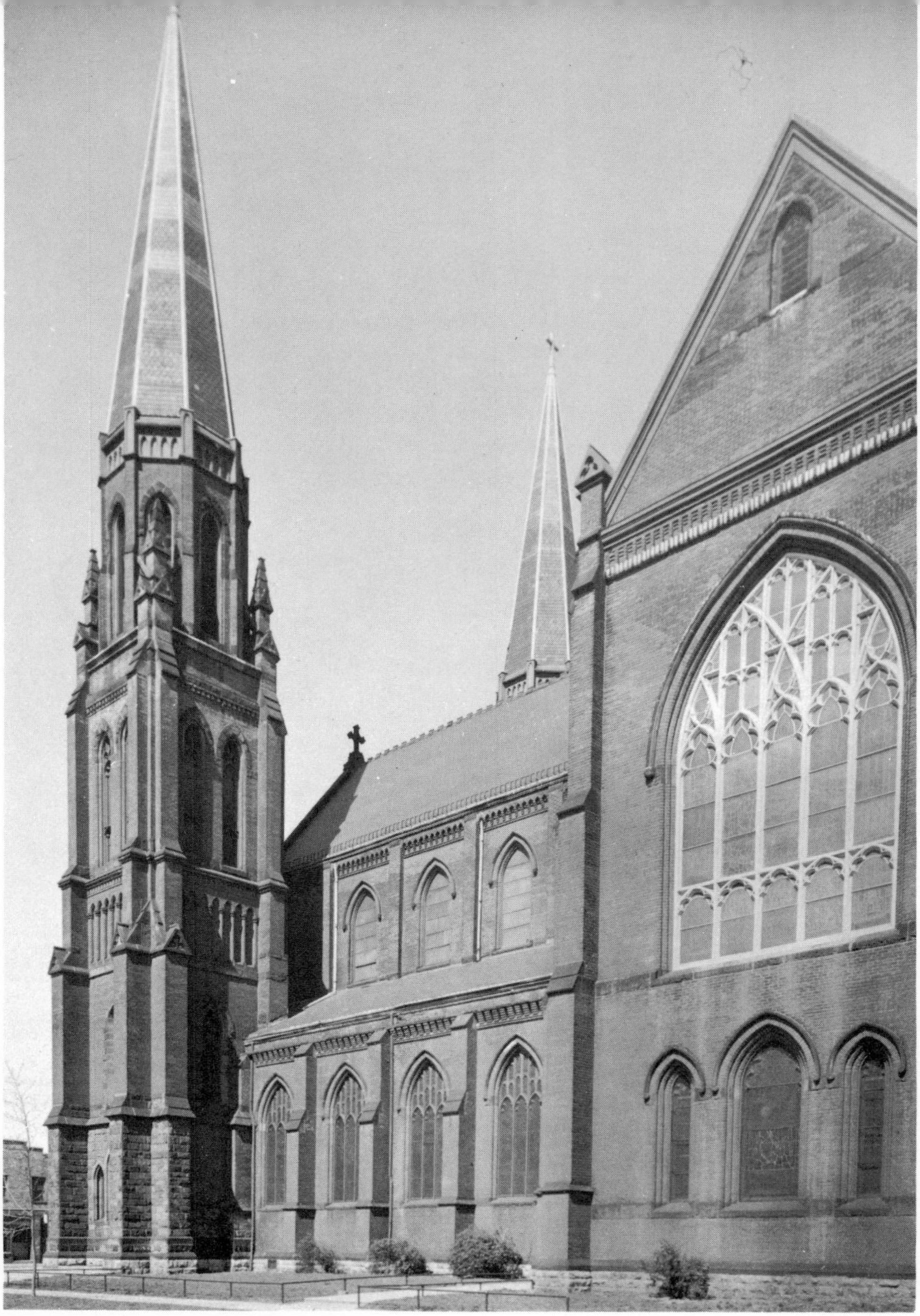

Photograph by Henry Leung

St. Anne's, 1958. A side view from Ste. Anne's Street facing east. The church, which fronts north on Howard Street, was erected in 1887. Most of the descendents of Father Richard's parishioners have long since dispersed into the surrounding population, and French is no longer heard after mass on Sundays. The parish is now composed mostly of families of Mexican descent.

Chapter 5

The Statesman

PILGRIMAGE

ARRAYED in their best bib and tucker, the worthy burghers of Detroit gathered on March 24, 1815 in Ben Woodworth's Steamboat Hotel for a Grand Pacification Ball, celebrating the end of the War of 1812. To demonstrate that the era of good feelings had arrived, the officers of the British garrison were invited, and for a few gay, happy hours all recollection of hostility, massacre and hardship was forgotten. With recovery from the effects of the war came better times for Michigan Territory. The next decade and a half was a period of unprecedented growth and development. In this, Gabriel Richard had his part.

Under the vigorous, far-sighted administrative leadership of Lewis Cass, Michigan Territory assumed the status of a progressive American community. Cass quickly wiped out the last roaming bands of hostile Indians and he settled the border controversies with the British. In 1817, the *Detroit Gazette,* the first regular and permanently established newspaper, began publication. President Monroe, in the same year, paid a visit to the Territory, thereby fixing national attention on this hitherto little known part of the country. By threats, pleading and cajolery, Cass prevailed upon the government to survey the public domain and place interior lands on the market. On August 27, 1818, the first steamboat to sail the lakes, the *Walk-in-the-Water,* chugged up the river to the delight of the populace and the amazement of Richard's Indian friends who were solemnly assured that it was towed by a school of harnessed sturgeon. When it tied up at Mr. Austin Wing's dock at the foot of Bates Street, a new type of swift, comfortable and economical transportation linked Buffalo and the western lake ports.

Then, in 1825 the Erie Canal was opened to Buffalo. This tremendous event, combined with steam navigation, drew thousands of settlers to Michigan during the next few years. The stream of western-bound Yankee and foreign migrants which hitherto had by-passed Michigan, in favor of Ohio, Indiana and Illinois, now was increasingly attracted to the Territory.

"The State of Michigan is certainly destined to be a flourishing region," Richard commented in 1825 as he observed all of this progress and activity. "The air is pure and salubrious, the land excellent. That the Federal Government recognizes its importance is evident from the fact that at the last session of Congress a resolution which I proposed was adopted namely, the opening of a highway from Detroit westward to Chicago, a settlement lying at the southernmost point of Lake Michigan. Three commissioners named by the President, and two surveyors, have explored this vast solitude, 260 miles, and have laid out the course of this important route which will open the interior of our Territory to the immigrants who have been crowding in this last season.

"Three steamers and more than 150 sailing-vessels plying our lakes have brought us 6 or 7 thousand immigrants who came to buy land. The great canal, 365 miles long, from Albany to Buffalo on Lake Erie has been completed. . . . This summer, in our little city of Detroit, seventy-two houses were built, some of them having two stories, and quite elegant. We expect that a hundred more will be built next summer, and that the canal will bring us twelve thousand immigrants from the East to clear our vast timber lands. It is true that there are few Catholics among the newcomers, but that is all the more reason why we need sterling priests to work for their conversion. . . . Much could be done by having priests travel among the Americans, holding friendly conferences in their homes during the long winter evenings, and answering questions—Americans are inquisitive. . . ."[1]

Political maturity accompanied this economic and social development. The incoming Yankees, accustomed to a degree of local self-government, brought new ideas with them. The old system of the Governor and Judges became outmoded and there was a demand for political advancement. In 1818, the boundaries were adjusted and all that remained of the old Northwest Territory, after the three new states of Ohio, Indiana and Illinois had been set off, became Michigan Territory.

This was, as Richard stated, a vast empire, including all of present-day Michigan, Wisconsin and a piece of upper Minnesota. On July 16, 1819, Congress authorized Michigan to send a territorial delegate to Washington, and the following September 2, William Woodbridge was duly chosen for that post in what may be regarded as Michigan's first general election. Meanwhile, the agitation for home rule continued, and on March 3, 1823, Congress was prevailed upon to pass an act transferring the government of the Territory from the Governor and Judges to a Governor and Council. Under this arrangement, the people would elect eighteen persons. From this list, the President, with Senate confirmation, would select nine to constitute the territorial Council. When the news of this advancement reached Detroit, it was greeted by the firing of cannon, a band concert and the inevitable civic banquet. The election was held in September, and it appeared that just about every male citizen aspired to a seat on the Council. There was a total of 123 candidates, including Gabriel Richard. It is not likely that he was an active campaigner, or that he really sought to be elected. He finished number 107 on the list with a total of only ten votes, receiving one vote in Mackinac and the other nine from the residents of the River Raisin, by this time designated as Monroe County.

When the Council met for its first session in the Council House on June 7, 1824, Gabriel Richard, by invitation, offered the invocation, praying that with divine guidance "the legislators may make laws for the people, and not for themselves"—or, as one citizen remembered the accented admonition, to "make laws for de peops, and not for demselves."[2]

To facilitate migration and provide farms for the settlers, the government once again started to negotiate land acquisition treaties with the Indians. The first was the one of 1817 which so greatly benefited Richard's church and the university. In 1819, Cass gained title to an area comprising about the eastern half of Michigan's lower peninsula. In 1821, another great treaty council was held at Chicago between American commissioners and the Pottawatomies, the object being to effect the purchase and sale of Indian lands in the southwestern part of the peninsula. The Pottawatomies invited Richard to be present to assist them in setting up a mission; and also in arranging educational facilities, now a standard provision in such agreements. Richard eagerly accepted, and he left Detroit on July 4 aboard a sailing vessel. He had been requested by Bishop Flaget to report on the condition of the northern settlements, and a trip around the lakes to Chicago would give him the opportunity to make the survey.

He stayed three weeks at Mackinac; it was the first visit by a member of the clergy since Dilhet's trip in 1804. Moving on, Richard wanted to visit his old friends, the Ottawa, at L'Arbre Croche, but stormy weather prevented a landing. Instead he went ashore at the mouth of the Marquette River, near the present city of Ludington. There he found a small settlement of about ten Ottawa families and he induced them to show him the spot where Father Jacques Marquette, the famed Jesuit missionary and explorer, had died in 1675. Although Marquette's remains had long since been taken to St. Ignace for reburial, the Ottawa recalled the location of his first grave.

"The spot pointed out to me by the Indians," Richard noted, "is about

2400 feet from the actual shore of the lake on the southern bank of the old bed of the river named after Father Marquette, which is 2800 feet north of the river as it is today. There I erected a cross in the presence of eight Ottawas and two Catholics, Frederich Countryman who made the cross, and Charles Rousseau, a young Canadian from Montreal. . . . I placed it directly over the spot where the Indians told me a cross had been standing, erected by the Canadians, until blown down by the winds three years ago. With my pocket-knife I carved the following inscription in English: Fr. J. H. Marquet died Here 9 May, 1675."[3]

Richard lingered in the locality for a few days, conducting services at the site of the grave. Continuing his trip, his progress down Lake Michigan was slowed by foul weather and he did not reach Chicago until after the treaty had been signed. To his chagrin, he learned that when he failed to appear on time, arrangements to conduct the mission were made with a Baptist minister who had accompanied the negotiating party. Nevertheless, he took an opportunity to conduct services in the home of a trader and to preach to the members of the Fort Dearborn garrison. He was the first priest to celebrate mass at Chicago since a Jesuit mission was abandoned there in 1700.

It was his intention to return to Detroit by the same route he had followed going to Chicago. But he discovered he could not obtain passage for nearly two months. It occurred to him that he could make faster time by going down the Illinois River to the Mississippi and then to follow the old route up the Ohio and Wabash to Detroit. It can be imagined that Richard found no difficulty persuading himself of the advantages of that route. It would give him a chance to visit his old haunts in the lower Illinois country.

Spending a few days at St. Louis, he renewed acquaintances at Cahokia, Kaskaskia and Prairie du Rocher. He then set out for Vincennes on horseback. The first day on the trail, his mount threw him, causing severe injuries. He managed, despite his pain, to struggle on and reach Vincennes where he spent two weeks recuperating. When he was enough recovered, he went down into Kentucky, making his first pilgrimage to the see of his diocese at Bardstown, and visiting his old friend Bishop Flaget. There he participated in the consecration of Edward Fenwick, who had but recently been named bishop of the newly-created diocese of Cincinnati and administrator of Michigan Territory.

The stop at Bardstown was productive in more than one way. While there, he met a young priest, Father Anthony Ganilh, and a recent seminarian, Francis Vincent Badin. They expressed an interest in going to Detroit to work with Richard. Bishop Flaget gave his approval; the party stopped long enough in

Cincinnati for Badin to be ordained by Bishop Fenwick. Richard needed help, and the assistance of two young, energetic and enthusiastic priests was greatly to be desired. The River Raisin parish had had no regular pastor since Dilhet left in 1804, and Ganilh was assigned there. Badin became the assistant at St. Anne's. From that time Richard was regularly referred to as vicar-general of Michigan.

Although he was engaged with the problems of his parish during all of this period, Richard still found time to carry his share of civic obligations. He seems to have had a keen interest in all public matters, particularly those which affected his parishioners or the French-Americans. His name continued to appear on petitions of one kind or another. As an example, he was one of a number who in 1827 asked the Legislative Council to abolish bridge tolls on the grounds that they "are a grievous burthen upon the people. A person, by going from Detroit to Monroe [as Richard often had occasion to do], the distance of only thirty-six miles, if in a single carriage with one horse, has to pay for toll at the several bridges, the sum of two dollars; and if in a double carriage, four dollars."[4] This assessment, the Council was reminded, was levied on travelers using the public road on which the United States had spent twenty thousand dollars for improvements.

There were many indigents, paupers, disabled veterans and plain ne'er-do-wells in the Territory after the War of 1812. Their support from public poor funds, or private charity, put a heavy burden on the taxpayers. Again Richard joined with a group of leading citizens, suggesting that a tract of public land be set aside and the proceeds from it be used to build and support a poor house, thereby relieving the citizens from burdensome demands for charity and a heavy tax load.

Richard also appeared on a list of names, mostly French, of persons asking Congress for compensation for damage to private property suffered during the war, both at the hands of enemy and United States troops. Apparently having heard that residents of Washington had been reimbursed for losses when the city was burned by the British in 1814, the Michiganders pointed out that "however great may be their distance from the seat of the Federal Government, and however few may be their political rights and privileges as Inhabitants of Michigan, under their present provincial form of Government, yet as Citizens of the United States of America they claim as full and perfect a right to the protection of the Constitution of the United States, as far as regards their personal liberty & private property, as their more fortunate fellow citizens who may dwell at the foot of the Capitol."[5]

Richard's activities were not confined to signing petitions and resolutions. He continued to attend regular meetings of the board of trustees of the University of Michigan. His name appeared on the general tax rolls, giving evidence that he paid, as did every male citizen above the age of sixteen, the one dollar head tax. He was also on the general county rolls, indicating that he was a property owner. He was a member of a group, which included Cass, Henry Rowe Schoolcraft and C. C. Trowbridge, that met in 1828 in the new territorial capitol to found the Michigan Historical Society. When, a year or two later, he was invited to deliver the annual address, he declined the honor, saying: "I regret that the extent of my correspondence, the multiplicity of my clerical functions . . . and several other pressing and uncontrollable circumstances, do imperiously prevent me from accepting a task which I consider a duty in all good citizens, to assist in preserving for the benefit of the Society the facts of the early transactions which have taken place in our Territory." He described what, in his opinion, should go into such an address: a summary of all known facts, an inventory of the records bearing on the subject, a treatment of antiquities of the Territory with attention to geography, customs, arts and traditions. Such an undertaking, he affirmed, would require at least six months of intensive preparation.[6]

Some of the new settlers arriving in the Territory brought with them a prejudice against the Catholic faith. Most of these were from New England or New York state; behind them was a Puritan tradition of fear and distrust of "papists." Because these newcomers were aggressive and rapidly becoming a majority of the population, a new problem arose and Richard foresaw the danger of the old French element being discriminated against, socially, politically and economically. To offset the possibility, he increased his activities in the field of public relations, seeking to establish a basis of reasonable understanding.

He directed his efforts along several lines. It was the custom, on days having special meaning to the church, to stage religious processions through the town. These had a semi-official character. An order of the adjutant-general in 1820 summoned the militia officers to turn out "on the General Parade ground in the rear of the city, on Saturday next at 2 o'clock p.m., with a view to prepare your men to attend as a military escort at the celebration of the anniversary of the institution of the feast of the blessed sacrament of our Lord Jesus Christ."[7]

On this, as on similar occasions, Richard caused a notice to be published, inviting persons of all denominations to take part, and he gave a short address, explaining the significance of the event. The spectacle of a procession of vested priests and acolytes bearing candles and religious insignia, wending its way through the town, did not sit well with some of the Protestants. Richard tried to offset this feeling by inviting Governor Cass and General Alexander Macomb, the army commander, to parade with the Catholics. They were assigned posts of honor in which they held the ribbons of the canopy under which the Blessed Sacrament was carried. Some of the parishioners were not edified by the spectacle of Protestants participating in the ceremony, as well as the appearance of the military. But Richard justified inviting them with the explanation that he sought "to do towards Protestants all that might draw them to the Catholic Church."

To further better understanding, he also renewed his former practice of Sunday afternoon lectures to Protestant audiences in which he explained Catholic principles. These meetings, he said, were sufficiently well attended "so as to give me hope that truth will not be preached in vain."

Richard was following the principle that familiarity breeds tolerance. Protestants always were welcome at St. Anne's, and many attended—some, unfamiliar with the Catholic service, out of curiosity. The latter group sometimes went away with reactions which probably would have distressed Father Richard. Henry Rowe Schoolcraft, for instance, attended service at St. Anne's on March 31, 1831 and recorded his impressions in his journal that evening.

"I went to the Catholic Church to hear Mr. Richard preach a sermon on the anniversary of the institution of the Lord's Supper," Schoolcraft said. "This is the first time, I ever heard the catholic service baring the burial service of an Indian at Butte du Morts. He was about two hours in addressing the audience in very bad English. Many went away, before he got through, but I determined to stay. The first part of his sermon related to the sufferings and divinity of Christ. He declared distinctly that Christ was God, and said that no part of his words were addressed to anyone, who did not think so. All this part of his doctrine was purely Calvanite and I was happy to hear it. I thought of a unitarian, who was present, and was pleased to have him hear, that both Catholics and Protestants agreed on this point."

The second part of the sermon, Schoolcraft felt, left much to be desired. It was a discourse on transubstantiation, and Schoolcraft thought Richard expounded his doctrine "with arguments that should not satisfy a child, and with vehemence that should disgrace a preacher." He left, feeling "the whole service was without impressiveness and before it was ended, I regretted having gone there for I came away in no bettered, but rather a lowered state of mind and heart."[8]

Despite Schoolcraft's feelings, the Reverend Noah M. Wells, an early

Presbyterian minister, was a friend and frequent caller on Richard and spoke of him as a sound and learned theologian.[9]

Richard sought at all times to ingratiate himself with the leaders of the government and passed up no opportunity to honor them with attention. When visiting church dignitaries graced the town with their presence, he staged receptions and dinners. When Bishop Plessis of Quebec was in Detroit in 1816, he was presented to General Macomb, who received him in dress uniform, with a guard of honor and the garrison band. At the dinner which followed in Richard's quarters, Macomb and Cass were both present. Plessis proposed a toast to the President of the United States and was a trifle dismayed when no one responded with one to the king of Great Britain. Cass offered a toast to the Pope, and Macomb followed with another to the prosperity of the Catholic clergy. The dinner was a notable success despite a storm of rain which blew in and sprinkled the guests. They would have liked to have had the windows closed, Plessis observed, but that was not possible; they had been removed in advance to provide more air. Much the same protocol was followed a few years later when Bishop Flaget appeared in Detroit.[10]

At this period, Richard was still occupying the Loranger farm which, according to contemporary account, "is directly opposite the Church of the Assumption [on the Canadian side of the river]. . . . The house being spacious, Mr. Richard has changed one of its apartments into a sanctuary, using another as a sacristy. A third and fourth form the nave, without counting that a certain number of parishioners can attend service at the windows, at least during the fine season, by means of a covered gallery in front of the house."

Obviously, this was at best a makeshift arrangement. So after Bishop Flaget succeeded in settling the quarrel with the Northeasters, and with the land at peace and the Territory prospering, it became time to do something about the construction of a new church. This now became Richard's principal interest.

TOWERS OF ST. ANNE'S

When Bishop Flaget went to Detroit in 1818 to settle once and for all the factional disputes which had plagued Gabriel Richard's life for a dozen years, he made a gesture symbolic of unity by laying the cornerstone of the new St.

Anne's, located on the generous government grant at Larned and Bates. The site had long lain idle, waiting for peace within the parish and the end of war in the Territory.

In the years following the destruction of old St. Anne's by the fire of 1805, Richard went ahead with rebuilding plans. It was part of his purpose when he went east in 1808–09 to solicit funds for the church, and no doubt he was successful. In 1814, John R. Williams, a leading member of the congregation and the man destined to become Detroit's first mayor, was in Albany. He wrote Richard, offering to solicit donations in that city, and it is again safe to assume that he received the priest's approval. The result was that by 1818, when conditions made it possible to start the new building, Richard had a fund at his disposal, sufficient, at least, for a beginning.

Looking over the site, he planned a structure about eighty-seven feet in length and sixty in width. Flaget, however, felt these plans were too modest and directed Richard to increase the length of the church to 116 feet. Somewhat flabbergasted, the priest could see his original cost estimates soaring. "God alone knows what straits this excessive size left me in," he declared. But Flaget's recommendation was followed. Flaget felt that a bigger church was needed because in time "it would be the cathedral of the proposed diocese of Michigan," which, in truth, it did become.

The cornerstone was laid on Tuesday, June 9. Later that day, while returning from dinner at General Macomb's quarters, the bishop's horses took fright, his carriage was overturned, and the hapless prelate was thrown down the high river bank. He suffered a painful injury to his right shoulder from which he never fully recovered.

Almost immediately the work on St. Anne's was well under way. On August 18, the following advertisement appeared in the *Detroit Gazette*:

"Great Bargain! Offered by Gabriel Richard, rector of St. Anne, 200 hard dollars will be given for twenty toises of long stone, of Stony Island, delivered at Detroit, on the wharf of Mr. Jacob Smith, or two hundred and forty dollars, if delivered on the church ground. 100 barrels of lime are wanted immediately. Five shillings will be given per barrel at the river side, and six shillings delivered on the church ground."[11]

There is a tradition that much of the building material was floated on scows up the Savoyard River, a small creek which meandered past the church property, but Silas Farmer, in his history of Detroit, denied it. The stone was furnished by J. B. St. Amour and Louis Desolcour, probably from limestone quarries on one of the islands in the lower Detroit River. Timber was purchased from Messrs. Young and St. Barnard and was cut from the stands of pine along the Pine River in St. Clair County. Originally, says Farmer, it was planned to have a row of pillars around the outside of the church, apparently in the style of a Greek portico. A few of the pillars were made and delivered, but the plan, for some unstated reason, was changed and they were not used.

Exactly how the work progressed is not entirely clear. The plans called for twin steeples, rising from cupolas which, in turn, surmounted a pair of truncated square towers in the front. The steeples, which were covered with tin, were completed in the fall of 1820, although they may not have been lifted immediately into place. It was said that while putting on the tin, the workmen used a brazier containing live coals to heat their irons. Through carelessness one steeple caught fire from these coals one night. When someone summoned the watch, who doubled as the town fire-fighter, that worthy refused to get out of bed to answer the alarm. "Never mind," he is supposed to have stated, "it's all green timber and won't burn much till morning." He was right; the damage was negligible, and the steeple was still standing sixty years later.

Gradually the stone walls rose to a height of six or eight feet above ground, or to the level of the top of the basement. That was roofed over, and by Christmas, 1820, services were being held in the basement. It would appear that funds began to run out before that time. Richard resorted to almost any device that would swell his building fund. He started a fishery, using seines. The enterprise is said to have been successful, and for a time he regularly packed and shipped salted fish to the eastern markets.[12]

Richard acted as his own contractor, and due to a shortage of currency in Detroit, he followed the example of local businessmen and issued his own script, or shinplasters, with which to pay his workmen. These shinplasters were printed for him in the office of the *Detroit Gazette*. One of the printers, a man named Cooper, surreptitiously appropriated the type, ran off a large number of the bills and counterfeited Richard's signature on them. He then proceeded to flood the countryside with them, to a total amount of several hundred dollars. Printer Cooper escaped punishment by enlisting in the army and being transferred before his crime was discovered. What it meant to Richard can well be imagined! With a heavy heart and uncertainty as to the extent of his loss, he set out to redeem the worthless money. Most accounts say he took care of all of it, but Farmer reports that he refused to redeem some—for what reason he does not state—and thereby incurred the lasting enmity of some townspeople. All evidence points to the fact that he acted honorably and with the utmost candor, even to the extent of pledging, if necessary, the assets of the church. This is shown by the following notice which he had published in the *Gazette*:

"The Undersigned returns his thanks to the merchants and other citizens of Detroit and its vicinity for the liberal assistance given him in erecting the Church of St. Anne, and having given free circulation to his small notes.

"With sorrow and displeasure he has discovered that many of his small notes are counterfeited, and that several of his neighbors have suffered by reason of the counterfeit. It appears that more than 200 fifty cent bills have been within the past fortnight put in circulation in this city. . . .

"The public are warned that every possible exertion will be made by the undersigned to redeem his bills without delay, and in order to do away with any fears that may exist as to his capability to do so, he deems it proper to state that besides three sections of land of the finest quality, and three valuable lots in the city, the Corporation of St. Anne holds a very valuable and extensive spot of ground which surrounds the Church, worth ten times more than the whole amount of the bills now in circulation. . . ."[13]

Despite vicissitudes and chicanery, the superstructure went up bit by bit. Finally the roof was put on, the finishing touches added, and on Christmas Day, 1828, ten years after the work was begun, the congregation joyfully held its first service in the new St. Anne's.

The new church steeples dominated the surrounding area and provided a landmark for mariners and a focus of attention when viewed from the Canadian shore. In the center of the ceiling was an octagonal dome, thirty feet in diameter and thirty feet high, surmounted by a representation of the sun upon which was embossed a human face with a cock above it. At the rear, on either side, were two small cupolas supporting representations of the moon and a fish. At first, the towers were open and the front façade was plain. Eventually the former were enclosed and a porch was added to the latter. Inside, installed as cherished mementos, were the pulpit and two side altars from the old St. Anne's which had escaped destruction when the church burned. At one point in the construction, Richard experimented by embedding empty bottles in the masonry to improve the acoustics.[14] The old bell, too, was saved and hung in the new structure. The church was surrounded by ample grounds which, in time, were landscaped and made park-like. In 1822, a two-story wooden rectory, adjoining the church, was completed and occupied.

St. Anne's stood, the mother church of Michigan, until the changing pattern of the city of Detroit made it advisable to sell the property. In 1886 it was disposed of and a new St. Anne's was built at Howard and Nineteenth (later Ste. Anne's) streets on the city's west side, not far from the spot where, years before, Father Richard had his church and school on the Loranger farm.

Richard's church was built up in another way after 1818. When Bishop

Flaget visited him that year, he stayed in Michigan, except for a couple of side excursions into Canada, until May, 1819. He was accompanied by two young priests, John Bertrand and Philip Janvier. When he finally departed on the *Walk-in-the-Water*, he permitted the two priests to stay with Richard to assist him with the outlying missions. In 1821, on his return from Kentucky, Richard brought back with him, as has been noted, Fathers Ganilh and Badin. During the next ten years, still others were added to his staff, including such well-remembered men as the Reverend Pierre Dejean, who spent several fruitful years with the Ottawa at L'Arbre Croche, and Father Frederic Baraga, who later became the first bishop of the diocese of Marquette. There was, naturally, some turnover; some of the priests who were sent to Michigan remained only a short time. By the end of 1830, there were eight priests in the Territory, serving not only the old churches and chapels at Detroit and Monroe, but also supervising such far-flung outposts as Mackinac, Sault Ste. Marie, Prairie du Chien, Green Bay, and others.

A report made by Richard in 1826 on the extent and condition of the church in Michigan listed eleven major settlements outside of the Detroit area with six churches or chapels; and a total of 1049 families and nearly seven thousand individuals making up the Catholic population.[15]

Although he fretted because he still lacked missionaries to send out to all the Indians, the burden of his regular work was lightening, enabling him to devote more of his time and attention to St. Anne's.

POLITICO IN CASSOCK

Having acquired the services of a delegate in Congress and a Legislative Council at home, Michigan became extremely politically conscious. Observing the privileges, emoluments and prestige attached to public office, more and more of the Territory's leading citizens aspired to positions on the public payroll. As a result, political factions, if not parties, began to form; elections were vigorously contested, and campaigns became raucous, bitter and highly personalized.

William Woodbridge went to Washington in 1819 as Michigan's first congressional delegate. He retained his local posts of territorial secretary and collector of revenue. He found that long absence from home was not to his taste, so after a year as delegate he resigned. He was succeeded by Solomon Sibley, who filled out Woodbridge's unexpired term and was then elected in 1821 for the full term which ran into 1823. That was enough for him and he let it be known that he would not again be a candidate at the election called for September 4, 1823. That started a scramble, and by late spring a number of hats were in the ring. Leading candidates who began early to solicit support were Austin Wing, sheriff of Wayne County; John Biddle, a scion of the Philadelphia Biddle family, who had gone west as a soldier and Indian agent; John R. Williams, a prominent member of Father Richard's parish; and two or three others. By May it appeared that the contest would narrow down to a three-sided match between Wing, Biddle and Williams.

Then something happened. Whether the French-speaking element thought they were not having enough voice in political matters, or whether some faction thought it saw a way to steal French support from one of the other candidates, is not known. But, unexpectedly, two eminent citizens—"Canadians"—identified as militia colonels, appeared on Richard's doorstep with the suggestion that he become a candidate.

Up to that time Richard had taken only a mild and rather objective view of politics. He was interested in public affairs, but he had neither sought office nor openly backed any candidate in previous elections. The proposal made by his two callers was wholly surprising and, at the moment, it struck him as ridiculous. His first reaction was one of anger.

"Such a suggestion," he said testily, "was so utterly unexpected that I bid them be off, telling them that it was folly to think of such a thing."[16]

Indeed, it was folly. Richard was not even a legal citizen of the United States; he could not qualify as a voter. But the two gentlemen who proposed his candidacy must have had a large share of political acumen. They planted an idea in Richard's mind and then went away, leaving it to mature. The priest's initial anger at the proposition quickly passed. He began to look upon it as a joke, and he and his assistant, Father Badin, talking about it, found it highly amusing. Then their amusement began to change to sober reflection as the possibilities came to them. As a delegate to Congress, Richard would be in daily contact with, and have the ears of, the most highly placed officials of the Federal government.

What better opportunity to press his plans for educational facilities and missions to the Indians? The salary of a delegate was eight dollars a day. That was substantial income; if it could be applied to St. Anne's building fund, how much faster would the walls of the new church rise! Suddenly the idea of becoming a candidate did not seem ridiculous at all.

The first thing to do was to sound out his colleagues and superiors and find out what they thought about it. He sent a letter to Bishop Louis Dubourg, at St. Louis, an old friend of his days in France. A prompt reply was forthcoming.

"Everything well considered, I believe that you should not hesitate to accept the nomination that has been proposed to you. It seems to me that Providence designs to use this extraordinary means to help you and the Church in your district. I hope that you have decided in the affirmative, and I would rejoice if my letter arrived in time to allay the fears that you might feel in accepting, and to inspire you with the confidence that such duties demand."[17]

That decided Richard, and he announced his candidacy. He must have felt that his chances of election were bright. He could count on the support of the French-Americans in Wayne and Monroe counties, particularly the latter where there still was a predominant French population. The upper districts, Mackinac, Green Bay and elsewhere, would have to be cultivated. He had been contemplating a trip to the northern missions; he could combine that duty with some electioneering. He set out for the north and spent some time at Mackinac, L'Arbre Croche and Green Bay.

Meanwhile, the other candidates turned upon him as an interloper who had no business invading their private domain—the field of politics. They assailed him with every attack they could devise. John R. Williams was particularly outraged; he could see what Richard's candidacy meant to his own chances, which were based largely on the French vote. Williams took himself to the printing office and bought some broadsides which he spread around the Territory. Couched in bombastic language, they stated exactly what Williams thought of a priest, whether his own pastor or not, meddling in political affairs.

Richard, declared Williams, was seeking to grasp the bishop's mitre with one hand and a seat in Congress with the other. At the same time he was attempting to get both hands on the salary of the delegate.

"It is reserved for you," stated Williams with an air of offended propriety, "to give the most austere rules, in words and sermons, against the honors, riches, and distractions of this world, and to add by example the ablest political manoeuvre to clothe yourself abundantly with them all."

Richard was out of his element in politics, Williams averred: ". . . the turf which now appears to you covered with flowers and riches, only to gather thorns and brambles. . . ."

"Believe me," he said concluding his tirade, "you have a talent for preaching the Gospel; confine yourself to that and the French language, and you will assuredly be useful to many good Christians; but I do not believe you can be in the House of Representatives at Washington where they speak English only. . . ."[18]

Having delivered himself of these sentiments, the disgruntled Williams, in the highest dudgeon, stalked out of the Catholic church, never to return. He was followed by his uncle, Joseph Campau, the wealthiest citizen of Detroit.

His other opponents, Wing and Biddle in particular, launched a more effective attack. Between them, they subsidized the *Gazette* which was careful to avoid mention of Richard's candidacy and did its best to keep his campaign a secret from the public. Then, the word was quietly circulated that it made no difference whether Richard ran or not. The voters were reminded that he was not a citizen and would not be eligible for a seat in Congress if he were elected. Therefore, it would be a waste of effort to vote for him.

This was a telling blow and was something Richard had overlooked. It was true that he had never applied for citizenship. That was not unusual. A good many immigrants of that day likewise did not understand about the process of naturalization and were not much interested in finding out. Richard had gone into the west where only the most primitive kind of government existed and the sovereignty of the United States was pretty remote. He had gone to Michigan at a time when governmental authority was just beginning to be asserted; in a sense he grew up with the country and undoubtedly took his citizenship for granted.

He took immediate steps to correct the oversight. Early in June he appeared before Judge Fletcher, presiding judge of the county court, with his citizenship application. The learned judge ruled that the county court lacked authority to grant it and suggested he apply to either the district or the supreme court, knowing full well that neither was in session. That this was plain subterfuge becomes evident when it is learned that Judge Fletcher was Austin Wing's campaign manager. The decision did not sit well with the public which recognized it for what it was—a political trick. Judges Witherell and Lecuyer, the other two members of the county court, overruled Fletcher. Richard was granted American citizenship on June 28.[19]

Fletcher's action confirmed in the minds of the French-Americans their belief that they were being discriminated against. The result was that they began to organize solidly behind Richard. To offset his growing strength, the other candidates began making alliances and deals, each trying to outpromise the other with inducements of backing for various appointments.

Each vilified Richard and the French generally, thereby forcing the latter to stand together more firmly than ever.

Actually, Richard did not campaign very actively himself. He left things in the hands of his friends who promoted his cause by word of mouth, and by a single circular which they distributed, reminding the electorate that "the zeal and integrity of Mr. Richard is so firmly fixed in your minds as to render you incapable of changing your sentiments, knowing that he has no greater wish than to serve you."

As election day approached, the "friends of Mr. Richard" were "invited to come to his house where they will have the goodness to conduct themselves with all possible order and quiet until they have given in their votes. . . . As your enemies say maliciously that one can buy 20 French votes with a bottle of whiskey, show them on that day that it is a black calumny."[20]

Apparently the idea was for Richard's supporters to march in a body to the Council House which was the polling place in Detroit. It is unlikely that Richard marched with them. A check of the poll list fails to reveal his name among those who voted.

In Wayne County he rolled up a comfortable lead over the other contenders and in Monroe County he swamped them. It was obvious that if Richard was to be beaten, it would be the outlying districts that would do it. The *Gazette* delayed publication for three days, hoping for returns from the north that would swing victory either to Wing or to Biddle. They came in slowly, and it took nearly a month before the result was known. Oakland County, which was almost 100 per cent Yankeefied, did not report a single vote for Richard. Neither did Brown, Crawford nor, surprisingly, Michilimackinac. Nevertheless, Richard clung to the lead which Wayne and Monroe gave him, and on October 24, William Woodbridge and Robert Abbot, as the board of canvassers, issued him a certificate of election. He had won with 444 votes, to 421 for Biddle and 335 for Wing. John R. Williams received only fifty-one votes.[21]

But Richard's troubles were not over yet. Biddle promptly announced that he would contest the priest's right to office and demanded a certification of the vote from the election commissioners. It was his contention that Richard did not qualify for office under the law because he had not been a citizen for a full year before his election, and that the county court lacked authority to grant him citizenship. When the Eighteenth Congress convened for its first session in December, Richard was on hand, having left Detroit in November. So was Biddle, who got to Washington about the same time as Richard. He laid his protest before the House. Richard was permitted to take his seat on December

8, while the committee was still investigating his eligibility. Meanwhile, Biddle was confident that Richard would be denied a permanent seat, and he began acting as if he had already been made the delegate. He advised government officials about appointments in Michigan and tried to assume other prerogatives of office. His brother, Nicholas Biddle, of Philadelphia, president of the Bank of the United States, wrote the Secretary of State on John's behalf.

"My brother . . . who is contesting the seat of delegate from Michigan," he said, "having a decided majority of the people of that country interested in his success, already feels towards them the good wishes & and also the duties almost of their representative. In that capacity he would have considered himself bound to communicate to you his views in relation to some appointments about to be made at Washington. . . ."[22]

The dispute was decided by the House committee on January 13, 1824. It was in Richard's favor. A delegate, it was pointed out, was not a bona fide member of Congress; therefore the laws governing the qualifications of a representative did not apply to a delegate. It found the canvass of the election to be proper and declared Richard elected and eligible to hold his seat.

By that action, Gabriel Richard became the first and only Catholic priest in American history to sit in the Congress of the United States.

CUP OF BITTERNESS

Gabriel Richard was no stranger to Washington, but as the territorial delegate from Michigan Territory new prospects were opened up to him in the capital city. The Washington of the early 1820's was not a prepossessing place. The streets between the Capitol and the White House were muddy quagmires or pots of stifling dust, depending on the season and state of the weather. There were relatively few residential buildings, although of necessity the town had a liberal quota of taverns and boarding houses for the convenience of congressmen and others who needed accommodations while transacting business with the government. A profusion of brickyards and stoneyards, furnishing the materials for the unfinished Capitol and other public buildings, were about the only evidence of industrial or commercial enterprise. One of the few imposing structures was St. Patrick's Church where Richard frequently celebrated mass. While most members of Congress boarded near the Capitol and took their meals at "messes"—private dining or boarding houses—Richard usually made the long trek each day to and from Georgetown where he had lodgings in the college.

If the city of Washington was still rather primitive, its general atmosphere, as the nation's capital, was stimulating. Great names and figures occupied the center of attention, and Richard had every opportunity to rub elbows with some of the greatest men of American history and to establish an easy intimacy with some of them. The stage was held by such men as Henry Clay, Daniel Webster, Thomas Hart Benton, John Calhoun, John Quincy Adams and Andrew Jackson, to mention but a few who had already made their mark and who would help shape the nation's destiny for years to come.

James Monroe occupied the White House, or President's Palace, as it was still referred to. He was serving his second term; it was still the Era of Good Feelings; the country, having recovered from the effects of the War of 1812, was prosperous. The Federalist Party had given up the ghost and to all outward appearances—deceptive appearances, to be sure—everybody was united under the political principles of Thomas Jefferson. An air of strong nationalism prevailed. The great western movement was beginning; it would soon find expression in the emergence of Andrew Jackson as the great leader. There was a natural tendency toward expansionism and much talk in Congress, familiar enough to Richard, about disposal of western lands and of internal improvements intended to further open up the interior.

During the first session of the Eighteenth Congress which ran into the spring of 1824, Richard did nothing that was outstanding or which gained him any particular distinction. That is not surprising in view of the fact that he had no vote as a delegate and hence no political influence in Washington. He did not qualify for any committee appointments. His real position was that of agent, or lobbyist, for the Territory; he was hardly expected to do much more than bring to the attention of the proper Federal authorities those matters which interested or concerned his constituents. Because much of this was done informally, or behind the scenes, his activities were seldom noted in official records.

He had a multitude of errands to perform for the folks back home, and he attended to them with diligence. His constituents sought his favor, and some of those who had opposed his election with vehemence and venom made conciliatory gestures. Typical of these was Ebenezer Reed, one of the co-proprietors of the *Detroit Gazette*. He wrote a friendly letter which implied that Richard bore no post-campaign ill will and was desirous of being of service to friend and opponent alike.

"The result of the contested election is what was anticipated by a great portion of the public," Reed wrote, "and although it was contrary to my individual wishes, yet I shall use the freedom you have politely offered to *all* the citizens of the Territory, of all political parties, of writing to, and corresponding with you, as cheerfully as if I have voted for you. It is a happy circumstance that, in our elective government, after the turmoils and angry feelings of an election have subsided, and the fortunate candidate is once invested with the delegated power of the people, he must in order to fulfill his duties honorably, become the representative of the *people*, and not of the party which elected him. . . ." Reed suggested that one of the first things Richard might properly do would be to propose a law more clearly defining the qualifications of territorial delegates.[23]

Richard was, at first, something of a curiosity in the Capitol and on the streets of Washington. His accented speech and his personal appearance attracted considerable attention. According to Catlin, "His appearance was as foreign as possible and like that of the men of a long past generation. He wore knee breeches, silk stockings, a long black coat, very short in the waist, very voluminous in the collar and with a huge skirt extending almost to his ankles. He listened eagerly to all that was said and took enormous quantities of snuff."[24]

A contemporary account given by an unidentified Washingtonian offers a further glimpse of the quaint and picturesque appearance of Richard. This observer, a young man, was presented to the priest by a mutual friend when they met on the street near the Capitol.

"My attention," he said of this encounter, "was attracted to a singularly odd-looking gentleman. He was of middle age, sharp features, and wiry frame. His low-crowned, broad-brimmed hat was thrown back from the crown of his head, and a pair of large goggles set enthroned on the uppermost of an expansive, bulging forehead. He had on the nicest fitting and best polished shoes man could ever wear, with silver buckles but—no stockings. He was tapping a fine gold snuff box, and he appeared in the act of offering a pinch to a friend whom he seemed to have just met. . . . Much I enjoyed the good man's conversation that winter, and it was the sweetest reminiscence of my life that I served his Mass at Old St. Patrick's; ay, good Father Mathew bestowed on me the distinguished honor of dining on Christmas Day with the honorable and reverend Gabriel Richard, M.C.!"[25]

Others found his company equally attractive. President Monroe and Secretary of War Calhoun received him cordially several times and they listened fascinated to his stories about the Indians and examined with interest the "hieroglyphic signatures" which various chiefs had affixed to treaty papers and other documents. Calhoun encouraged Richard to talk about his ideas for Indian schools and missions, thereby raising Richard's hopes that something would be done.

Of his activities, Michigan's delegate gave occasional accounting to his friends back home. "I have written a great many letters since I am here," he reported on February 10, 1824. "I may say more than 60 in less than a month. My object is to render service to my constituents, not to court their popularity. I might, as perhaps too many do the same, I might offer Resolutions which I would know would not, and could not pass, if I would calculate only to please. But I aim at something more useful, I omit such acts in order to devote more time in paying visits to the members of the committees, before whom I have Business, and I may say, perhaps, that I tease the committees by calling too often in order to awaken the petitions that are at rest. . . ."[26]

Congress recessed in the spring and Richard went back to Detroit. If he expected to be greeted with gratitude and approval he was soon disillusioned. His return found him in the center of a storm of trouble which had been brewing for seven years. It had its beginning back in 1816 when François Labadie, a native of the Montreal region, appeared in Detroit and became a member of St. Anne's Church. It was no secret that he had left a wife, Apolline, behind him. He had simply packed up and deserted her, some said. He replied that he left her upon discovering she had been unfaithful to him. François applied to the Michigan courts for a divorce, and as soon as it was granted, he married a comely widow, Marie Anne Griffard.

Father Richard made some inquiries and found the facts about as reported. He warned Labadie to leave his newly acquired wife and bring Apolline, whom the church regarded as his lawful spouse, to live with him. Three times the warning was given with fair intervals between. Each was ignored. Richard gave the details to Bishop Flaget and asked his advice. An order came back from Bardstown stating that if Labadie did not repent and obey, he must be excommunicated. On the bishop's authority, Richard pronounced Labadie an adulterer and issued the excommunication edict.

The records pertaining to the case, both official and unofficial, reveal that Richard resorted to strong language in reprimanding Labadie.

"This François Labadie is a scandalous sinner," one account quotes him. "He commits adultery. Having a wife yet living, he married yesterday evening, another woman; and caused himself to be married by a Protestant magistrate. The marriage, which he has contracted, is neither good nor valid. It is concubinage."[27]

Levi Dolsen, who claimed to have been present when the excommunication was pronounced, later recalled:

"I have never heard such a curse uttered before or since. It rings in my ears still. He cursed Labadie when he was awake and asleep; when he was well and when he was ill; lying down or standing up; feasting or fasting; cursed his head, body and soul; and condemned him to hell everlasting."[28]

Many of the parishioners shunned Labadie because of his being excommunicated; and John S. Roby, in whose store Labadie was a clerk, felt obliged to discharge him in order not to lose the Catholic trade. Labadie complained he himself was thereafter unable to employ members of the parish as laborers or to work in his garden.[29]

Labadie was outraged and declared he had been libeled. He started suit against Richard in 1817, asking damages of five thousand dollars. Richard was advised by his attorneys that the case would be quashed if he shifted the blame for the excommunication to Bishop Flaget, pleading that he had only been acting under orders of his superior. Recognizing that a principle was involved concerning the privilege of a clergyman to admonish a member of his flock where there had been a violation of church law, Richard refused to take the easy way out. The case came to trial, but dragged along without any conclusion being reached for the time being. This was probably due to Judge Woodward. His friendship for the priest caused him to do all he could in the latter's behalf. Although Woodward remarked that the language Richard used in the excommunication was libelous, "words are spoken before Ecclesiastical Jurisdictions, or in the exercise of ecclesiastical discipline, which cannot be made the subject of a suit for slander, although they might be actionable if spoken without such cause or occasion, and maliciously."

Finally, not even Woodward could stall matters any longer, and in 1821 a verdict was given in Labadie's favor with a judgment of $1,116.00. Richard was represented in this suit by the most eminent members of the Michigan bar. His counsel appealed for a stay of judgment, which was granted; the case was to be reviewed during the next term of the court in 1823.

The rehearing was held on October 4; it has been hinted that it was scheduled for that time as part of a political plot to interfere with Richard's candidacy as territorial delegate. Whatever the reason, one of the judges was absent; Woodward and Witherell took opposite views, which resulted in a deadlock and another postponement.

When Richard first went to Washington he carried Woodward's opinion which stated, in essence, that the priest's remarks "meant only to impute to the plaintiff that which the Roman Church considers an offense and not that which the municipal law regards as such." He passed this around among the brightest legal minds in Washington and won concurrence from such men as Henry Clay, Daniel Webster and Edward Livingston.[30]

While Richard was still attending the first session, Woodward's term expired and all of his political foes, of whom he had many, joined forces to make certain he would not be reappointed. All kinds of charges were made against him; he was accused of everything from treason to chronic drunkenness. One of the points raised against him was that he had conspired to protect Richard. In a letter to President Monroe, a deputation of Detroit lawyers (each of whom hoped to win appointment in Woodward's place) declared:

"To obtain the favor and support of Gabriel Richard, the delegate from this Territory, the said A. B. Woodward stopped the course of justice by refusing to suffer a judgment. . . . the said Gab. Richard did in open church on the Sunday succeeding the said argument, declare to his congregation that Judge Woodward was his friend and had saved him!"[31]

Richard certainly did feel obligated to Woodward. Interceding with President Monroe, he sought to prove that the charges against Woodward were malicious and without foundation. But it was too late. The new appointments for Michigan did not include the judge's name. The best Richard could do was to persuade Monroe to give his friend a new judicial post in Florida.

Accordingly, when Richard got back home in 1824, he was summoned before the court and the original verdict was confirmed. About the time he prepared to return to Washington for the second session of his term in the late summer of 1824, Sheriff Wing stepped up, served a writ of body execution and escorted him to jail.

It was September 21 when Sheriff Wing slammed shut the iron door of Richard's cell, thereby accomplishing what neither the anticlerical forces of the French Revolution nor the British army of occupation had been able to do. He could have won his release any time merely by paying the judgment. But that he would not do. There was a principle involved and he would not compromise with his own conscience. To have done that would have meant, in his eyes, the acknowledgment of the power of the civil authority over purely ecclesiastical concerns. So he remained in the town lockup for more than three weeks while his friends tried to arrange bail or obtain his release in some other way. There is a tradition that the first public knowledge of his imprisonment came when a parishioner, passing the jail, heard Richard singing a sacred song.[32] He was prevented from attending mass or conducting services in the church. His only means of reaching his parishioners was by letter, written in his cell. One such communication was read on Sunday in St. Anne's. In it, he said:

"No doubt you have all been informed that on September 21 of this year, a judgment was rendered against me in favor of François Labadie for having excommunicated him by order of Monseigneur, the Bishop of Bardstown, because having a lawful wife, Apolline Girardin, still living, he married another woman before a civil magistrate, which action is pronounced by the Church as adultery. One hour after the judgment was rendered I was served with its execution by the sheriff, who demanded that I immediately pay the eleven hundred and fifty-four piastres, more or less, or be imprisoned. Persuaded that the judgment is unjust and contrary to the law, besides my inability to procure such a large sum in a moment of time, I chose to come to prison where I am still today, the tenth of October, 1824, at this time of writing. More than six days ago, a sworn surety that I would remain within the limits of the County of Wayne was signed by three worthy citizens of this parish. But, although approved by two justices of the peace, this writing was rejected by the plaintiff's attorneys, who demanded one of a different form. So it has happened that by special dispensation of Providence I find myself still detained, and although this is the Holy Sabbath Day I shall not have the happiness of offering the Holy Sacrifice, and you will be deprived of assisting thereat. We should, each of us, be resigned to the will of God who rules all things in his wisdom for his greater glory, and for our greatest good.

"But although I am held a prisoner, I would say to you in the words of St. Paul when he was a prisoner like me for having done his duty: 'The word of God is not bound.' *Verbum Dei non est alligatum*. And although I am separated from you by these walls of four foot thickness and by these iron bars, in which I glory, I can still continue to address to you the word of God. . . ."[33]

The following Tuesday, bond was finally approved and posted, and Richard was released. Under the provisions of the bond, he was restricted by the court to remain within Wayne County.

This posed a new problem. Congress was about ready to convene and Richard's presence was required in Washington if he was to fulfill his obligations to the electorate. Did the terms of his bond apply to Richard, the delegate, as they did to Richard, the private citizen? Was he entitled to claim congressional immunity and leave Wayne County in his official capacity? His attorneys and Labadie's could not agree. He wrote to Henry Clay, speaker of the House for advice, and was assured that he could safely claim immunity and attend to his official duties at the capital.

From then on, for the rest of his life, this law suit continued to plague Richard. Except for the few months he was in Washington in 1824–25, he was never again allowed to pass the bounds of Wayne County. Labadie assigned his claim to judgment to several people; these thus gained a hold over Richard. One of them was Joseph Campau, uncle of his arch-foe, John R. Williams. It is doubtful that Campau, a wealthy man, was as much interested in getting the money as in the opportunity to harass the priest.

Richard got back to Washington in 1824 in time to take part in the official welcome tendered the Marquis de Lafayette on the occasion of the old hero's grand tour of the United States. The second session was more productive for Richard than the first. His performance as delegate was never spectacular, but it was useful to Michigan. He adhered to his rule of speaking only on rare occasions; most of his activity was devoted to lobbying for measures of benefit to the Territory. He did a great deal of business with the Committee on Public Lands, seeking to speed surveys and get additional lands on the market to meet the demands of the steady stream of new settlers entering Michigan.

One of the principal resources of the young nation at this time was the vast public domain which comprised the greater part of the western territories. The sale of these lands to immigrants was producing more revenue than the government needed to meet its obligations and provide for its general operations. Public land was a common topic of discussion in Congress. There was a steady stream of bills introduced and plans discussed for exploiting them for public purposes. Richard entered this debate because he saw how the public domain could be used to advance his pet project—education. He added his voice to a proposal to increase the grant of a township, made to Michigan in 1804 for "a seminary of learning," by the addition of a second township. He also worked for legislation which would permit these two townships to be split up into various differently located parcels. This act was passed in 1826 when Richard had ceased to be a delegate, but the credit for it is usually given to him. This land, together with the Indian donations of 1817, became the basis of real financial aid to the University of Michigan.

As a member of the university's board of trustees in 1826, he urged that the parcels be located immediately. This resolution was adopted. Some of the donation land was in the heart of present-day Toledo, but unfortunately it was disposed of long before that city's development. Had it been held a few years longer, it would have provided a rich endowment source for the university.

Largely at the request of Governor Cass, Richard promoted a judgeship for Solomon Sibley, whom he characterized as a man possessing "talents, integrity and long experience." He worked hardest to obtain justice for the dismissed Woodward. Before he finally was able to secure the Florida appointment for him, and when Woodward's prospects appeared least encouraging, Richard offered him philosophic comfort. "I wish you health and happiness," he said. "Do not be disheartened by this unfortunate accident, which teach you in a forcible manner, that all things of this world are nothing else but *vanitas vanitatum* &c and no true comfort is ever to be expected of them."[34]

Richard pushed his pet project to aid the deaf. In January 1825, he was successful in having a bill introduced to provide federal funds "for the benefit of the Asylum for teaching the Deaf and Dumb of Kentucky, New York, Pennsylvania, and of the territory of Michigan." Like so many of his other dreams, this one failed, too; his bill died in committee.

Richard's major accomplishment in Congress was in promoting Federal road building in Michigan. Highways were one of the Territory's greatest needs. Until 1817 there was no real road in the entire Territory. In that year, Governor Cass persuaded the government to build one between Detroit and the Maumee Rapids as a military necessity. Richard obtained some additional grants to improve what became known as the Toledo Road.

But there was a crying need for a route that would tap the interior of the Territory and link Detroit and Lake Michigan and also thereby tie together the scores of small villages, towns and farms, that were springing up in southern Michigan. The old Sauk trail ran between Detroit and Chicago, and territorial leaders sought to have it surveyed and made into a road. Richard worked diligently for this measure, and on its behalf he delivered the only important speech he ever made in the House.

Pointing out that the Chicago road would be of more than local importance, he described it as a western projection of the Erie Canal which would connect the heartland of continental United States with "the battery in New York." He drew attention to the military advantages by which troops could be moved to the western posts in winter when navigation on the lakes was closed. But primarily he stressed the meaning of the road in human terms.

"Make this road now," he told the House, sitting as a committee of the whole, "when you have the full sovereignty over the Territory of Michigan, before it becomes an independent State, and you may easily anticipate how beneficial this road will be to your finances. There are more than seventeen millions of acres of generally good and fertile land in Michigan proper (without speaking of the 94,000,000 acres in the Northwest Territory). Without a road to go to these lands they have no value. We are credibly informed that on our inland seas, I mean Lakes Erie, St. Clair, Huron and Michigan, no less than one hundred and fifty vessels are plying up and down, on board of which whole families do come sometimes with their wagons, horses, sheep and milk cows, land in Detroit, ready to go in search of good land, to settle on it, and having their money ready to give to the receiver of the land office. No road to go into that immense wilderness: What disappointment. . . .

"If you ask me what will this road cost? I beg leave to answer it will cost nothing to the government. I might say it will cost less than nothing. The half of the land along the road only will, after the road is made, sell for a great deal more than the whole would without the road. What an immense profit for your treasury you can derive from the sale of this immense wilderness, which remains entirely unprofitable if you have no road to come at it. This road is, therefore, to be beneficial to your finances, your military operations and to all parts of the Union as well as to Michigan itself, as it will afford all kinds of encouragement to the citizens of the Eastern States, who wish to emigrate to the beautiful and fertile lands of the West."[35]

Congress listened attentively and nodded approval of Richard's argument. On March 3, 1825, the bill was passed and an appropriation of three thousand dollars was made to finance the initial stages of the work. While Richard observed all this with the utmost satisfaction, he also warned the government to take measures that would prevent speculators from picking up choice land adjacent to the right-of-way at public sale.

Here at last was a significant and far-reaching legislative achievement, and Richard went home when Congress had completed its business, feeling that he was entitled to another term. He announced that he would be a candidate for re-election in 1825.

Once again Richard's competitors were Austin Wing and John Biddle, and the campaign of 1825 closely followed the pattern set by that of 1823. Because he expected to receive the solid French vote, with the American vote being split between the other candidates, his prospects appeared very favorable.

Attempts were made as early as 1824 to forestall Richard's second term candidacy. A letter to John R. Williams, written by Father Ganilh who had left the River Raisin for a pastorate at Wheeling in west Virginia, was widely circulated among the Michigan Catholics. Ganilh urged "you and all other influential Catholicks of Detroit, to use all your means of prevailing over Dear Mr. Richard that he may resign his post of Delegate to Congress. . . .

"In spite of all his learning, he was not calculated for the office. he knows nothing about the laws and his inaptitude to speak english well, makes him altogether unfit. He cutts but a poor figure in the house, and is at best but a kind of merry andrew, to congress: the very children running after him in the streets crying out: 'the black priest.' He is a walking Lampoon on the catholick ministry and we all wish most ardently that he may not appear in that caracter anymore."[36]

Judge Witherell, in a letter to Solomon Sibley, contemptuously referred to Richard as "the Pope of Congress."[37] Richard's opponents concocted some other new tricks that had not been used in 1823. Election day was moved up to May 31, a time when many of the French trappers were still in the woods. When Richard's friends appeared at the polls they found the opposition organized against them. Many of the voters had failed to pay their head tax. Those who favored Richard were challenged on that score and denied ballots. Those who were known to support one of the other candidates were allowed to vote regardless of whether their taxes were paid. Some of Richard's friends were forcibly prevented from voting. Robert Marsac swore "that he was driven from the poll by constables confederated with others who struck many of the french population with a Club over the head." Gabriel Chene testified that while on his way to the polling place he met a crowd of French who told him that fighting was going on and that "it was prudent for them to remain at home."[38]

Members of the Legislative Council were voted for on the same day. When the ballot boxes were opened, territorial delegate votes were found to have been erroneously deposited in the Council box. When these ballots were for Richard, they were rejected; those for his opposition were counted.

The outcome, even so, was surprisingly close. Despite intimidation and thimblerigging, Richard led in Detroit and Monroe with heavy majorities. But these were offset in the other districts with the result that the final canvass showed Wing the winner with 728 votes, while Richard trailed him with 724. Biddle was a close third with 684.

Now it was Richard's turn to cry foul and protest Wing's right to the seat. Even in that he was handicapped. His congressional immunity no longer served him, and the terms of the Labadie bond prevented him from going to Washington to present his case in person. His attorneys argued for him, eloquently, but to no avail. A congressional committee looked into the matter with more than ordinary attention, but was not impressed by the charges of fraud. Pointing to Richard's total vote which so closely equalled that of each of the other candidates, the committee decided there could not have been any serious intimidation of the voters.

If the outcome was a blow to Richard, it was not because of any personal loss; he felt and feared his French-American supporters were being discriminated against and being denied their rights by the aggressive Yankees.

The election of 1827 saw Richard beaten even more decisively. The vote was —Wing, 1,039; Biddle, 1,034; and Richard, 815. His name was on the ballot again in 1829. Feeling against the Masons was running high at that time, and someone got the idea that Richard would make a strong and perfectly logical candidate for the anti-Masonry party. Henry Whiting viewed this maneuver with some disgust and told his friend Henry Rowe Schoolcraft that Richard was a "man disqualified in the highest degree."[39] Actually, there is no evidence that Richard was privy to this plot, and it is doubtful that he would allow his name to be used in such a connection. Records fail to show that he made a serious campaign; his candidacy was pressed more by a few unorganized supporters than by himself. Wing declined to run again, so in 1829 Biddle had a clear field and finally achieved his ambition to be a delegate to Congress.

As for Richard, the campaign of 1829 marked his last venture into politics.

NUNC DIMITTIS

Gabriel Richard was one of those ill-starred individuals who almost achieve the pinnacle of their hopes and desires and yet are never quite able to grasp it. To have climaxed his career of service in Michigan by becoming its first bishop should, in the light of his labors, have been perfectly natural. But though Rome nominated him to be bishop of Michigan, the honor and distinction of the office were withheld from him.

The suggestion that his huge diocese be split up and a separate see be established at Detroit was made by Bishop Flaget as early as 1819, and the idea had undoubtedly been discussed for some time before that. The proposal was laid before Archbishop Maréchal, of Baltimore, who had succeeded Bishop Carroll. The matter was widely and thoroughly talked over, and a number of possible candidates for the bishopric were considered. At first Richard's name was not mentioned. Then the diocese of Ohio was created, and Bishop Edward Fenwick was given supervision of Michigan, perhaps as the first step in making it a diocese.

Fenwick went to Detroit on a visit in 1822 to determine when steps could be taken to detach Michigan from Bardstown. Following his inspection, he concluded that the time had arrived, and he wrote the archbishop, stating: "Nothing could afford me more pleasure and relief of mind than the erection of the bishop's See in Detroit, whose jurisdiction should extend over the Michigan and Northwest Territories, containing an extent of country equal to all Europe. . . ." He noted with approval that St. Anne's Church, then in the process of being built, was "well calculated for a cathedral."

The following year, Fenwick went to Rome, where he laid the plan before the proper church authorities. It was he who first proposed that Richard should be Detroit's bishop. He referred to him as a man "of great learning, piety, and zeal." Fenwick carried with him recommendations from others, including prominent laity in support of Richard. One such endorsement was by John R. Williams who had not yet broken with Richard and the church over political differences.

"Your diocesans being likewise informed that it is in contemplation to create a separate Bishopric in the Territory of Michigan," declared Williams, "beg leave respectfully to mention the name of our Reverend and well-beloved Pastor, Gabriel Richard, and humbly recommend him as a suitable person to fill that distinguished station. His long and pious services, indefatigible zeal, and charitable character entitle him to our sincere admiration, respect and eternal gratitude. He has labored faithfully during a period of upwards of twenty-five years, and would consequently be highly acceptable to his flock when clothed with higher dignity and powers. . . ."[40]

Despite such eloquent advocates, Rome was not to be hurried. For nearly seven years the Congregation of the Propaganda, the church agency charged with weighing the necessity for new dioceses in missionary areas, carefully examined all facets of the matter. Nevertheless, Bishop Fenwick considered it settled, and Richard, himself, confidently expected to hear almost any day of his appointment.

"I have seen Bishop Fenwick. . . ." He wrote from Washington to an acquaintance in Detroit. "He says that every day the official nomination from Rome may arrive directed to the Archbishop of Baltimore by which I may be found to give up running candidate as delegate. . . ."[41]

To another churchman he confided some of the arrangements he would make relative to his diocese and the kind of priests he hoped to have under him "if I have to be the BP. of Mich." But the expected word did not come; new pleas for action were sent by the archbishop and by Fenwick. One of the things that caused delay was Rome's uncertainty about the exact state of affairs in Michigan. Reports concerning a candidate for bishop who had served a prison term were disquieting; so were the stories of past parochial turbulence. Rome wanted more facts and asked for a report from a Jesuit who had spent much time in America and was supposed to be familiar with conditions in Michigan. His opinion of Richard was favorable; he characterized him as zealous, blameless, well-versed in theology, and as being held in high esteem. Imprisonment had not damaged his reputation.

Still the church authorities hesitated and delayed action. Not until 1827 did they authorize that Michigan "become a distinct diocese whose see shall be at Detroit." In the same order, Richard was nominated bishop and commended for his piety, integrity, ministerial zeal and long service. On March 4, Pope Leo XII confirmed the nomination, and on March 20 the diocese of Michigan was officially created. But at the last moment it was decided to withhold the orders. Another evaluation of the situation was made; testimony was heard from an American priest, formerly of Bardstown, who had just arrived at Rome. He thought the action was unwise; Michigan was not ready to be made into a diocese, he said. Its Catholic population was still too small and could not properly support a bishop. While he conceded that Richard was capable in most ways, he pointed out that he was under the handicap of large debts.[42]

In view of this and similar information, it was decided to do nothing further; and matters were allowed to stand as they were on March 4 and March 20.

"Detroit remained a diocese without a bishop," Paré explains, and, "the nomination of Father Richard was suppressed. Apparently the Congregation decided to let this anomalous situation stand until his death should make a new beginning possible. . . ."

One reason for Rome's hesitation was the Labadie case, the details of which were not clearly understood so far away from Detroit. Even at home, Richard was not too certain of how and where he stood. When he returned from Washington in 1825, he learned to his dismay that the construction which Henry Clay put upon congressional immunity was not the same as that of Detroit authorities. The record is not entirely clear, but there are indications that he was called before the court for having violated the terms of his bond by leaving Wayne County. At least his bond was cancelled. He began to have disturbing doubts of his ability to win his case and avoid paying the judgment which, because of accumulating interest, was growing in amount, year after year.

The case was finally appealed to the United States Supreme Court, but even then Richard had his troubles. His attorney refused to represent him further until a fee of fifty dollars was paid. Richard had difficulty raising the money. He was also unable to post the triple-damage bond which the court required. Actually, no final decision was ever made. Richard died before the high tribunal could reach a determination.

There was a hint of despair in Richard's suggestion to Bishop Fenwick in 1830 that his assistant, Father Badin, be assigned elsewhere, permitting Richard to save the salary which could be applied on the judgment should he be required to pay it. Moreover, he was not in good health, having reached the age of sixty-three pretty well worn out by his worries and his labors.

"I can do a great deal of work provided I can see the prospect of discharging debts that are sacred," he said, somewhat plaintively. "For that object I must remain alone for a few years. Then I will have great deal less trouble and will be enabled to pay five or six hundred dollars every year at least by economy."[43]

Despite this plea, Father Badin remained with him, helping to carry the load of St. Anne's and the neighboring parishes. After all, there was no point in paying the judgment until the Supreme Court decided he was obligated to do so. Some of his parishioners proposed selling, or leasing, the old Malcher farm on the Northeast Coast and using the proceeds to settle accounts with Joseph Campau, Labadie's assignee. But Richard dissuaded them from arranging such a deal for the time being, although he admitted that eventually it might be necessary. There is reason to suspect that the transaction may have been suggested by Campau, who regarded it as a means by which he could pick up a choice piece of property at small cost.

"My constitution is broken and much weakened," Richard wrote again in May 1832. Badin, by that time, was busy at other stations, and Richard felt the need of additional assistance. "I have much to do. I cannot stand it," he said. But he was still able to deliver lectures "by candlelight to Americans," and to supervise the printing of one thousand "small alphabets for the Indians" which had been requested by Father Baraga. He also clung tenaciously to his hope of establishing a seminary, and he wrote the superior-general of the Sulpicians at Paris, requesting not only financial aid, but also that his nephew, the twenty-nine-year-old son of his brother Charles, serving as a priest at La Rochelle, be sent to assist him.

"I have many things wherewith to begin a college, even on a grand scale," he pointed out: "an electrical machine, a pneumatic machine, an organ for the church, an extensive, well-chosen library, a printing press with 800 pounds of type, a farm of 300 acres adjoining the second city of Michigan [Monroe], 400 acres of land near Kaskaskia in the state of Illinois, etc."[44]

Bishop Fenwick came to Detroit in May 1832, and he advised Richard to settle his lawsuit and offered to provide some of the money. But despite this generous offer, Richard did not know exactly what to do. There were moments of dark despair when he talked about retiring to L'Arbre Croche and living out his days with his Ottawa friends.

But the time for making decisions, had he known it, was all but passed. Events, which would soon affect him, were being shaped far from Detroit on the Iowa bank of the Mississippi by Black Hawk, the Sauk chief. This old ally of Tecumseh in the War of 1812 was gathering together the remnant of his band of braves to challenge the white man's intrusion on his tribal lands in Wisconsin. Alarmed at the prospects of a new Indian war on its vulnerable frontier, the United States mobilized its forces to crush the threat. What followed found its place in the history books as the Black Hawk War, the last major Indian uprising in the original Northwest Territory.

Michigan made ready for battle. The militia turned out and there was general uneasiness among many of the settlers that the war whoop would ring out in the clearings of the interior. In Washington, the government ordered troops westward to reinforce garrisons along the Mississippi. Detachments of dragoons and infantry were sent to Buffalo, loaded aboard lake transports and sent around to Chicago. Some of them carried with them an enemy more deadly than Black Hawk's braves. It was the Asiatic cholera, which had been originally imported into the United States by immigrants arriving from Europe.

On July 4, the steamer *Henry Clay* docked in Detroit on its way to Chicago with several companies of infantry aboard. While the ship took on fuel and supplies, one of the soldiers became sick and died. The diagnosis was cholera. Several other cases immediately appeared among the *Henry Clay's* passengers, and the frightened ship's surgeon deserted. The people of Detroit cringed in terror, and health authorities ordered the steamer to clear immediately.

Moving up stream, the *Henry Clay* anchored off the tip of Belle Isle. As she lay there, the disease spread and her captain then took her up to Fort Gratiot (Port Huron). By this time there had been several more deaths and the situation was out of control. The soldiers were ordered ashore and told to make their way back to Detroit as best they could. Many of them died along the road, but about one hundred and fifty reached the town, bringing the disease with them.

Within a few days the cholera cases in Detroit reached epidemic pro-

Photograph by Joseph Klima Jr.

Clay study model for the Leonard Jungwirth sculpture of Father Richard. The statue itself is in Detroit's Gabriel Richard Park on Jefferson Avenue east of the Belle Isle Bridge.

Statue by Julius Melchers on the Woodward Avenue façade of the old Detroit City Hall building, corner of Woodward and Fort, across from Cadillac Square. It commemorates his far reaching influence on the city's life in its early years. Richard's birth is usually designated as 1767 rather than the 1764 shown on the base of the statue, and the city has recently changed it to 1767.

Photograph by Henry Leung

Photograph by Henry Leung

Richard's impact on early Detroit and Michigan is remembered and commemorated to this day. Pictured here are three public educational institutions which derive their name and heritage from this priest whose overriding interests were always centered in fostering democratic educational endeavors of any type, from grammar school to university level. Above is the Père Gabriel Richard School in Grosse Pointe, an elementary school at 176 McKinley Street. To the left is Detroit's Gabriel Richard School. It is also an elementary school, located at 13840 Lappin. Below is the Detroit Public Library's Gabriel Richard Branch, situated on the corner of Grand River Avenue and Stoepel Street.

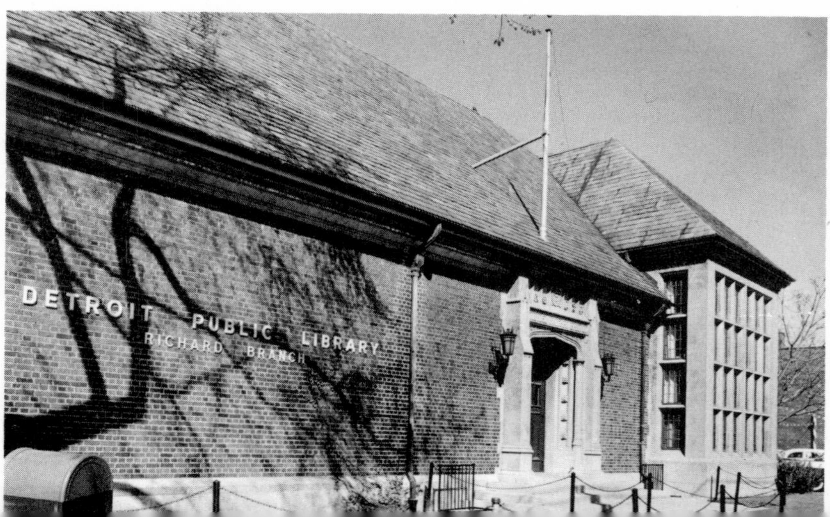

Photograph by Henry Leung

portions. Danger from the Indians was forgotten; people sought only to escape the ravages of the cholera. It was not easy. Those who fled the town found that the inhabitants of the interior villages had thrown up road blocks, forcing the refugees at gun point to turn back.

Detroit's half dozen doctors pitched in and worked heroically around the clock to help the stricken. Citizens who managed to keep their wits formed a nursing corps and Father Richard joined this band, giving all of his physical resources to caring for the sick, comforting the bereaved, ministering to the dying and burying the dead. The Capitol was turned into a hospital and Richard spent more time there than in his church.

"During all the excitement and consternation for two months after its appearance here," a Detroiter, R. E. Roberts, said about the cholera epidemic, "Gabriel Richard might be seen clothed in the robes of his high calling, pale and emaciated, with spectacles on his forehead and prayer book in his hand, going from house to house of his parishioners, encouraging the well, and administering spiritual consolation to the sick and dying."[45]

The disease continued to spread throughout July and into August. Those who were stricken experienced violent vomiting, diarrhea, cold extremities, chills and, finally, an almost imperceptible pulse. The next stage was death. Medical authorities administered opiates and stimulants, whichever was at hand. They advised against eating fresh fruit or vegetables. Efforts were made to cleanse the air by burning pitch, tar and sulphur in the streets. No one could tell exactly how many died. One doctor complained that "it is impossible to ascertain the exact number as the papers publish no reports on account of the continued fears of the inhabitants of the interior." Another declared that "scarce a person who is much exposed to the night air escapes a severe attack of cholera moribus or diarrhea."[46] Richard wrote at one stage of the epidemic that "since July 6 there have been 51 deaths, nearly all from cholera, in my parish St. Anne alone."

For the time being, Richard was leaving most of the work of his parish to others. Bishop Fenwick was still in Detroit, and in the midst of the epidemic he confirmed thirty-six persons. Father Badin, Richard reported, contracted the disease. Fortunately it was a mild case and he recovered quickly. Fenwick remained until early September when he departed for the East. He apparently carried the infection with him, because on reaching Canton, Ohio he was stricken. He died there on the twenty-fifth.

Meanwhile the epidemic was running its course in Detroit, although in mid-August there were still enough people sick and enough new cases being reported to keep Richard busy. "Two persons died of the cholera during the night and this morning," he said, "and several others have been recently attacked. Fear seems to be the principal cause in many cases." Gaunt, bone-weary, so pale his skin was almost transparent, Richard continued to make his sick rounds, an example of devotion which did not pass unnoticed by the grateful people of his town.

Gabriel Richard was now sixty-five years old. His strenuous, self-sacrificing life had left its mark on him. He had complained for more than a year before the epidemic struck of his physical weariness and general poor health. It was inevitable that a toll would be exacted for his uninterrupted care of the cholera victims. The disease had all but disappeared by the second week of September; as Paré says, only one more victim was to be taken. Before the beginning of September Richard knew the cholera was planted in his own system. In his final letter, he indicated an awareness of symptoms which could only have meant one thing. "I am better," he said, "because I take no supper no breakfast; I take only cold liquids. Warm drinks go down immediately and stir up the diarrhea."

"Completely worn out with fatigue, and seized with the unmistakable symptoms, he was forced to yield," Roberts stated. "The day he was stricken down, I saw him in a court yard in which were a number of tenament houses, going hurriedly from house to house, and looking more fit for the white than the black gown he wore."

A "martyr of charity," as someone described him, his resistance gradually wore down; at last he could do no more. Lovingly, tenderly, Father Badin and other friends watched over him, doing what they could to ease his pain and discomfort. But it was no use. Richard, and those about him, knew that the course was run, that the end was approaching. On Saturday, September 8, by almost superhuman effort, he got up briefly, went into the town to transact some business and later heard some confessions. Sunday he was too weak to get up. On Monday, high mass was sung for his recovery, and St. Anne's was crowded with well-wishers from all walks of life. Badin was absent at the moment, and when another priest offered to hear Richard's confession, he refused. Badin, he said, was his confessor and he would have no other. A wagon was sent Tuesday morning to the chapel on the Huron River to bring Badin back.

"At noon I was back with my venerable, dying friend," Badin said. "I had much difficulty in hearing his confession." Fully conscious, Richard received communion from Badin, assisted by Baraga. "We as well as the small number of persons present were extremely edified by his sentiments regarding the

August Sacrament of the altar, for he wished everything done in silence. He desired that Extreme Unction be put off until later."

He was reconciled to death and prepared for it, in worldly as well as spiritual matters. He had made a second will years before—it was dated at St. Genevieve, Missouri, October 31, 1821. His estate consisted principally of three tracts of land, his library and such personal items as clothing (including a suit of buckskins), a pair of spectacles (valued at inventory at one dollar), a set of billiard balls and a game of checkers. The value put upon his estate at probate was $3,671.03.[47]

The doctor continued to come regularly. He had prescribed doses of calomel, but by Tuesday afternoon it was evident this drug was having no effect, so a mild stimulant was ordered. Badin and Baraga administered it at half hour intervals through the night. Richard slept comfortably except when he was aroused for his medicine. Wednesday morning he seemed better "and a ray of hope animated" his friends. But by nine o'clock he took another turn for worse. Badin, who was preparing to sing mass, was hastily called from the church, and he and Baraga administered the last rites. As Richard received them, he spoke in Latin, according to Badin, murmuring "Now, O Lord, let thy servant depart in peace according to Thy word." They were his last recorded words.

"Towards noon it became impossible to make him take anything," Badin stated, "and all we could do was to wet his tongue with a feather until the moment when his happy soul winged its way to the bosom of God."[48]

That occurred at ten minutes past three on the morning of Thursday, September 13, 1832.

"His remains," according to J. A. Girardin, "dressed with the robe of his sacred office, lay in state in the sanctuary of his church, with his face exposed to the view of his congregation. From early morn until dark was the church filled with the multitude who had come from all quarters to take a last glimpse of him. His remains were followed to the grave amid the solemn tolling of all the bells of the city, and followed by a large concourse of citizens of all classes and denominations who evinced the deepest sorrow at this afflicting bereavement."[49]

The funeral was held at four o'clock in the afternoon, Thursday. Father Baraga delivered the eulogy; William Woodbridge was to have spoken, but the lateness of the hour prevented. The *Detroit Free Press* noted that the funeral was attended by more than two thousand persons—a throng larger than the population of the city.[50]

Gently they took him up. Wrapped in the shroud of his faith, warmly covered by the pall of his love for his fellow men, they carried him to the burying ground north of St. Anne's. The last comforting words of the church were spoken over his grave, and the mourners departed. The bells ceased to toll. Inside St. Anne's the candles flickered and the shadows grew deeper.

The long adventure had come to its end.

KEEPER OF THE FLAME

A century and a quarter have passed since Gabriel Richard's life of service to his fellow citizens of Detroit and Michigan ended. That span of time has witnessed many changes. The little river front village has become one of the great metropolises of the world. The places and scenes which were so familiar to Richard have a different look now; virtually nothing has been left by the inexorable hand of progress that he would recognize.

He lies no longer in the little cemetery which was on the outskirts of the town. The church which he labored so long and so hard to build has disappeared. Another structure today bears the name of St. Anne's, continuing in an unbroken sequence of years, the parish—one of the oldest in the United States—which once encompassed hundreds of thousands of miles of frontier wilderness. In this newest St. Anne's Church, in a tomb under the main altar, are enshrined the mortal remains of Gabriel Richard. They were moved, first from the cemetery to a crypt in the old church and, when that was abandoned in 1886, to their present resting place.

No longer is the French patois heard in the streets of Detroit. No more do the Pottawatomies set up their lodges at the Spring Wells. The old fort which dominated the town has long since been razed; its sunset gun no longer barks from the ramparts, starting the echoes across the strait. The brash Yankee pioneers have faded into history; new migrations have brought alien tongues into Richard's city.

Yet, despite change and progress, the spirit of Gabriel Richard lives on. Of all the pioneers, he is, perhaps, the best remembered; certainly the most beloved. Two statues in public places preserve his likeness. A park and a library bear his name. The city of Detroit and one of its suburbs each has a modern school named after him. Of all his monuments, he undoubtedly, would cherish these the most.

What vital spark was there in the spirit of this man which today makes him almost as real and vivid a personality as he was when he walked through the streets of Detroit; when he thundered from the pulpit; when he taught their letters to little French and Indian children? Great soldiers and lords of industry, bishops and ministers, wise men and good men, have come and gone and are but dimly recalled. Yet Richard's name is universally known; he is loved and venerated. Why?

"His life," says Paré, "was a succession of failures. There is no enterprise in the diocese today which traces back to him. The state university which he helped to found has, until recently, striven to disclaim relationship with him. Years of agitation could not give his name to the great highway through the state which he fathered. For thirty years as pastor of St. Anne's, sometimes in seeming dishonor, often in the midst of discord, always in extreme poverty, he struggled for the betterment of a backward and lethargic community that would not follow where he led."[51]

But who is to gauge failure; who is to assign success? Though Richard was denied the trappings of bishop of the diocese he created, there has risen a great archdiocese upon the humble foundations he laid. If the university he helped establish has withheld recognition from him, it is no less great a university. Richard would be satisfied with what it has become and would feel no sense of failure. He would not agree that the people of his parish occasionally failed him. On the contrary, he would contend that he had failed them.

"His renown," Paré continues, "need not suffer from his failures; they prove only that he was ahead of his time and superior to his setting." Therein, undoubtedly, lies the key to his present-day fame.

Richard was a humble man, and humility has a durable quality about it. The life of the Master whom he served offers glowing proof of that. Richard was a man of the common people and he expressed the hopes and yearnings which lie deep in the human heart, but which faltering tongues find difficult to articulate. What the people felt but could not express, Richard said for them.

In spite of the dissension and controversy in which he was involved, Richard's qualities of heart and mind were recognized during his lifetime. Few men, actually, were more honored and respected in life.

"He is undoubtedly one of the most learned men in the United States," William Woodbridge wrote to a friend in 1820. "He possesses a wonderful controll over the minds of the Canadians, & also over the Indians of whom many are Roman Catholic;—During the late war he was of singular service to this government & especially to the distressed & miserable inhabitants of Michigan after they were thrown at the feet of their vindictive enemies—

"He at all times enforced both by his precepts & his example the necessity of continuing firm in their fidelity to this Govt."[52]

Judge James V. Campbell, a later justice of the Michigan Supreme Court, knew Richard personally, and described him as "not only a man of elegant learning, but of excellent common sense, and a very public spirited citizen. . . . His quaint humor and shrewd sense, in no way weakened by his imperfect pronunciation of English are pleasantly remembered. . . ."

With reference to the role he played in early Detroit—he has been called the "second founder of the city"—it was said: "He came strong in young manhood and well-educated, enthusiastic and wide reaching in his appreciation of the scope of his new field and prepared both as a priest and civilian to do all that could be done by devotion, intelligence and earnestness towards raising the religious, educational and social status of his people. The prosperity of the town and the interests of the Territory at large, he made his own interests, and while strictly consistent and earnest in his religious work, he was also a hard and effective worker in a worldly way. Being a man of firm purpose, good executive ability and gentle nature, his coming to Detroit proved a continuous benison to the people during all of the thirty-four years that he lived here."[53]

Within a year after his death, the *Detroit Courier* spoke of him in these words: "Though a European by birth, he was an American in feeling, always evincing a firm attachment to American institutions and republican principles. The influence he exerted and the part he took in the late war evinced in an eminent degree the extent of his patriotism and the value he placed on American liberty."

It is significant that each of these tributes came from a non-Catholic source; an indication of the high esteem in which he was held by the non-Catholic part of the population. The reason is not difficult to understand. He lived in an era of intense nationalistic fervor. His attachment to the United States was demonstrated beyond question; his example helped to remove any doubts about the true allegiance of the French whose loyalty was at first a question to the American element. In repayment for his patriotic service, he won for the French a tolerance which has been a valuable community heritage ever since.

To understand Richard's status, it is necessary to understand the frontier as it was when he appeared upon the scene. To say that, by modern standards, frontier society was rough and crude, is almost an understatement. Lacking close contact with a more developed and refined civilization, it was, in many respects, close to the savage state. This was the raw material with which Richard had to work in Michigan.

For many years, Richard was the sole exponent of Christian doctrine in an area which now comprises in whole, or part, four American states. He was the only representative of formal religion of any denomination in that vast territory. The handmaiden of religion is education, and when he appeared in Michigan there were no schools and virtually no means of instruction. The attitude of the people toward education was one of almost complete indifference. Not until the influx of New England and New York settlers was well underway was there any popular demand for schools. In the interim only one man advocated the principles of general education and provided, to the extent of his limited physical and financial resources, by the sole weight of his persuasiveness, the means by which the lamp of learning was lit. He attempted to provide both religious and secular education, and if his efforts and the results were imperfect, at least he kept alive such aspiration when no one else cared. His hope, ambition and sense of duty ultimately flowered into a great state university and a system of universal education which, in many respects, provided a pattern for the rest of the United States to follow.

In 1787, when Richard was still a seminary student in France, the American founding fathers created a political organism known as the Northwest Territory. For its governance, they wrote an ordinance which is recognized as one of the world's great charters. In the preamble to this charter, they ordained as a basic requirement of association with the American commonwealth, three things—religion, morality, knowledge. These, they said, "being necessary to good government and the happiness of mankind, schools and the means of education shall forever be encouraged."

To Gabriel Richard, who spent forty fruitful years in the Northwest Territory, those words were a mandate, written in his mind and heart in burning letters.

Religion, Morality, Knowledge! These were the precepts to which his life was dedicated. As a priest, he built and tended the altars of Christianity in a part of the world which did not know the Word except as he proclaimed it in his Master's name. He implanted morality in the community by the pure example of his own private and public life. Through his introduction of the printing press and the medium of Michigan's first newspaper, he spread enlightenment; by unwavering devotion he encouraged schools and the means of education.

Adhering to the three great principles which the Ordinance of 1787 laid down, he fostered good government and the happiness of mankind.

He was, in his humble way, an empire builder.

Down through the ages, he will be remembered by a grateful people.

Notes and References

ABBREVIATIONS USED:

MPHC *Michigan Pioneer and Historical Collections* (Lansing, 1877–1929), 40 volumes
TP *The Territorial Papers of the United States,* C. E. Carter, editor, (Washington, 1942)
BCA Baltimore Chancery Archives
BHC Burton Historical Collection, the Public Library, Detroit.

FOREWORD

1. George Paré, *The Catholic Church in Detroit, 1701–1888* (Detroit, 1951); Sister Mary Rosalita, *Education in Detroit Prior to 1850* (Lansing, 1928).
2. Louis Untermeyer, in the Introduction to Robert Frost's *Come In and Other Poems* (New York, 1943), p. 3; quoted with the permission of the publishers, Henry Holt and Company, Inc.
3. Rosalita, *op. cit.*, p. 62.
4. Wilfred B. Shaw, "Some Sidelights on the University's First Years" (a recent address before the University of Michigan's Azazels, a faculty club).
5. See Frank E. Robbins, *Records of the University of Michigan, 1817–1837* (Ann Arbor, 1935).
6. Rosalita, *op. cit.*, p. 62; quoted from Richard R. Elliott, "Sketch of the Life and Times of Rev. Gabriel Richard."
7. Chase S. Osborn, "Father Gabriel Richard," *Michigan Alumnus Quarterly Review XXI* (1937).

INTRODUCTION

1. Except for an informal letter book transcript of Richard's writings, to which Clarence Burton, Father George Paré and I have contributed, a compilation of Father Richard's writings has not yet been seriously attempted. One of the reasons is that scholars are still in the process of discovering new materials. Through the good offices of the Reverend P. M. Tonnellier, pastor near Saintes, I have acquired an important collection of documents bearing on Richard's family, youth and education, as well as a portrait in oil of Richard painted at the time of his ordination. In addition to all this, I have come into possession of the manuscript of Tonnellier's unpublished biography, *L'Abbé Gabriel Richard, Missionaire aux États-Unis d'Amerique.*

The cathedral archives of the archiocese of Baltimore contain many letters written by Richard to Bishop John Carroll, who from 1789 to 1808 had ecclesiastical jurisdiction over all territory within the boundaries of the United States, and to his successor, Archbishop Ambrose Maréchal. St. Mary's Seminary, a Sulpician seminary near Baltimore, whose faculty Richard once intended to join, also has some of his letters. The St. Louis chancery archives contain his letters to Bishop Joseph Rosati and parish records written while Richard was laboring in the Illinois missions. The chancery archives of the archdiocese of Quebec possess many Detroit, and a few Richard, documents. There are not many original letters of Richard in the Louisville (Bardstown) chancery archives, or in the archives of the archdiocese of Cincinnati. Some letters are to be found in Mount St. Joseph College in Cincinnati.

In Detroit, the Public Library's Burton Historical Collection has the largest accumulation of Richard materials, including a photostat of the St. Anne "Registre," imprints of the Richard Press, as well as background material. The chancery archives of the archdiocese of Detroit contain some of Richard's writings and also the original St. Anne "Registre" (from 1704 to 1850). However, some of the material the scholar would expect to find in the Detroit chancery is in the archives of the University of Notre Dame, Indiana. An attempt has been made there by Librarian James Farnham Edwards to establish a depository for all source materials relating to the Catholic church in the United States.

At St. Mary's of Redford parish in Detroit, there is a collection of letters pertaining to Richard's youth and his education at Saintes, Angers and Issy. Photostats and transcripts of documents and a few of Richard's possessions and those of old St. Anne's have also been gathered there over the years. At Marygrove College, Detroit, Sister Mary Rosalita has acquired many photostats and transcripts and microfilms of documents pertaining to the educational work of Richard and his Indian missions. Much of his library is now housed in the Sacred Heart Seminary in Detroit and at St. John's Provincial Seminary, Plymouth, Michigan. Some of the autographed volumes formerly in this collection are now in the Burton Historical Collection and in the Michigan Historical Collections at the University of Michigan. Recently, a Detroit imprint collector, Dr. Norman E. Clarke, presented a fine collection of Richard imprints to Central Michigan College of Education in Mt. Pleasant.

The archives of the Michigan Historical Commission in Lansing are looked to as a central repository of official and personal documents, as are the National Archives. In addition, the library of the United States Supreme Court at Washington, D. C. contains material on the *Labadie* vs. *Richard* litigation. The Bishop Baraga Association of Marquette, Michigan, is now engaged in reproducing all the original Baraga documents from European and American collections as a prerequisite to his possible canonization. Only a few Richard items have turned up in this connection, but it is inevitable that more will be unearthed.

The roads of scholarship also lead abroad. In Rome are the archives of the Sacred Congregation of Propaganda Fide. Here is found correspondence regarding the earliest years of our colonial history: the establishment of dioceses, ecclesiastical boundaries, the appointment of bishops, the opening of seminaries, religious houses and colleges, the foundation and extension of missions, and related matters. The Society for the Propagation of the Faith with its central councils at Paris and Lyons has important Richard letters describing the great need of the infant church of Detroit and begging for assistance in obtaining men and money. The Sulpician Seminary at Issy and the Sulpicians in Paris also possess a few pertinent documents.

In passing it should be mentioned that in Richard's library there are nineteen bound manuscript volumes. The majority of these are unmistakably written in his hand and deal with the natural sciences, mathematics, history, literature, philosophy and theology. However, their actual authorship is in doubt. Did Richard originate them, or do they represent culled lecture notes and wide reading? If these writings represent his own individual thoughts and reflections, then Richard approaches genius. It will take time and the critical judgment of experts to answer this question.—E. J. H.

2. Letter of Gabriel Richard (Detroit, December 22, 1825) to M. Didier Petit, secretary, Oeuvre de la Propagation de la Foi, Lyons. It is quoted in Pierre Guérin, *Le Martyr de la Charité* (Lille, 1850), p. 81.
3. John A. Russell, "Gabriel Richard. Address on the Occasion of the Opening of Gabriel Richard Branch Library, April 23, 1923," *Detroit Historical Monthly,* I (1923), 49-53; T. A. E. Weadock, "A Catholic Priest in Congress," *MPHC,* XXI (1892), 432-447; Richard R. Elliott, "Sketch of the Life and Times of Rev. Gabriel Richard," *American Catholic Historical Researches,* XVI (1899), 155-176.
4. George Paré, *The Catholic Church in Detroit, 1701–1888* (Detroit, 1951).
5. Sister Mary Rosalita, "Four Women Lay-Apostles of the Old Northwest," *United States Historical Records and Studies,* XXXI (1940), 119-137; "Gabriel Richard, American," *Catholic World,* CL (1939), 89-92; "A Page from Pioneer Politics," *Michigan History Magazine,* XXIII (1939), 377-390; "The Spring Hill Indian School Correspondence," *Michigan History Magazine,* XIV (1930), 94-149.
6. See Albert Hyma, "The Scholarly Work of Gabriel Richard," *Michigan Alumnus Quarterly Review,* LVIII (1952), 222-231.
7. The results of this research have not yet been published.
8. Some recent publications by Mildred Connely include "Gabriel Richard, Man of Action," *The Catholic Directory and Guide of the Archdiocese of Detroit, 1950* (Detroit, 1949), pp. 6-14, and "Gabriel Richard, Educator," *The Newman Review,* I (1950), 4-5, 22-24.
9. Randolph G. Adams, *Gabriel Richard: Address at the Unveiling of the Gabriel Richard Statue* (1940); Chase S. Osborn, *Father Gabriel Richard* (1936); George W. Paré, *Gabriel Richard, 1767–1832* (Detroit, 1947); Stanley Pargellis, *Father Gabriel Richard* (Detroit, 1950); Andrew A. Polscher, *Father Richard* (Detroit, 1948); Milo M. Quaife, *Gabriel Richard, Pioneer* (Detroit, 1934). For article listings of Mildred Connely, Albert Hyma and Sister Mary Rosalita see preceding footnotes 8, 6 and 5.
10. Norman E. Clarke, *The Richard Press, 1809–1823* (Detroit, 1951); A. H. Greenly, *A Bibliography of Father Richard's Press in Detroit* (Ann Arbor, 1955); Douglas C. McMurtrie, *Early Printing in Michigan, with a Bibliography of the Issues of the Michigan Press, 1796–1850* (Chicago, 1931).

CHAPTER I

1. The official birth certificate is in the National Archives, Paris. The records at Issy, which contain the biographies of important men who formerly studied and taught there, also have this information on file.
2. Léonce Grasilier, "Un Saintongeais missionnaire chez les Illinois, Gabriel Richard (1767–1832)," *Bulletin de la Société des Archives Historiques. Revue de la Saintonge & de l'Aunis,* XXII (1902), 182-186. This valuable article contains a letter written in 1793 by Richard to his father in which he describes his trip from Baltimore to Illinois and conditions in Illinois at the time.
3. Pierre Guérin, *Le Martyr de la Charité ou Notice sur Mr. G. Richard, Missionaire* (Lille, 1850), pp. 1-10. This book contains several quotations from letters written by Richard to his parents, including the one given above. These letters were transcribed by Abbé P. M. Tonnellier, who lived near Saintes, in a biography, *M. L'abbé Gabriel Richard de Saintes, La jeunesse d'un grand franco-americain.* It deals with Richard's youth. In the summer of 1952 Father George Paré, acting on behalf of Msgr. Edward Hickey, obtained all the original letters that Richard wrote to his parents.
4. P. Guérin, *op. cit.*, p. 15.
5. *MPHC,* XXII, 338.
6. A. Fournet, "Saint Sulpice," *The Catholic Encyclopedia* (New York, 1912), XIII, 380.
7. N. E. Dionne, *Gabriel Richard Sulpicien Curé et second fondateur de la Ville de Détroit* (Quebec, 1911), p. 2. See also Tonnellier's work and the nineteen manuscripts by Richard at the Sacred Heart Seminary and at St. John's Seminary mentioned in Msgr. Hickey's Introduction and footnote 1 appended thereto. Richard studied under D. Labrunie and J. B. Richard.
8. Gabriel Richard Papers, *MS* in St. John's Seminary, Plymouth, Michigan. In the sixth volume of Richard's theological works, written at Angers and Issy, in the section on Penance, in an insert facing p. 23, Richard observed that the relation between church and state should follow the pattern set by papal authorities, notably that of Pope Pius VI in his bull of April 13, 1791. See also Richard's *Annotationes theologicae praecipué autore D. Labrunie,* II, pp. 14-15, which is also at St. John's Seminary.
9. Between July 7-15, 1792, Richard wrote a long letter to Father Duclaux, saying at the outset that he was fulfilling his promise to tell him about his trip and arrival in the United States. From April 12 till June 19 he had not seen any land. For at least ten days the passengers had to endure the results of a severe storm, rendering Father Matignon very ill. Reverend Maréchal, who had taken some medicine along, found little relief from his illness, but Richard and Ciquard did fairly well. On June 23, Saturday evening, Ciquard and Matignon left the vessel and spent the night with a "Lord Anglais." The other two men waited until Sunday morning to go ashore. They were delighted to observe that in a "land of heretics" the French Catholics could worship freely. Unfortunately many Frenchmen in the United States were worldly, especially in Baltimore, but less so in Philadelphia. Levadoux and Flaget had become missionaries among the Illinois, but Richard found Badin and Baret in Balti-

more. On July 8 he had "for the first time exercised his duties as a deacon at the mass administered by Mr. Maréchal."

CHAPTER II

1. John Francis Fenlon, "Sulpicians in the United States," *The Catholic Encyclopedia* (New York, 1912), XIV, 329-332.
2. Léonce Grasilier, "Un Saintongeais missionnaire chez les Illinois, Gabriel Richard (1767–1832)," *Bulletin de la Société des Archives Historiques. Revue de la Saintonge & de l'Aunis,* XXII (1902), 184-186.
3. Letter by Richard to his father in L. Grasilier, *op. cit.,* 184-185.
4. George Paré, *The Catholic Church in Detroit, 1701–1888* (Detroit, 1951), p. 267.
5. Letter of Gabriel Richard (Prairie du Rocher, January 24, 1796) to Bishop John Carroll, BCA.
6. *Ibid.*
7. *Ibid.*
8. Jean Dilhet, *État de l'Église Catholique ou Diocèse des États-Unis de l'Amerique Septentrionale* (Washington, D.C., 1922), p. 219.
9. Paré, *op. cit.*, p. 268.
10. Letter of Richard to Carroll, January 24, 1796.
11. Paré, *op. cit.*, p. 270.
12. *Ibid.*, p. 270.
13. Letter of Richard (Prairie du Rocher, March 23, 1797) to Carroll, BCA. The main letter was written in French, but the postscript in English.
14. Paré, *op. cit.*, p. 279.
15. *Ibid.*, p. 270.
16. *Ibid.*, p. 270.
17. Paré, *op. cit.*, p. 274.
18. *Ibid.*, p. 280.
19. A June 29, 1798 letter from François Pepin to François Navarre (Michigan Historical Collections, University of Michigan) discloses that Dilhet had first arrived at Detroit only two days before. (See also Paré, op. cit., p. 281.)
20. F. Clever Bald, *Detroit's First American Decade* (Ann Arbor, 1948), pp. 125-127.
21. *Ibid.*, p. 100.
22. Paré, *op. cit.*, p. 277.
23. Bald, *op. cit.*, pp. 100-102.
24. Letter of Richard (November 6, 1799) to Carroll, BCA.
25. *Ibid.*
26. *Ibid.*
27. Paré, *op. cit.*, pp. 283-285; also Bald, *op. cit.*, p. 156.
28. Letter of Richard (July 28, 1803) to Carroll, BCA.
29. Paré, *op. cit.*, p. 292.
30. Dilhet, *op. cit.,* pp. 111-112.

31. For further account of the fire of 1805 see Bald, *op. cit.*, pp. 239-241; and Frank B. Woodford, *Mr. Jefferson's Disciple: A Life of Justice Woodward* (East Lansing, 1953), pp. 3-6.

CHAPTER III

1. George B. Catlin, *The Story of Detroit* (Detroit, 1926), p. 118.
2. George Paré, *The Catholic Church in Detroit, 1701–1888* (Detroit, 1951), p. 297.
3. Frank B. Woodford, *Mr. Jefferson's Disciple: A Life of Justice Woodward* (East Lansing, 1953), p. 39.
4. C. M. Burton, *Proceedings of the Land Board of Detroit* (Detroit, 1905).
5. Richard Papers, BHC. See especially Richard's petition of April 27, 1807.
6. Richard Papers, BHC; microfilm No. 60.
7. Paré, *op. cit.*, p. 304.
8. *TP*, X, 264.
9. Letter of Jean Marchand (December 8, 1808) to Bishop Joseph-Octave Plessis, Quebec Chancery Archives.
10. Paré, *op. cit.*, p. 320.
11. Frank B. Woodford, *Lewis Cass—The Last Jeffersonian* (New Brunswick, 1950), p. 98.
12. *The Detroit Gazette*, August 8, 1817.
13. *MPHC*, I, 443, 484.
14. F. Clever Bald, *Detroit's First American Decade* (Ann Arbor, 1948), p. 141.
15. *TP*, X, 138 ff.
16. *TP*, X, 266 ff.
17. Letter of Gabriel Richard (October 8, 1807) to Bishop John Carroll, BCA.
18. *MPHC*, I, 484.
19. *MPHC*, XL, 350.
20. Letter of Richard (November 6, 1799) to Carroll, BCA.
21. *TP*, X, 130.
22. *TP*, X, 132.
23. Paré, *op. cit.*, p. 317.
24. *Encyclopedia Americana*, VI, 95. For another description of printing in early Detroit see Colton Storm's pamphlet, *Regulations for the Indian Department printed at Detroit in 1814, by Theophilus Mettez, at the direction of Lewis Cass* (Portland, Maine, 1953).
25. Letter of William Woodbridge (December, 1823) to Henry Clay, BHC, Woodbridge Papers.
26. *MPHC*, XL, 159.
27. *MPHC*, XII, 338.
28. Paré, *op. cit.*, p. 316.
29. *Ibid.*, p. 316.
30. Glenn Tucker, *Tecumseh, Vision of Glory* (Indianapolis, 1956), p. 274.
31. Paré, *op. cit.*, p. 317.
32. Tucker, *op. cit.*, pp. 273-274.

33. Letter of A. B. Woodward (March 5, 1815) to acting Secretary of War, National Archives, War Department.
34. Paré, *op. cit.*, p. 314.
35. Silas Farmer, *History of Detroit and Michigan* (Detroit, 1884), p. 288.
36. *MPHC*, XXXVI, 383.
37. Paré, *op. cit.*, p. 315.

CHAPTER IV

1. Richard Papers, BHC. These books are housed in the Michigan Historical Collections, University of Michigan; St. John's Seminary, Plymouth, Michigan; and the Burton Historical Collection.
2. George Paré, *The Catholic Church In Detroit, 1701–1888* (Detroit, 1951), p. 619.
3. *TP*, X, 249.
4. Will of Gabriel Richard, October 1, 1806, Detroit Chancery Archives.
5. Paré, *op. cit.*, pp. 621-622.
6. Letter of Secretary of War (April 30, 1808) to General William Hull, National Archives, War Department.
7. Letter of Thomas Jefferson (April 29, 1808) to Secretary of War, Jefferson Papers, Library of Congress.
8. *TP*, X, 261.
9. *TP*, X, 262.
10. *TP*, X, 300.
11. *TP*, X, 340.
12. *MPHC*, I, 493; also XXII, 338.
13. Sister Mary Rosalita, "The Spring Hill Indian School Correspondence," *Michigan History Magazine*, XIV (1930), 94-149.
14. Paré, *op. cit.*, p. 633.
15. John Monteith, *Diary*, Michigan Historical Collections, University of Michigan.
16. Frank B. Woodford, *Mr. Jefferson's Disciple: A Life of Justice Woodward* (East Lansing, 1953), p. 157.
17. Thomas M. Cooley, *Michigan* (Boston, 1885), p. 310.
18. Burke A. Hinsdale, *History of the University of Michigan* (Ann Arbor, 1906), p. 162.
19. Cooley, *op. cit.*, p. 313.
20. *Ibid.*, p. 313.

CHAPTER V

1. George Paré, *The Catholic Church in Detroit, 1701-1888* (Detroit, 1951), p. 361.
2. *MPHC*, II, 366.
3. Paré, *op. cit.*, p. 332.
4. *TP*, XII, 1127.
5. *TP*, XII, 11.
6. *MPHC* I, 493-494.
7. Silas Farmer, *History of Detroit and Michigan* (Detroit, 1884), pp. 533-534.
8. Henry Rowe Schoolcraft, *Journal*, March 31, 1831, BHC.

9. Richard Papers, BHC, microfilm No. 60.
10. Paré, *op. cit.*, p. 319.
11. *The Detroit Gazette*, August 19, 1818.
12. *MPHC*, I, 490.
13. *The Detroit Gazette*, August 18, 1818.
14. *MPHC*, I, 490.
15. Paré, *op. cit.*, p. 362.
16. *Ibid.*, p. 341.
17. *Ibid.*, p. 342.
18. Etienne Dubois, in a broadside dated August 31, 1823, BHC, answered the broadside issued by Williams, which is also in the *BHC.*
19. *MPHC,* XXI, 438-440.
20. Paré, *op. cit.*, p. 344.
21. *TP*, XI, 483.
22. *TP*, XI, 498.
23. *TP*, XI, 510.
24. George B. Catlin, *The Story of Detroit* (Detroit, 1926), p. 270.
25. *The Illustrated Catholic Family Almanac for the United States, for the Year of Our Lord 1871*, p. 49.
26. Letter of Richard (February 10, 1824) to Alexander Fraser, Richard Papers, BHC.
27. Richard Papers, BHC, microfilm No. 60.
28. *MPHC,* XXVIII, 608-609.
29. W. W. Blume, *Transactions of the Supreme Court of the Territory of Michigan* (Ann Arbor, 1940), III, 603. Details of many aspects of *Labadie* vs. *Richard* are to be found in various references in the *Transactions.*
30. A June 17, 1824, letter to this effect is located in the Detroit Chancery Archives (I, 55). It is signed by Henry Clay, Daniel Webster and Edward Livingston, among others.
31. *TP*, XI, 494, 541.
32. *MPHC*, XXI, 437.
33. Original letter in Detroit Chancery Archives. By a remarkable coincidence the difficulty between Father Richard and François Labadie has found a contemporary parallel in Prato, Italy. See *Time* magazine, LXXI, No. 10 and 11 (March 1, 1958, and March 17, 1958).
34. *TP*, XI, 538.
35. *Congressional Debates* (Washington) I, 374.
36. Letter of Anthony Ganilh (July 15, 1824) to John R. Williams, Richard Papers, BHC.
37. Letter of Benjamin F. Witherell (January 19, 1824) to Judge Solomon Sibley, Richard Papers, BHC.
38. *TP*, XI, 822.
39. *TP*, XII, 46.
40. Letter of John R. Williams (May 29, 1823) to Bishop Edward Fenwick, John R. Williams Papers, BHC.
41. Letter of Richard (February 9, 1825) to Alexander Fraser, Richard Papers, BHC.
42. Paré, *op. cit.*, pp. 363-365.

43. *Ibid.*, p. 371.
44. *Ibid.*, p. 382.
45. *Medical History of Michigan* (Minneapolis, 1930), I, 691-700.
46. Account by R. E. Roberts in Richard Papers, BHC, microfilm No. 60.
47. Richard Papers, BHC.
48. Letter of Francis Vincent Badin (September 22, 1832) to Louis Grignon, Richard Papers, BHC.
49. *MPHC*, I, 495.
50. *MPHC*, I, 495; also XXI, 435; and *Detroit Free Press*, September 20, 1832.
51. Paré, *op. cit.*, p. 289.
52. Letter of William Woodbridge (March 31, 1820) to Secretary of War, National Archives, War Department.
53. *MPHC*, XIII, 490.

Index

Manuscript edited by Alexander Brede, Francis T. Majeske
and Georgiana Ward Strickland

Design by Richard Kinney

Typography by G. Alden Smith

Set in Linotype Granjon with Bankscript and Bulmer Display faces. The engravings are by The Scranton Engraving Co. The illustrations are printed by offset on Ticonderoga Text paper, the text composed and printed on Ticonderoga White Wove Offset and bound in Terek Book Cloth Class C by the Haddon Craftsmen, Inc., Scranton, Pa.

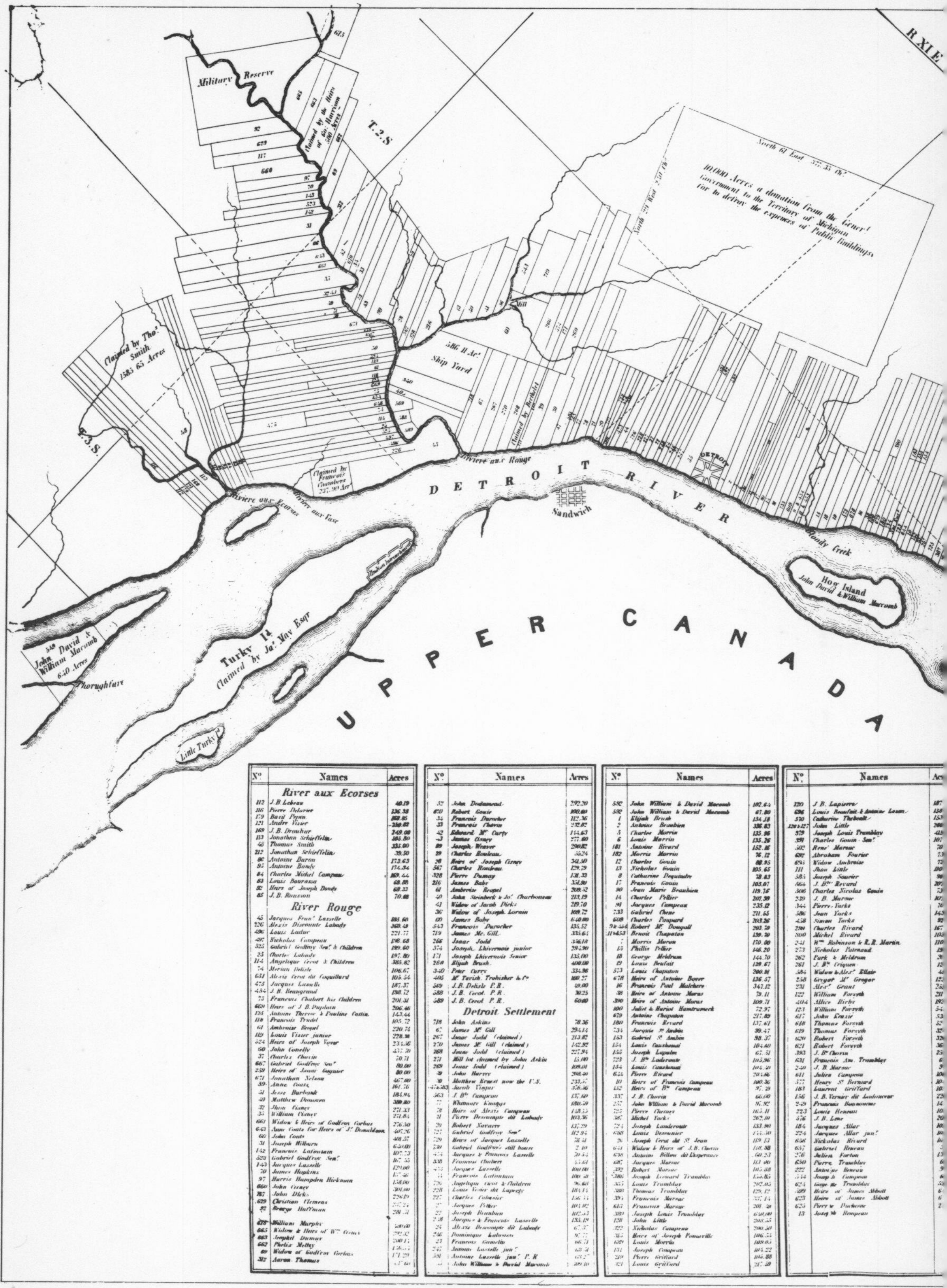

No.	Names	Acres
	River aux Ecorses	
112	J. B. Lebeau	40.19
116	Pierre Delurier	136.38
179	Bazil Pepin	168.85
121	Andre Vizier	250.82
169	J. B. Drouhar	249.00
113	Jonathan Schieffelin	385.80
48	Thomas Smith	335.00
212	Jonathan Schieffelin	39.50
86	Antoine Baron	173.63
95	Antoine Bondy	174.34
84	Charles Michel Campau	169.44
83	Louis Bourassa	68.88
92	Heirs of Joseph Bondy	68.33
85	J. B. Rousson	70.68
	River Rouge	
45	Jacques Franc. Lasselle	595.60
226	Alexis Discomte Labady	360.49
496	Louis Laduc	221.77
497	Nicholas Campeau	198.68
325	Gabriel Godfroy Senr. & Children	199.60
25	Charles Labady	197.80
114	Angelique Cerat & Children	385.82
74	Merian Delisle	106.67
651	Alexis Cerat dit Coquillard	105.54
475	Jacques Lasselle	187.37
454	J. B. Beaugrand	198.72
75	Francois Chabert his Children	201.31
669	Heirs of J. B. Puplain	206.46
125	Antoine Therese & Pauline Cattin	143.44
118	Francois Trudel	105.72
61	Ambroise Reopel	220.74
119	Louis Vizier junior	228.38
524	Heirs of Joseph Voyer	234.56
50	John Conelly	457.70
37	Charles Chovin	70.71
667	Gabriel Godfroy Senr.	80.00
259	Heirs of Isaac Gagnier	80.00
671	Jonathan Nelson	467.00
59	Anne Coats	161.76
51	Jesse Burbank	184.94
29	Matthew Donoven	389.80
32	Jhon Cisney	271.33
35	William Cisney	271.84
661	Widow & Heirs of Godfroy Corbus	276.50
643	Anne Coats for Heirs of Jn. Donaldson	407.26
66	John Coats	401.57
31	Joseph Wilburn	640.00
142	Francois Lafontain	107.73
523	Gabriel Godfroy Senr.	167.55
143	Jacques Lasselle	129.00
70	James Hopkins	157.46
97	Harris Hampden Hickman	158.00
660	John Cisney	304.00
767	John Dicks	226.19
629	Christian Clemens	257.24
92	George Hoffman	281.31
673	William Murphy	580.00
665	Widow & Heirs of Wm. Gener	292.32
663	Josephil Dumay	200.14
662	Phelix Melley	156.44
69	Widow of Godfroy Corbus	171.29
312	Aaron Thomas	157.60

No.	Names	Acres
32	John Dodameaul	292.20
670	Robert Gouie	100.60
34	Francois Durocher	112.36
33	Francois Chovin	232.82
42	Edward Mc. Carty	144.63
43	James Cisney	277.60
89	Joseph Weaver	290.82
29	Charles Rouleau	55.24
28	Heirs of Joseph Cisney	341.50
567	Charles Rouleau	129.79
328	Pierre Dumay	131.33
216	James Baby	351.90
61	Ambroise Reopel	209.52
40	John Steinbeck & Jos. Charboneau	213.19
41	Widow of Jacob Dirks	219.70
36	Widow of Joseph Lorain	109.72
60	James Baby	640.00
543	Francois Durocher	135.52
719	James Mc. Gill	335.64
266	Isaac Jodd	356.18
574	Joseph Lhivernois junior	294.90
171	Joseph Lhivernois Senior	135.00
260	Elijah Brush	400.00
340	Peter Curry	334.96
405	Mc. Tavish, Frobisher & Co.	100.27
569	J. B. Delisle P. R.	49.00
588	J. B. Cerat P. R.	30.25
589	J. B. Cerat P. R.	60.00
	Detroit Settlement	
718	John Askins	78.36
67	James Mc. Gill	294.14
267	Isaac Jodd (claimed)	213.82
270	James Mc. Gill (claimed)	142.92
268	Isaac Jodd (claimed)	227.94
271	Mill lot claimed by John Askin	15.00
269	Isaac Jodd (claimed)	109.01
39	John Harvey	208.40
30	Matthew Ernest now the U.S.	233.57
47 & 583	Jacob Visgar	376.56
563	J. Bte. Campeau	137.60
77	Whitmore Knaggs	180.59
78	Heirs of Alexis Campeau	148.75
21	Pierre Descompte dit Labady	103.36
20	Robert Navarre	137.29
727	Gabriel Godfroy Senr.	112.94
729	Heirs of Jacques Lasselle	78.41
730	Gabriel Godfroy's still house	2.10
474	Jacques & Francois Lasselle	70.54
338	Francois Chabert	55.61
473	Jacques Lasselle	100.00
44	Francois Lafontain	100.48
726	Angelique Cerat & Children	96.60
228	Louis Vesier dit Laperty	184.14
227	Charles Cabassier	156.74
27	Jacques Peltier	104.02
22	Joseph Beaubien	102.53
248	Jacques & Francois Lasselle	135.19
24	Alexis Descompte dit Labady	67.57
246	Dominique Labrosse	97.77
23	Francois Gamelin	66.71
247	Antoine Lasselle junr.	68.51
591	Antoine Lasselle junr. P. R.	63.27
4	John William & David Macomb	380.10

No.	Names	Acres
592	John William & David Macomb	102.64
592	John William & David Macomb	67.80
1	Elijah Brush	134.18
2	Antoine Beaubien	336.83
5	Charles Morrin	135.96
6	Louis Morrin	135.26
181	Antoine Rivard	152.16
182	Morris Morrin	76.12
12	Charles Gouin	88.95
13	Nicholas Gouin	105.65
8	Catharine Dequindre	78.83
17	Francois Gouin	105.07
90	Jean Marie Beaubien	119.76
14	Charles Peltier	207.39
91	Jacques Campeau	235.12
733	Gabriel Chene	211.55
609	Charles Poupard	203.26
9 & 454	Robert Mc. Dougall	203.70
11 & 453	Benoit Chapaton	139.30
7	Morris Moran	170.00
15	Phillis Peltier	146.20
18	George Meldrum	144.70
19	Louis Beufait	139.67
573	Louis Chapaton	200.91
678	Heirs of Antoine Boyer	136.57
16	Francois Paul Malchere	347.12
38	Heirs of Antoine Moras	79.11
390	Heirs of Antoine Moras	109.71
100	Juliet & Hariot Hamtramck	72.97
679	Antoine Chapaton	217.89
180	Francois Revard	137.61
734	Jacquis St. Aubin	99.47
153	Gabriel St. Aubin	98.37
154	Louis Caushouai	104.40
155	Joseph Lapalm	67.51
723	J. Bte. Laderoute	105.96
154	Louis Caushouai	104.40
644	Pierre Rivard	204.05
10	Heirs of Francois Campeau	100.36
152	Heirs of Bte. Campeau	97.39
337	J. B. Chovin	66.00
257	John William & David Macomb	97.92
725	Pierre Chesney	165.11
387	Michel Yacks	262.10
724	Joseph Landeroute	133.90
688	Louis Desounier	144.50
26	Joseph Cerat dit St. Jean	119.13
641	Widow & Heirs of J. B. Chovin	148.88
698	Antoine Billow dit L'esperance	60.23
687	Jacques Marsac	113.00
392	Robert Marsac	105.88
386	Joseph Leonard Tremblay	155.85
385	Louis Tremblay	202.05
388	Thomas Tremblay	129.12
394	Francois Marsac	237.14
613	Francois Marsac	201.29
389	Joseph Louis Tremblay	640.00
128	John Little	208.55
322	Nicholas Campeau	200.50
345	Heirs of Joseph Pouarville	106.54
689	Louis Morrin	109.05
131	Joseph Campeau	103.22
249	Pierre Griffard	105.88
321	Louis Griffard	217.59

No.	Names	Acres
120	J. B. Lapierre	
696	Louis Beaufait & Antoine Louse	
570	Catharine Thebault	
126 & 127	John Little	
379	Joseph Louis Tremblay	
391	Charles Gouin Senr.	
502	Rene' Marsac	
692	Abraham Fourier	
695	Widow Ambroise	
111	Jhon Little	
585	Joseph Saurier	
564	J. Bte. Revard	
506	Charles Nicolas Gouin	
239	J. B. Marsac	
344	Pierre Yacks	
586	Jean Yacks	
458	Simon Yacks	
299	Charles Rivard	
300	Michel Rivard	
241	Wm. Robinson & R. R. Martin	
273	Nicholas Patenaud	
262	Park & Meldrum	
261	J. Bte. Criquen	
584	Widow & Alexr. Ellair	
258	Gregor Mc. Gregor	
231	Alexr. Grant	
122	William Forsyth	
404	Allice Richy	
123	William Forsyth	
617	John Kenzie	
618	Thomas Forsyth	
619	Thomas Forsyth	
620	Robert Forsyth	
621	Robert Forsyth	
393	J. Bte. Chovin	
631	Francois Am. Tremblay	
240	J. B. Marsac	
611	Julien Campeau	
577	Henry St. Bernard	
183	Laurent Griffard	
156	J. B. Vernier dit Ladouceur	
249	Francois Bonhomme	
223	Louis Reneau	
576	J. B. Lene	
184	Jacques Allar	
224	Jacques Allar junr.	
656	Nickolas Rivard	
657	Gabriel Reneau	
276	Julien Forton	
650	Pierre Tremblay	
222	Antoine Reneau	
344	Joseph Campeau	
624	George Tremblay	
599	Heirs of James Abbott	
623	Heirs of James Abbott	
625	Pierre Duchesne	
13	Joseph Rempeau	